PUNK USA

THE ROOTS OF GREEN DAY & THE RISE & FALL OF

UPDATED AND EXPANDED

KEVIN PRESTED

FOREWORD BY JESSE MICHAELS

PUNK USA
THE ROOTS OF GREEN DAY & THE RISE & FALL OF

UPDATED AND EXPANDED

KEVIN PRESTED

FOREWORD BY JESSE MICHAELS

PORTLAND, OR / CLEVELAND, OH

Punk USA

The Roots of Green Day & the Rise & Fall of Lookout Records

Second Edition, August, 2022
First edition first published December 1, 2014

For a catalog, write or visit:
Microcosm Publishing
2752 N Williams Ave
Portland, OR 97227
www.Microcosm.Pub
ISBN 9781648411267
This is Microcosm #159

Edited by Alexis Orgera
Cover by Christopher Applegren

Photos courtesy of Anna Brown, Frank Portman, Dan Schafer, and Chris Appelgren.

Microcosm Publishing is Portland's most diversified publishing house and distributor with a focus on the colorful, authentic, and empowering. Our books and zines have put your power in your hands since 1996, equipping readers to make positive changes in their lives and in the world around them. Microcosm emphasizes skill-building, showing hidden histories, and fostering creativity through challenging conventional publishing wisdom with books and bookettes about DIY skills, food, bicycling, gender, self-care, and social justice. What was once a distro and record label was started by Joe Biel in his bedroom and has become among the oldest independent publishing houses in Portland, OR. We are a politically moderate, centrist publisher in a world that has inched to the right for the past 80 years.

Table of Contents

Foreword to the second edition: An Interview with Jesse Michaels of Operation Ivy

I was asked to write a foreword for the second edition of this book and also interviewed for it. During the process, we realized the interview probably covers anything that would be in a foreword anyway. If it feels more skeptical than celebratory about the East Bay in the period between 1986 and 2000 or so, that wasn't intentional but, you know, we are all doing the best we can. —Jesse

Going back to the beginning here. What brought Operation Ivy together, and more importantly, did you know you had something special, a rare synergy, from the start?

There was a big youth culture in the Bay Area. Perhaps like many other places, I don't know, but in the Bay Area there was this remnant from the hippie days, plus normal kids, plus eighties-type new wave, plus the punks, plus the indie rock people, plus the goths, then the college crowd, and so on, so it just seemed like there was a huge party scene in general. I reconnected with Tim at a Crimpshrine band practice (I knew Tim from around town and through Aaron Cometbus) and later at a party where they were playing. Anecdote: Tim taught me how to pump a keg at that party; for some reason I had never pumped one before, although I had been to many keggers. That was one of our first interactions. It's just kind of ironic because we are both sober now. Later, he introduced me to Matt, and they found Dave. I did not know that we had a special synergy from the start. I just knew that I thought our songs were to my own liking.

What about the early days at Gilman Street? Did it feel like a special place, tapping into a particular energy of an era? What was that energy?

Gilman was great and also super lame and annoying at the same time. It was both those things. The intentionality of it took away from some of the spontaneity because it was very carefully and methodically organized by a bunch of older, far-left punks. There was this whole narrative where Gilman was the place all the nerds and outsiders and weirdos went, and it was fairly true and that was great, and it was also at times a little bit too much. There were a lot of people who showed up who were kind of the type of people I went to punk shows to get away from—like weird hippies and artsy, sex-cult freaks.

At the same time it was literally physically safer than other venues. It was sort of like a free box, which of course was great in some ways, but it got messy. Some nights you would see a play, a poet, a weird rock band, two punk bands, and a speech about toxic waste. But the scene in general was at a low ebb in 1986 so it represented a new phase of people defining punk/counterculture for themselves. Over the next few years it gradually settled into being more of a standard punk club with occasional outliers. Frankly, once that happened, I actually liked it better. But that's just me. Everybody has their own memories of that time, and I honestly would not argue that mine are more accurate than anybody else's.

And onto Lookout!, this book's subject. From your perspective, what's the significance of Lookout! Records then, and now, in the landscape of American punk rock? What made it and the scene it documented special and important? Does it have a lasting legacy?

There are kind of two answers to that. The Bay Area scene around Lookout! Records and Gilman Street has been elevated in public history, but in many ways it was not particularly special, and in fact, less interesting than what had come before. The success of Green Day and Rancid and Jawbreaker have a lot to do with the whole historical revision where the Bay Area scene has been canonized as "important." If you don't believe me, just do a search for "early punk in________" and add any major city in virtually any country with a fairly open society. Then listen to the music that was produced. There is so much spectacularly good stuff that nobody has ever heard of. I am not taking anything away from what we did by saying that. It's just the truth. So the word "special" is a little bit loaded. For just one example, listen to the EP by the band Rebel Truth. They are one of the best punk bands that ever struck a note, and most people have never heard of them. There are hundreds of other bands like that.

The other answer to your question is that there was something very special about the East Bay scene, but it's not what people think. It was one of the first scenes that I have seen where people stopped worrying about being "cool." They were a little bit less pretentious, a little bit less uptight, and a little bit less concerned with appearing tough or fashionable (in the punk sense) than things that had happened before. I think that is significant. People worry too much about that shit. There is something to be said for having style and not being a wimp—kind of like that tough New York or LA sensibility—that is also special and important, so I'm not saying the Bay Area was better than anybody else. But we did do this thing where people were able to just relax for a second, and I think that was a good thing. We laughed at people who were overly concerned with fronting and welcomed the socially awkward outsiders a little bit more than other places. That's my hallucination anyway.

Lookout! Records, specifically, documented a portion of the bands that were happening in the Bay Area between 1987 and whenever the label folded.[1] In terms of popular music history, it is probably mainly important because of the more well-known bands that were exposed through the label—Operation Ivy, Green Day, Neurosis, and so on. I am very skeptical about how rock writers use the word "important" because it is usually based on commercial factors. For example, to me, the record called *Is This My World?* by Jerry's Kids is one of the most important records ever made, but it does not have broad commercial or influential significance. Any rock critic will tell you that some Weezer or Pixies record is more "important," but I don't agree. Personally, I thought Lookout! put out some great records including some very underrated ones like the Nuisance record. They also put out a lot of crap. In terms of my own life, they were the main platform for Operation Ivy until we folded, and I am grateful for that. I am still on good terms with all of them.

In a more general sense, the era of punk music from the late 1980s to early 2000s was a time when underground music continued expanding into the mainstream. I have no judgment about that; it's just the way things go, and Lookout! was positioned to be a huge part of that. They were probably largely responsible for the pop punk thing.

1 Lookout! closed its doors for good in 2012

What were the early experiences of working with those founders at Lookout! and of being part of that early enterprise?

It was a real DIY set up with people doing mail order in a very small and somewhat run-down Berkeley flat. They were always great guys, and we had a lot of laughs and fun hanging out. Larry Livermore famously could be contrarian and difficult, but he also really believed in the scene and the bands, and he got the stuff out there long before there was any guarantee of financial reward. I think he was a smart guy, and he knew from the beginning something was happening. But the bottom line is he took a risk and put in the hours. David Hayes was the organizational backbone of that project from the beginning, and I think he gets left out of the story too much. Overall, for me they were pretty fun and easy to deal with, although I think there are other people who had a different experience with the label. The success of our record and band probably made it easier for us in terms of dealing with the label and so on.

Toward the end of Lookout Records, when things got pretty dicey, what was the last straw that made you pull your catalog?

I didn't really have much input in pulling the catalog. Matt Freeman was sort of like the "dad" of our band, and he more or less just announced that we were pulling our shit and moving it to Epitaph. I had no objection to that because the house of cards was clearly falling, and I agreed it was important to secure our rights and masters before the shit completely hit the fan. Lookout! was tied up with bigger distributors and entities, and there was some danger of getting into legal bullshit so we decided to get out while the going was good. We had loyalty to Lookout! to pretty much the last minute, but honestly this was mostly because nobody really wanted to deal with sorting it all out until it became very clear that the ship was sinking.

I still have a lot of love for those guys, including Chris, who got unfairly blamed for a lot of stuff. He was a very young guy, practically a kid, who received a huge pile of responsibility and complicated business obligations before he had any experience running an organization of that size. If you look at many of the labels of the eighties and nineties that experienced a little success, the majority of them ended up tanking. They all made the same mistake: they had a few popular records and then they took on a bunch of expenses that they couldn't back up. Even Sub Pop, which was a juggernaut, only survived by being rescued, if I'm not mistaken. Chris was and is a good person who made a few mistakes, but as far as I can tell no more than me or most other people I know have made. Unfortunately, the stakes and repercussions were higher for him because of the position he was in.

What's it like now to have made something so lasting?

I am very grateful to have participated in something that has grown and that people appreciate. I know that I am very fortunate in that way. At the same time, I never reflect on my art in a historical context because if you do that you go from being an artist to being an old, boring, self-referential asshole. I am trying to avoid that for as long as possible, although I'm sure it's coming for me. It is hard to do something in this world that people actually care about so I am grateful to have landed that. Also, at times the whole thing feels like a simulation.

Boil it down, and Op Ivy songs are full of heart and social consciousness. One of your most prescient and poignant lyrics is, "To resist despair in this world is what it is what it is what it is to be free." What were you thinking about when you wrote it, and how can we enact "resisting despair" right now when there's a veritable shit ton of it?

In that song and in several other songs, I was trying to capture this idea that the euphoria one feels in music is part of a bigger kind of spiritual principle. Most people, myself included, live in a mental rat race of personal suffering, mixed behavior, shame, disappointment, anger, striving, and anguish. Good moments and music give you a little freedom from that. My idea was that this occasional sense of freedom is actually more "real" than the daily madness and bullshit we all go through, and it is a kind of window into how life "should" be, that is if we were not all so fucked up. The thing about song lyrics is once you explain them you are already overthinking them in a way. The meaning is in the feeling of the song.

You're a musician, visual artist, writer...how do these art forms fit together in your life and with each other? What brings you satisfaction in day-to-day life?

The fact that I am so multi-directional has been a curse in my life. I wish I was more like one of these people who does one thing and goes far with it, but that's just how I'm wired. I guess the thing that ties the different creative outlets together is an interest in trying to do things that are a little rough around the edges, things that have "soul." In terms of what brings satisfaction, I like the creative process when it's working, I get a lot of meaning from spiritual things like meditation, and I enjoy my friends and local animals. When I have a productive day creatively where I also have social contact and not too much clinical depression, it is a win. Exercise also helps a lot and may be the key to everything. I know that is sort of mundane, but if you are fucked in the head and problematically antisocial, exercise is often the main answer.

Can we change the world through art? Does it matter?

Art is an end in itself. Everything that happens afterwards is a side effect. Everybody who makes things has one job: make the best stuff you can, whether your name is Cal from Discharge or Mozart or Eve Libertine or Taylor Swift.

Introduction

On April 10, 2010, the musical *American Idiot* opened on Broadway at the St. James Theatre. The musical was created by Green Day, based on their 2004 album of the same name and expanded on the album's concept, including the addition of a recurring character called Jesus of Suburbia. This connected two generations of fans and asserted Green Day's return to form after their 1994 major label debut, *Dookie*. On its release, *Dookie* hit number two on the *Billboard* charts and went on to sell over twenty million copies. The *New York Times* had chided the album, saying its pop sound only remotely resembled punk music. But it was that blend of pop and punk that spread awareness about the previously marginal, underground scene in the East Bay.

At the end of the 1980s, punk was stubbornly hobbling on one leg. Its first generation was over, and punk in the US had never gotten as popular as it had been in England. Bands were continuing to tour in broken-down vans along the same trade routes that punk pioneers Black Flag had established. Young punks still had feelings to express to each other and needed enclaves in which to communicate them. But the institutions that had united them appeared to be dissolving. By 1986, Dead Kennedys dissipated while their singer fought an obscenity trial for artwork used inside their album *Frankenchrist*. By 1991, underground stalwart SST Records, who had brought Black Flag, Hüsker Dü, and the Minutemen to the national limelight, was caught up in an extensive trademark lawsuit over Negativland's album *U2*. DIY venues closed as fast as they had opened, and punk shows were relegated to rental halls. Punk appeared to be on the verge of becoming a historical footnote as its participants faded or turned into crossover metal bands.

Green Day's sudden stratospheric success did more than line the pockets of the band members; it raised the tide for US punk bands of all stripes. A sprawling network of kids with fanzines, dirty venues, and closet record labels become known around the world. Even kids in the most isolated suburbs with little access to their own punk subcultures found out about Green Day, and through them, a larger movement.

Green Day's story started back in 1989 when the teenage band members met David Hayes and Larry Livermore, founders of the then-tiny record label Lookout! Records. Lookout! released Green Day's first two albums, which went on to put the label on the map. By the mid-1990s, pup-punk fans hungrily devoured all of the label's other in-print records as they sought more bands like Green Day. Bands like Screeching Weasel, Operation Ivy, and the Mr. T Experience were launched into success by this association, with many more reaping the benefits.

The relationship between Green Day and Lookout! offered something much more than just sound: they opened an accessible avenue into underground music, allowing kids to discover music that was never going to be on the radio and shared an ethos and aesthetic that might otherwise have stayed obscure outside of certain scenes in California. Lookout! Record's presentation implied a participatory culture, something young people across the world craved, some even starting bands of their own inspired by this democratic aesthetic. Looking at many of their products, it felt like you could probably make a record too. And while Green Day was mainstream, Lookout! was not, so it felt like you had discovered something special that was your own. A new wave of punk was born.

It was an opportune time for the previously not notable San Francisco Bay Area scene to take the limelight, and the punk fanzine stalwarts at *Maximum Rocknroll* were there to document it all.

In mid-2010, I began work on what would become *Punk USA* after being a big fan of Lookout! Records for close to twenty years. I was motivated to create a book that I would want to read—the ultimate history of the label, along with the backgrounds and stories of every band and release. Over the next two years and thousands of hours of interviews and writing, I came close, exceeding 178,000 words. I have always been one for more details, so I put great emphasis on covering the minutiae of every release and band in chronological order. As I began to edit this epic story, I realized how much needed to be cut for the benefit of the work as a whole. So, I shifted gears and relaxed a bit, and as a result this book focuses specifically on the story of the label.

Huge chunks ended up being trimmed. As much as I love Brent's T.V. or Surrogate Brains, the casual reader might not be interested in five or six pages of writing on each of these 7-inch releases. While I set out to write the entire story of the label and its releases—and I think I succeeded—what you hold here is the "theatrical cut," with about half of the original material.

I apologize to anyone who wanted to know the ins and outs of the recording of the debut Crumbs album or the backstory on the Spitboy 7-inch. I feel your pain! But I think what you are about to read will function better as an entertaining ride through capturing the world of Lookout! Records. You can find the "deleted scenes" on my site, punk-usa.typepad.com, which will duly serve the completest nerds with your quests for the ultimate overview. Also, as much as I strove to write this book in complete chronological order, due to the editing process, some pieces of the story may overlap here and there, so please bear that in mind when reading. All of the interviews are original and exclusive to this book. Thanks for taking the time to pick this up, and I hope you have a fun ride.

—Kevin Prested

1

The Early Days

Larry Livermore and the Lookouts

With a population of under 1,500 people Laytonville, California—located in Mendocino County—is an elevated town founded in 1874 by one F. B. Layton, who built the first house where the town is now located. A little over one hundred years after Laytonville's founding, a new resident by the name of Lawrence Livermore arrived at a house off of the winding and remote Spy Rock Road. Lawrence—or Larry—was born in Detroit on October 28, 1947, and the thirty-six-year-old hippie movement supporter made the jump from San Francisco to a new life in the country outside of Laytonville with his then-girlfriend, Anne.

The summer of 1984 marked both a time of personal discontent and an important first step in what would become an unexpected journey for Livermore. With finances low and a messy situation that would ultimately end his four-year relationship, he hatched the idea for *Lookout Magazine*. Using skills he'd learned writing for underground presses in the sixties, Livermore released the first issue in October '84—fifty crudely assembled photocopies filled with his vocal opinions—which, once read by residents of Laytonville, caused local outrage, including within the hippie community, and led to boycotts. There were even instances of locals destroying the magazine on sight. Initially, Livermore had covered local issues in the free magazine, naming and discussing actual incidents or events in and around Laytonville, but with local threats forthcoming, *Lookout Magazine* began to widen its horizons and focus on subjects aside from the Laytonville pot harvest—namely punk rock.

Although Livermore's interest in the punk scene can be traced back to the seventies, the birth of the radio program *Maximum Rocknroll*—founded by Tim Yohannan—reignited Livermore's interest. In fact, it inspired him to start a new band named after his magazine. Livermore had salvaged the drum kit left behind by his now ex-girlfriend and ex-drummer. In an early incarnation of the Lookouts, Sue Rhine took over the empty drum stool. Rhine had met Livermore at the gay club, The Stud, in San Francisco, and after sharing some dance floor moves, they'd reconvened outside to get better acquainted.

Sue Rhine (The Lookouts): Behind his smile, I sensed that Larry was an interesting and complex character. When he suggested that I ought to consider being the drummer for his punk band, I laughed out loud. I had never even thought about playing drums before. Was this a joke or maybe a very strange pickup line? He insisted that he was indeed quite serious about this and explained that, based on my dancing, he could detect some sort of natural rhythm. He told me that he had a drum set, a rehearsal space, and that he could easily show me what to play. Key elements already in place, I figured, why not give it a try?

Getting together to play their only gig at a small venue Livermore had booked himself, Rhine became immediately concerned with the idea that they had already graduated to headlining status.

Sue Rhine: There was some relief in that the audience was quite small. I was relieved that we made it through our set without any major fuckups, as if anybody would've noticed anyway. Still, I felt inadequate about my wimpy drumming and lack of stamina. My insecurities had gotten the best of me. I was done. I don't remember how I left the band, probably over the phone. Soon thereafter, I moved away to Maui not knowing whether Larry continued with his vision for a band or not.

By 1985, Livermore's dream of the Lookouts finally came to fruition when he asked a couple of local tweens to join the band. He recruited twelve-year-old Frank Edwin Wright III on drums and fourteen-year-old Kain Hanschke on bass guitar. The German-born Wright had never played the drums, which raised some concern for Hanschke who wanted to be taken seriously. But, after several get-togethers, Wright proved his natural rhythm abilities. Wright quickly became Tré Cool—Tré a family nickname and Cool a Livermore addition—and Hanschke was renamed Kain Kong.

The Lookouts rehearsed through the spring of 1985, with some unsuccessful local live appearances. While Livermore continued building the circulation of *Lookout Magazine*, the Lookouts recorded for the first time, making the *Lookout! It's the Lookouts* twenty-six track demo, featuring a good helping of oldies and seventies rock covers. After distributing the demo via mail order, the Lookouts started playing around the Bay Area. Traveling back and forth between San Francisco and Laytonville over the next year, Livermore was spending more and more of his time in the punk community and getting involved in the live scene. The three-piece team of Tré Cool, Kain Kong, and Livermore were some of the first seeds sown—musically speaking—in what became one of the most important and influential scenes in American punk music of the 1990s.

A Scene Is Born: 924 Gilman Street

Kamala Parks (Kamala & The Karnivores): I used to book gigs at various places with Victor Hayden, and we were looking for a permanent place to have gigs when we found 924 Gilman and a very accommodating landlord. It was a bit trying at first because Victor and I didn't have money saved up. Timmy Yohannan of *Maximum Rocknroll* (*MRR*) was looking for a place to have shows in San Francisco but wasn't finding anything. So, Victor convinced him to come look at Gilman. Tim saw the place, met with the landlord, and decided that it would work. But, he had a different idea for running the place than Victor and I did. Victor and I had wanted it to be our jobs to run the place, whereas Tim wanted to run it like *MRR*, as a collective, volunteer-run place. So there were some conflicts between us. Nonetheless, I stayed involved with Gilman whereas Victor dropped out. I regularly went to shows, volunteered, booked some shows.

Paul Curran (Crimpshrine, Monsula, Go Sailor): In 1987, when the Gilman Street Project opened, it felt as if punk had reinvented itself. All of a sudden going to shows was (a) possible if you were underage, (b) fun, (c) welcoming, and (d) safe. It has been hashed over many times, but it's true that skinhead violence was a regular part of Bay Area shows in the mid-eighties, and scrawny little kids like myself were easy targets for getting pummeled in the pit and jumped on the street.

So many bands would find their footing in the premises of 924 Gilman, and along with the musical revolution came a new set of ethics, politics, and rules: no drinking, drugs, racism, sexism, homophobia, or violence; yet it could still be rock and roll with anything goes.

Kamala Parks: I remember Operation Ivy's first show, more in retrospect than anything. Jesse Michaels held his gut the whole time, but they were obviously a great band, even from the beginning. Isocracy always put on quite a show.

Jesse Michaels (Operation Ivy): Our first show was great. It was successful—meaning, we played fine and everybody liked it. I have always held the microphone the same way—I tend to lean way forward and clutch a bunch of the cord near my stomach. So I was holding the cord. I don't know why I do that. Probably because I'm a deeply wounded soul, and it represents holding my intestines from falling on the floor. Just kidding. I think there were about forty people at the show, tops, and construction was still going on. It did not feel like a real venue; it was very experimental at that time. For example, they did not advertise on flyers because they wanted people to just sort of show up because it was a kind of quasi-socialist artist community. There were lots of weirdos who were not strictly "punk." This diversity would come to characterize Gilman in the first few years. I don't mean it was like an early prototype of today's multiculturalism idea, more like you might see your weird mailman or acid-casualty aunt there.

Kamala Parks: One show in particular involved a guy named "Slither" throwing out bags and bags of cat litter during their set. We all had respiratory problems afterwards. Blatz would sometimes throw out very questionable items. In particular, I remember Jesse [Townley] one time, reaching into a furry animal toy and bringing out a handful of something that resembled dog food. I stepped to the back. I was at Gilman for the Feederz show when they threw a dead dog out into the crowd. That was pretty awful. The singer of the Feederz came on stage with cockroaches glued to his bald head and a dead German shepherd wrapped around his shoulders. He said something like "I guess Lassie isn't coming home" and threw the dog out into the crowd. Blood got spattered on a whole bunch of people, including my roommate Honey, who was a vegan and pretty upset.

Cammie Toloui (Yeastie Girlz): The day I met Kate [Yeastie Girlz bandmate] was one for the history books! She was manager of a band called the Feederz, and the night they came to play Gilman Street, the singer Frank Discussion decided to glue live grasshoppers to his head and throw dead animals out into the audience. Wow, were people shocked and pissed off! It was so punk and also really gross. Anyway, Kate was outside the club being shouted at by all the angry punks, and Jane and I were watching it all go down when she leaned over to me, pointed to Kate and said, "She's the one I was thinking would make a good Yeastie Girl." I always imagine how this would make a great scene in the movie someone will make about the Yeastie Girlz.

The first documentation of the new Gilman scene emerged in the form of a compilation record—the *Turn It Around!* double 7-inch compiled by David Hayes, a local punk scenester and eventual cofounder of Lookout! Records. The compilation served as the original authority on the Gilman scene and was released via the *Maximum Rocknroll* imprint, quickly adding to the legend surrounding the all-ages venue. Hayes had previously worked with local bands on his own cassette compilations. The *Turn It Around!* compilation, with its handmade cover, was an extension of these compilations, showcasing what was going on at Gilman in the form of seventeen tracks by bands including Corrupted Morals, Sweet Baby Jesus, Isocracy, No Use For A Name, Crimpshrine, Operation Ivy, Stikky, Nasal Sex, Yeastie Girlz, Rabid Lassie, Sewer Trout, and Buggerall.

Paul Curran: When the *Turn It Around!* record came out, it was quite a big deal. It was still kind of a mystical thing to put out a record back then, so to have all of your fellow Gilmoids' bands come out on vinyl was really exciting. Not only that, but to hear them recorded in a real studio was amazing! Some bands were revealed to be even better [than] you'd thought—especially Crimpshrine and Isocracy—and some bands, who I won't mention, when you got [to] hear what they really sounded like, you were like, "meh . . ." I don't know if that record was a huge success nationally, but it certainly was locally, and it was played to death. To this day, when "Another Day" ends I immediately expect to hear the Operation Ivy song right after it.

A Label Is Born

While David Hayes was busy working on *Turn It Around!*, Livermore had been gearing up his young cohorts for the first release bearing the Lookout! Records name: 1987's *One Planet, One People* (**LK 001**). The band's first "official" release was a collection of basic, yet charming songs with folk flavors. Shortly after the album's release, instead of supporting the album in the live scene, Livermore headed out traveling for a few months. When he returned, he started looking more closely at the exploding 924 Gilman scene and believed it warranted being documented as it emerged.

So, Livermore forged a business friendship and cofounded a record label with David Hayes. Hayes had been flirting with the idea of starting his own label, Sprocket Records, to release Corrupted Morals. The two were drawn together through *Maximum Rocknroll* and attending the same regular live shows. They created a partnership with Lookout! Records, winning out name-wise because it was already recognizable. Hayes brought comedic value and an identifiable, creative art style to the table, and Livermore held the reins on the business end, finding ways to save money. The initial sleeve printing, for example, was conducted at the regular *Lookout Magazine* printer for next to nothing—a perk secured because the shop manager was a fan of the publication. Even with differing personalities and tastes, as was proven over time with Hayes's

While a little sloppier and goofier, the art, humor, and design of the early Lookout! releases set the stage for the next ten years of the label as well as inspiring many other labels to take a similar approach.

referrals to Livermore as "the hippy," the formula was successful—if only in the short term.

Although they toyed with the idea of a split LP release between the Lookouts and Isocracy to follow up *One Planet, One People*, the second Lookout! release was the *Chet* (**LK 002**) 7-inch EP by Corrupted Morals. The band had already recorded two cassette demos in 1986 and 1987 by the time the debut five-track 7-inch came along in 1988, having developed a metal-tinged blend of speedy punk and American thrash. Although undeniably punk, the band's sound was rounded out with two guitarists and fast, metal-style blasts of lead soloing, bringing together something akin to an early Metallica or Bay Area thrash metal sound battling with early eighties hardcore pioneers like Minor Threat or the Circle Jerks. The mix worked, creating a cocktail of energetic and furious songs, which the five-piece recorded at the Art of Ears Studio in the summer of 1987. The colorful photocopied sleeves of *Chet* featured a folded pink sheet with wraparound artwork by Mark Tippin, based on the Bill Paxton Chet character from the John Hughes movie *Weird Science*.

Operation Ivy

Sharing stages with Corrupted Morals was Operation Ivy. As childhood friends, Tim "Lint" Armstrong and Matt Freeman had discovered English punk records like the Specials and the Clash, along with US punk heroes like the Ramones. After experimenting in a few prior bands, they formed Basic Radio, an early ska-punk blend. They played a handful of local shows until, after a couple of years, both were kicked out by their bandmates via letter. Discovering the Gilman scene as Basic Radio was falling apart, Armstrong and Freeman quickly found some other like-minded individuals and created a new band: Operation Ivy.

Returning to Berkeley after a stint in Pittsburgh, Jesse Michaels was brought on board as vocalist. Michaels already had roots in the East Bay punk scene, playing alongside local Jeff Ott in the band S.A.G. While Dave Mello, an Albany local—where both Freeman and Armstrong had grown up—was enlisted on drums following his time behind the kit for Distorted Truth. It wasn't long before Operation Ivy played at Gilman

Street—their second ever show after a show the previous night in Dave Mello's garage.

Following the band's appearance on *Turn It Around!*, Operation Ivy worked with Hayes and Livermore on the *Hectic* 7-inch EP (**LK 003**). Recorded in November 1987 with punk engineer Kevin Army in Oakland, the six tracks on *Hectic* captured an honest, raw, and original sound—the product of an unrepeatable time and place. Recorded in a day, the 7-inch sold out its initial run of one thousand copies within a month, surprising the band, even with its newfound local following.

Jesse Michaels: Kevin Army was a great engineer for this type of music, and it was easy and fun. The whole thing went by in a couple hours. After years of listening to bands, I still couldn't quite believe I was really in a real band, if you know what I mean. That status had always been for the older kids in the past, people cooler than me, in my mind. So I was very pleasantly surprised when it sounded not only good, but fairly original. The recording session was informal and very fast without feeling rushed.

Operation Ivy, May 21, 1989 at SF Women's Center by Murray Bowles, Courtesy of Anna Brown

Crimpshrine

Jesse Michaels's ex-S.A.G. bandmate, Jeff Ott, was also in another important East Bay band. The creation of Operation Ivy had driven an important stake into the ground, and Crimpshrine continued to develop the scene's foundations.

Guitarist and vocalist Jeff Ott and drummer Aaron Elliott (better known as Aaron Cometbus) attended summer camp together at age ten, along with John Kiffmeyer of Isocracy. Starting around 1983, they formed a piano and drums band that slowly evolved. By the mid-1980s the two had joined forces with another young local, Pete Rypins (replacing Tim Armstrong on bass), who went on to create the bass-run sound that was part of the band's identity.

Pete Rypins (Crimpshrine, Tilt): I got my folks to buy me [a] starter bass for under a hundred bucks. I got high every day and practiced in my room for three hours a day for two years, until I thought myself good enough to join a band. It was my plan all along to bring advanced and melodic bass to simple punk music.

They named the band Crimpshrine, a tribute to a high school music scenster by the name of Maya who frequently crimped her hair. The trio immersed itself in the 924 Gilman Street community, quickly becoming regulars on the scene, alongside Operation Ivy, Soup, and Isocracy.

Pete Rypins: All the Gilman bands were part of our crew, more so Operation Ivy and Isocracy than anyone. Operation Ivy and Crimpshrine shared a practice space in '87 and '88. We played dozens of gigs with them. The camaraderie was strong. However, there was envy towards Operation Ivy, because everyone loved them from the word "go" and for the rest of the bands it was difficult to establish fans.

Jeff Ott (Crimpshrine, Fifteen): There was a community feeling amongst the 924 bands as well as the people who worked there. It became somewhat stronger when *Turn It Around!* came out. Larry was always around the club, and I had seen the Lookouts a few times, so I already knew who he was, and Lookout! release number one was the Lookouts' 12-inch so I guess I already knew he was putting out records.

With the addition of Idon Bryant on second guitar, the product of the collaboration was *Sleep, What's That?* (**LK 004**)—a classic, late-eighties, sloppy punk masterpiece with Rypins's meandering melodic bassline, Ott's impassioned gravel voice, and Cometbus's machine gun snare blasts. There were some genius musical contributions from Rypins, such as his take on the riff of a-ha's "Take On Me." It is impossible to imagine Crimpshrine sounding any other way than they did on their debut 7-inch, scratchily recorded, at times off-key, running to keep up with each other musically, yet the blend stands the test of time as a perfect product of its environment. *Sleep, What's That?* set the tone for Lookout! over the next few years.

In support of the band's debut, they set out to spread the word on a self-booked US tour in 1988; however, the road was Crimpshrine's first test of friendship in and out of the band. Taking the band's roadie, Zack, with them, Idon Bryant and Pete Rypins left mid-tour, stranding Jeff Ott and Aaron Cometbus in Gainesville, Florida.

Pete Rypins: My leaving started long before the tour. I was drifting away from my early teen best friend Idon. In reality, he was drifting away from me, but I wasn't accepting of this. Idon played guitar and was into metalish stuff with long wanky solos. In an effort to keep our friendship close, I pushed hard for him to join Crimpshrine. There was eventually a culture clash. As a three-piece, Aaron, Jeff, and I were three different parts of the same punk band. With the addition of Idon we became two factions. The punks, Jeff and Aaron, and the rockers, Idon and Pete. I also wasn't the leader of anything, so I looked to Idon for guidance. He suggested that we leave the tour. The big mistake wasn't made that day. That likely made the remainder of it bearable for Jeff and Aaron. The error was in forcing Idon into the band in an attempt to save a dying friendship.

Ott hitched a ride from a friend across Florida and then took a Greyhound bus to Chicago, meeting Cometbus and a young musician named Ben "Weasel" Foster. Paul Curran, drafted to replace Rypins, also made his way to Chicago with his brother Jack in tow. Re-formed in Chicago, Crimpshrine played two live shows with Ben Weasel filling in on bass. Curran rounded out the rest of the tour with the once again three-piece band.

Paul Curran: It's true that when Pete and Idon left the band mid-tour that Aaron busted out his list of people he knew who played bass and started making phone calls. I didn't know Aaron very well but had known him since my earliest days of going to punk [shows]. My brother Jack and I got in my 1976 Ford Pinto and drove to Chicago to meet up with Aaron and Jeff. We arrived at the home of Ben Weasel and [John] Jughead of this band that I had only sort of heard of before: Screeching Weasel. I remember Ben making fun of us for bringing our skateboards on tour and them telling us about their shitty experiences trying to buy a tour van for Screeching Weasel. The rest of the tour was crazy long but with very few shows, many of which were booked as we went along, and the route made no sense whatsoever.

Isocracy

Isocracy, another regular in the 924 Gilman scene, came together when the band was in high school. Drifting through each others' lives from a young age, Martin Brohm, Lenny Johnson, John "Al Sobrante" Kiffmeyer, and Jason Beebout formed a bond through their love of music and skateboarding. Isocracy's performances at 924 Gilman involved anarchic displays of music and madness.

Lenny Johnson (Isocracy, Filth): We threw whatever trash and such we could when we played. Mostly for the bands from Berkeley and Oakland it was a venue, of which there were few, and for us and other bands from the surrounding areas it was a venue period.

The four young punks had been rehearsing in the back of Al Sobrante's workplace and had graduated to the live scene beside the Lookouts. Along the way they became acquainted with David Hayes, who offered them a 7-inch. It seemed like a no-brainer, and the band headed into the studio for four hours with Kevin Army to record the *Bedtime for Isocracy* 7-inch EP (**LK 005**).

Lenny Johnson: I guess it was all interesting to me and all new. Kevin was killer to work with, I think. I mean, what did we have to base anything on? For what we were, it still sound[s] pretty damn good to me. Working

Isocracy, June 14, 1987 at 924 Gilman by Murray Bowles, Courtesy of Anna Brown

with Lookout! was a breeze—again, what did we know? Although now that I do know and have been around DIY labels for so long, Lookout! was a pretty good template to work from.

Bedtime for Isocracy crammed ten tracks into just over ten minutes. Amongst those were several individual outbursts of teenage madness such as a self-made ad for Al Sobrante and Martin Brohm's favorite cigar brand, "Swisher Sweets," along with backwards masking and ridiculous juvenile shouting. The drums quite often tripped over themselves, while Jason Beebout—destined for punk stardom as the future voice of Samiam—shouted over the energetic riffs. The photo on the front was a cut-and-paste montage from an original Murray Bowles photograph, in which the longtime Bay Area punk scene photographer himself was featured.

Lenny Johnson: I don't really remember why we broke up. I think it had to do with me in some way. Al moved on to Sweet Children, what is now Green Day. Martin and Jason eventually ended up in Samiam, and my next thing was Filth. I can't speak for the others, but I had a killer couple of years with those fools, and I met a shit ton of people that I wouldn't have. Martin and I would go out to *MRR* radio every Tuesday and meet up with people in Berkeley. We seemed to hit the mark at the right time as far as the scene was concerned. All good times.

The Young Apprentice

Chris Appelgren (Lookout! Records): I got into punk with my elementary school best friend. I had just turned fourteen and had moved from the suburbs south of San Francisco to rural Northern California in the summer after seventh grade—actually about fifty miles north of Laytonville, the town where Lookout! Records' first P.O. box was located. I taped my friend's records, and whenever I found it at a record store or magazine shop, I'd buy *Maximum Rocknroll* magazine. I became aware of the Gilman Street Project music scene through *MRR*. Lawrence Livermore's *Lookout Magazine* was also available for free in the one small cafe / ice cream shop in the area where I lived. One of two other people at my high school who were aware of punk was this girl, Cia, who subscribed to *MRR* and was pen pals with Lawrence. He made her a cassette that had the *Turn It Around!* compilation on one side and on the other the tracks for the first four Lookout! EPs—Corrupted Morals, Isocracy, Operation Ivy, and Crimpshrine. Cia lent me the tape, which I promptly dubbed. It was pretty much a revelation. I didn't know which bands were which, but songs like Sweet Baby Jesus's *Turn It Around!* contributions seemed as amazing and important to me as The Beatles.

Soon, local punk bands became Appelgren's new soundtrack, but he felt he needed to explore deeper. Barely fourteen, Appelgren started to volunteer at KMUD, a new local community radio station, and hosted a show called *Wild in the Streets*. Originally cohosting with a friend, Appelgren quickly had the show to himself after his partner dropped out. The show, named after a Circle Jerks song, was armed with a copy of the *Turn It Around!* compilation, which Appelgren had picked up from a local record store, and he began spinning the tunes of East Bay punk on community radio.

Chris Appelgren: I found out about an Isocracy, Operation Ivy, the Lookouts, and Crimpshrine show to be held at nearby Humboldt State University. I made sure to be there. The show was amazing. I met Tim Armstrong—known only as Lint then—who was sweet and floppy and charming. For some reason—maybe that Jeff Ott had run away from home, Crimpshrine wasn't listed on the bill. My friends and I also met Lawrence that night and told him about our band, the Dirty Donuts. I wrote and asked Lawrence if he'd give me some promo copies of Lookout! releases for my radio show and he wrote back—neither of us had phones—suggesting he be a guest on the show. Lawrence divided his time between his home in Northern California and the Bay Area and, instead of being a one-time guest on my show, he became my cohost, driving the fifty miles or so every Saturday afternoon in time for us to get on the air at 1:00 p.m.

An alliance was soon formed between the two, despite an age difference of twenty-six years. Through the radio partnership, Appelgren was soon helping out with Lookout! by filling mail orders. On the weekends, Appelgren made the trek to Livermore's house, packing 7-inch records in marathon sessions. Livermore would then drive Appelgren back home in time for school on Monday morning. Also starting up his own fanzine,

Puddle, Appelgren found himself under the wing of Livermore as he contributed stories, helped out with photocopying, and offered the zine in the Lookout! catalog.

Chris Appelgren: I was an only child and had a single parent, so in many ways, Larry filled some of what a father should have been for me in my life. He helped me print my zine, encouraged me, hung out with my small-town circle of friends, and even almost started a student publication at my high school. He met my journalism teacher a few times to discuss it. Larry really professed an emotional attachment to me that I never really understood. I took it for an absent parental kind of approval and didn't really stop to think about what it might be or how appropriate it might seem. I think that Larry deeply cared about me, and he gave me some incredible opportunities.

The unconventional relationship didn't raise too many eyebrows.

Chris Appelgren: Larry was a super open-minded hippie in the sixties and had always been an underground character. It was an odd situation, and it's a weird thing you find in punk—at least in the Bay Area. People like Tim Yohannan, Larry, Jeff Bale—all much older than their social scene.

Around the time of the next release on Lookout!, Appelgren became a paid employee at five dollars an hour, and he noticed the ever-growing friction between Livermore and Hayes. The two partners often clashed over releases and began to separate their projects from one another. This would often divide the bands on Lookout! as "Larry bands" or "David bands." And as Livermore and Appelgren spent more time together, it became obvious Hayes wasn't excited about the pair.

Chris Appelgren: Once, when I was still in high school, I rode down the two-hundred-plus miles to Berkeley to go to a show at Gilman with Larry. We played basketball in the parking lot underneath David's apartment—the original Lookout! Records offices. I think at that time David was living with Martin [Brohm] from Isocracy and then later Samiam. We didn't go in, and I didn't talk to David, but we did sleep in the camper of Larry's truck that night after the show and basketball game.

Forming a Sound and Vision

Stikky

One of "David's bands" was the insane, humor-filled annihilation juggernaut known as Stikky, featuring brothers Chris and Todd Wilder and former No Use for a Name guitarist Chris Dodge. The Wilders grew up just north of San Jose, in Santa Clara, California, taking notes from mid-eighties punk and hardcore. While in high school, Chris Wilder also took in the best of the metal world, crossing swords with his punk loving sibling, Todd. With the combination of Chris's love of Venom and Exodus and Todd's punk diet, the two began playing together in bands. By 1984, they were opening for Social Distortion and the Faction.

Chris Wilder (Stikky): That's when I met Chris Dodge. He leapt up on stage and introduced himself and said he was the singer for a band called Legion of Doom. I told him I knew who the hell he was, because he was the South Bay Punk Flyer master. You couldn't walk into Sessions Skateboard shop or Tower Records without seeing one of his hand-drawn flyers. We became friends right away.

When the two Wilders decided to put together a new band, they had only one intention: to create the fastest, most extreme band around. Drawing influence from local bands like Verbal Abuse, Christ On Parade, and Violent Coercion, they enlisted the help of school friend and bassist Jamie Porter in 1985.

Chris Wilder: We were at every show we could get to in the Bay Area during that time and were lucky enough to be there at a time when the scene was really strong. GBH, 7 Seconds, Suicidal Tendencies, D.R.I., Black Flag—everyone came through touring, and the local bands always got to play. By 1986, Jamie wasn't that into playing gigs, and so Todd and I asked Chris Dodge to join . . . it took us ten seconds to think up Jamie's replacement. "Dodgeo" was perfect, and of course his contribution to making music obsolete is now the stuff of legend.

The band credits their off-the-wall shows for making them a perfect fit for playing 924 Gilman Street. It wasn't unusual for milk and cookies to be handed out to the audience during a Stikky set.

Chris Wilder: Bands that didn't get it about Gilman sort of became our "targets." Again, we never set out to be the band that made fun of all things stereotypically "punk" or "metal" or "straight edge" . . . it just made us laugh, and we hoped it would make others laugh too. When it didn't, like for skinheads or serious attitude punks or bands like Slapshot and Youth of Today, we poked fun at them. We would slam dance in slow-motion or while pretending to be our favorite animals. Once, Stikky played a set at Gilman while also engaging the audience in a rousing game of "Pin the Tail on Ray Cappo's Hand," à la Pin the Tail on the Donkey. One guy who always laughed at our shenanigans was David Hayes, a cool dude who made and collected comp tapes and really dug the nerdy aspect of Stikky, Isocracy, Crimpshrine, and other bands that refused to take themselves too seriously. David understood Stikky completely from the get-go, and would usually be there with us moshing in the Gilman pit to Corrupted Morals while pretending to be an elephant or wombat.

As Livermore and Hayes were releasing their first 7-inch records for the label, Stikky was recording their own selection of tapes. One came in the form of the band's demo, titled *We're Going to Keep Putting Out Shit Like This If We Don't Get Signed to a Record Label Soon*. Recorded "live" in Todd Wilder's bedroom direct to cassette in a couple of hours, all the tracks were literally made up on the spot.

Chris Wilder: "Here's a riff," I would say and string some chords together. "Who has a topic?" One of us would come up with some crucial social commentary like "Don't Lick My Leg"—about our dog who frequently did—or "I Love Fonzie"—who doesn't? We stuck in some cover tunes we liked, and the entire "Stayin' Alive" Bee Gees extended disco track, stolen from the *Saturday Night Fever* LP. To our complete surprise, lots of Stikky fans said it was their favorite, especially David. I think it's what led him to say "Lookout! would like to put out a Stikky LP, but there are a few requirements." We were all in a huddle at Gilman one night when he broke this news to us.

Hayes's requirements: some of the songs from the tape had to be included, including "I Love Fonzie." The terms were set, and with a handshake agreement between the band, Hayes, and Livermore, Stikky set out on the quest to create the most hilarious, ultrafast punk hardcore album ever to be released.

As Hayes worked on **LK 006,** Stikky's *Where's My Lunchpail?* LP, the tension between him and Livermore was palpable to Appelgren. A couple of months after the initial handshake, the band got a call from Livermore. The label had been receiving strong advice from someone—possibly outside of Lookout!—to create some kind of binding agreement for future projects, so a contract was drawn up for the label's second full-length release and passed on to the band to look over.

Chris Wilder: We reviewed the contract, which was pretty straightforward. The only term I remember was at the very end, which went something along the lines of "Over and above the preceding agreement, the two parties agree to work together in the spirit of mutual respect and friendship, in mutual benefit, to resolve any differences or concerns as we move positively forward." Twenty-three years later, as a nonprofit CEO, I still use language like that in any contract I write.

As one of "David's bands," Stikky spent a lot of time with Hayes, who essentially acted as coproducer, while giving the band free reign to do whatever they pleased in terms of album direction. Hayes reveled in the crazy, off-the-wall material that Stikky was producing, encouraging the band to include as much insanity as possible. Songs that were written in minutes or even seconds were urged to be part of the finished product.

Chris Wilder: David gave us *too* much artistic license. Perfection was *not* Stikky's middle name, and as long as we all thought it was cool or funny, it was included. This also included some jokes on the actual LP that would never have gotten approved had the label been bigger, more stuffy, or less naive. Not only did David love all these jokes and amazingly agree to let us do all of them, he did the layout for the lyric sheet/insert. In early 1988, he invited us over to the *Maximum Rocknroll* house—where he was living at the time, and working on the zine—and showed us his work in progress. It was a total mess of clip-art jokes and silly crap . . . exactly what Todd, Chris, and I would have done.

At twenty-two tracks, *Where's My Lunchpail?* was a vinyl-only release that sped along an insane highway. With their ultrafast beats and hilarious lyrics, Stikky soon became the root of the power violence musical phenomenon. Chris Dodge went on to create his label Slap-a-Ham Records (active 1989–2002), documenting a large portion of the extreme grindcore bands that emerged post-Stikky.

Plaid Retina

Not falling too far from the Stikky tree was another of "David's bands," Plaid Retina, from Visalia, California. Formed post–high school among high school friends in the throes of the Los Angeles metal scene, Plaid Retina was actively playing out, taking Bay Area punk influences and attaching them to their own brand of nihilistic, raging punk rock.

Hayes discovered them through his peers at *Maximum Rocknroll* and struck up a bond with the band. He agreed to release the already-recorded, self-titled debut 7-inch EP as **LK 007**. The twelve-tracks attacked the listener with furious blasts of punk energy, the longest track clocking in at just over a minute. As was the case with all of Lookout!'s 7-inch EPs at the time, the record was wrapped in the trademark fold-over, one-color, photocopied sleeve. Some of these early 7-inches began to appear on different colored paper. It wasn't unusual to see, for example, the Isocracy 7-inch for sale in a pink or a green photocopied cover from one store to the next depending on where the sleeve had been photocopied. This was due to short runs of sleeves printed on demand and not necessarily at the same printing outlet.

Don Hudgens (Plaid Retina): The early Lookout! 7-inches each had their own color and the covers looked similar. It was kind of like what Dischord was to D.C., Lookout! was to the East Bay scene. However it always had a "startup" feel. It never felt "arrived"—no sold out shows, no people lined up around the block.

Plaid Retina also sensed the mounting relationship problems Hayes had with Livermore and Lookout!. The Lookout! moniker was more convenient than parting ways, but each partner was handling his own projects more and more.

Don Hudgens: "[David] would let us know he was feeling down in the dumps, and we would party and cheer him up. We would see Larry on almost all of our Bay Area gig trips, but we weren't close, it was just like "Hi, how ya doin'!" I remember standing next to him quite a few times at the Gilman Street gigs, watching bands. Once I thought to myself, I need to communicate more with this guy, so I talked about an article he wrote that moved me in *Maximum Rocknroll*, and that wound up being as close to him as I ever got.

Sewer Trout

Two brothers, Hal and Jim MacLean, attended Gilman shows during this time. The MacLeans, along with guitarist Keith Lehtinen, formed Sewer Trout in 1985. With Hal on drums and Jim on vocals and bass, they'd already been kicking around the local scene for a couple years.

Hal MacLean (Sewer Trout): David had dug up our old Davis zine interview where I blurted out that it would be amazing if we ever got anything on vinyl, and he offered it up. We jumped at the chance. He also wanted us to record the entire 7-inch in one sitting, but our best songs were already recorded, so we took that as an opportunity to record the rest of our songs. Ultimately, we threw three different recording sessions onto the 7-inch *Songs about Drinking*. I think David was a little disappointed because the quality varied, but we were frugal and naive and that made sense to us.

Songs about Drinking (**LK 008**) was released in 1988—seven tracks of what became the classic Sewer Trout sound: sloppy, upbeat, and uptempo punk ditties revolving around Jim MacLean's meandering bass lines. It showcased the band's lyrical talent, mixing silly themes like those in the "Sex Trout" lyrics: "Vicious fish trout with tits and foot-long dicks," with genuinely moving, rambling, and loose tunes like those from "I'm a Hypocrite": "Screaming please someone help me, It's so damn cold I got nothing to eat, I just don't want to die in these unfriendly streets."

Hal MacLean: Many years later, when the Lookout! store was booming on University Avenue, I inquired about getting some more copies of Sewer Trout releases. I was told they were all out of print. I admit that I was a bit disappointed. I don't think Jim or Keith cared. After some stewing, I decided to make an all-inclusive Sewer Trout CD. If it wasn't for Lookout! letting *Songs about Drinking* go out of print, I probably wouldn't have put out the Sewer Trout complete discography. I asked Lookout! for the info on how many records were pressed. I explained my project and wanted a ballpark figure of how many CDs to make. Lookout! juggled me, and I was given the runaround for months. Finally, Jesse Luscious told me that he didn't think Lookout! had any records of pressings or sales of *Songs about Drinking*. He did set me up to get quarterly statements about how little we made off of [*The Thing That Ate*] *Floyd* [compilation], which was nice. Jesse was the only one who seemed to try to help me . . . they were over their heads with responsibility and record keeping, but they did release lots of awesome records that influenced a generation.

3

From Scenes to Ears

Finding a Distributor

For the early Lookout! releases, Hayes and Livermore had been working through a variety of sources for distribution—including Caroline, Rough Trade, and Systemic—and building a network of record store contacts. They were having mixed results and varying levels of success. In the midst of dealing with stores and indie distributors, the fledgling label was finding itself handling an increasing number of mail orders.

Chris Appelgren: When I first started working at Lookout!, basically Larry and I would do two-hour marathons of entering and fulfilling mail orders in the small office that he had in his home on Spy Rock Road. He'd collect a huge bundle of mail and sit at his desk, entering the orders into Microsoft Works and then would print labels for me. Each label had the address of the recipient and a two-letter code for each item they had ordered. We'd sit for hours and Larry would tell me stories of his life, gossip about the Bay Area punk scene, and discuss the orders or comments from letters people were sending to the label. The rest of the time we'd stuff 7-inches.

When approached by Lookout! in its earliest days, independent, friendly, and reputable Mordam Records—headed up by Ruth Schwartz, an original *Maximum Rocknroll* editor—passed on the opportunity to work with them. With some persuasion from Tim Yohannan at *MRR*, Schwartz had a change of heart and approached Livermore via Yohannan, forming one of the label's most important partners.

Ruth Schwartz (Mordam Records): We started [working] with Lookout! with the release of the Yeastie Girlz 7-inch. Typically, we wanted to see a label mature a bit before we would take them on. That was for two reasons. First, that we would not end up launching distribution for them, and they not be serious enough to keep going and fold up. Second, when we did launch a label, it could seriously overwhelm a label's ability to perform in financial terms with the volume of records needed for distribution and then be able to produce more releases. We generally asked to see a few albums before we'd take [a label] on. Lookout! at that time had two or three singles and really didn't qualify yet.

With organized distribution in place, Lookout! saw sales numbers increase and had the luxury of regular payments from Mordam—something that had been lacking when dealing one-on-one with varying sources.

Yeastie Girlz

Kicking off the relationship with Mordam was the ten-song EP *Ovary Action* (**LK 009**) by the Yeastie Girlz, an all-female group performing "live vaginacore acapella rap" about sex, poop, censorship, masturbation, bodily autonomy, and more. The original trio was Cammie Toloui, Joyce Jimenez, and Jane Guskin. Kate Razo joined the group soon after and performed on *Ovary Action*. Conceived at a Gilman Street Fourth of July barbecue in 1987, the band infamously jumped on stage to spontaneously perform the just-written lyrics "Yeast Power."

Cammie Toloui (Yeastie Girlz): We'd seen sexism in the male-dominated punk scene. Shows were usually all-male lineups, and the practice was to book the female bands together all in one night, as if mixing us in with the male bands would give them puss cooties or something. Once the Yeastie Girlz got going, we were booked in mixed shows with male bands as well as in the "all-girl-band" shows.

Jane Guskin (Yeastie Girlz): It was about recognizing that Gilman—a scene that I loved and felt deeply connected to—was still a heavily male vibe. Not macho, not a tough guy scene. It was a goofy GUY scene—emphasis on the word guy. Women were in support roles and basically ignored. Dudes were on stage getting all the love (from all genders). I don't remember there being many bands with women in them in the Gilman scene. Those few that existed—like Bitch Fight and Kamala and the Karnivores—didn't get nearly as much attention as the boy bands. We [later] booked one show ourselves that was mostly women bands (that was the show where we built the squishy / hairy vag doorway that people had to push through to get in!). But other than that one show, I don't remember any shows with mostly-women bands—whether grouped together or mixed in. There just weren't enough of us.

Robert Eggplant (Blatz): Two of the Yeastie Girlz I would see quite frequently at Gilman doing work and being a part of the audience. Cammie often had a camera and would work the door. Jane stage-managed or ran the door. Suddenly they were in a band. Since they were at the club every week, they had an attentive audience when they first took the stage. By the time they played with [sexist shock rock band] the Mentors, they had a very strong draw and the Mentors set was lackluster in comparison.

Cammie Toloui: There was a lot of build-up before the show that it was going to be some kind of showdown: Yeastie Girlz vs. the Mentors, the powers of good vs. evil, but what really happened is that we did a kick-ass set to a hungry audience of fans, and the Mentors weren't even there. They swaggered in late, totally drunk and played a lousy, sloppy set. There was no question who "won" that night, as far as a lot of people were concerned.

Joyce Jimenez (Yeastie Girlz): I don't really remember the show but do remember what a total dick El Duce was. I disliked him on and off the stage. And this feud, if you could call it that, was a reaction based on how vile and repulsive he was towards women. When I ran into him a few years later at the Chatterbox in San Francisco, he threw a beer bottle at my face and chipped a tooth.

The Yeastie Girlz unabashedly rapped about oral sex, the FCC, feces, misogyny, condoms, and healthy masturbation. Their songs included such works as "Put a Lid on It," where they explain their feelings about the scene:

I was hanging out at Gilman Street the other day.
I met a zine editor, he's a major babe.
But before I let my sloppy juices burst,
there's something I gotta say to him first.
I say "I wanna fuck you now, but first we better talk
about a little piece of rubber that fits on your cock.

Robert Eggplant: Their stage presence was almost an extended conversation—to *MRR* or the sound person or to the women who worked at Gilman and hung out there. The absence of amplified instruments drew us closer to the stage . . . and the messages of their songs. It wasn't as if we didn't get unusual arrangements at Gilman shows, but after two hours of maximum volume, it's cool that a group takes the stage that has the energy without blasting us.

Joyce Jimenez: Most of the people working at Gilman were super nice and welcoming. Once the YGs came about, we used our "Shock Therapy" on these dudes, and it worked on some, not all. But on the ones it did, we had tremendous support from.

Jane Guskin: I think it was a surprise to us—or at least to me—that people got into it. It was really spontaneous: we were just jumping on stage doing this thing because why not? We weren't actually thinking we were going to take it and run with it. But the response was pretty enthusiastic, so we just kept going wherever people invited us and taking the opportunities that came our way. At least that's how I remember it. But also, Cammie did a ton of work making all the cassettes and sending them out and communicating with people. So I'm sure that was a big part of it.

Cammie Toloui: I remember recording *Ovary Action* because we did it at my stepdad's recording studio at Diablo Valley College, where he worked. It was just bare-bones voices—no effects or anything but our

awesome lyrics and laughter. David Hayes and Larry Livermore were our friends at Gilman, and we were all really close and hung out there every weekend. I was dating David for a while. And I was living with Larry at the *MRR* house, and the Yeastiez were one of the very few female bands who were so immersed in the scene at the time (apologies to Kamala and the Karnivores, Bitch Fight, and others if I'm getting my timelines wrong). So maybe it was just a given that we would have a 7-inch on Lookout, but I do remember being really surprised and excited when they asked us to do it. Everything was so informal and DIY—I have a vague memory of folding the covers and stuffing the records in the sleeves, and I don't know if we signed any contracts. They were our friends, and we were all in it together, that's how it felt. And we were all so against the attitudes of the money-focused major labels that we very consciously did what we could to make it about the music and community. I know that was David's intention, anyway.

Kate Razo (Yeastie Girlz): I remember working with the Betty Dodson vagina drawings for our portraits—and laughing at the overall aesthetic, which was just so funny and silly and wonderful. At the recording, I remember Cammie's mother telling us, with a shake of her head, that one day we would be embarrassed about this recording. I remember thinking that was such an odd thing to say.

While the band didn't record past the EP, it archived a moment in the 924 Gilman Street scene and the true punk spirit of the early path of Lookout! Records. Twenty-five years later, the zine *Ovary Action*, published in Oslo, Norway, was inspired by the work of the Yeastie Girlz, continuing the worldwide discussion about feminism, gender, and nonconformity.

The Lookouts, March 28, 1987 at 924 Gilman by Murray Bowles, Courtesy of Anna Brown

What Ate Floyd?

Op Ivy: Legends in the Making

Since their debut EP release the year prior, Operation Ivy had maintained their rabid local fan base, becoming a thing of legend in the Bay Area in just under two years. Recording at Sound and Vision studios in January 1989, the band made history with the *Energy* LP (**LK 010**). In the time since their inception, Operation Ivy had crammed in an impressive number of shows—reputedly over 180—no small feat for a band with limited live options aside from Gilman Street, garages, and backyard parties. Their fresh musical approach was still striking a chord on the live scene, as were their anthemic, socially aware lyrics that were further explored on the nineteen tracks recorded for their first and only full-length album.

Jesse Michaels: The recording for the album was very similar to the recording for the EP, meaning we did it quickly, we were well-rehearsed, it flowed, and we were happy with it afterwards. I was very surprised at how good it sounded and impressed by my band mates. My only beef was that they rushed the intro to the song "Room without a Window," so I had to cram all those words into those stabs at the beginning of that song. On vocals, I tortured everybody by taking up to twenty minutes to do a song at times, which back then seemed like a lot. As usual, I was writing lyrics and fixing lyrics in the studio up to the very moment when I had to go in the booth and sing.

Energy shouted a message of unity and hit home with issues such as anti-war sentiments, local music scene politics and name-checks, overtaking corporate structures, and tales of life as an underdog. One of the most interesting parts of Operation Ivy's music was their mainly serious lyrical content crashing up against music that was so feel-good. Upbeat on record and on stage, the band found a die-hard following and made reverberations in the punk world, making them one of the greatest punk bands ever to stand together on stage.

Jesse Michaels: We actually didn't become what we are now til years after we broke up. It was the posthumous growth after the LP came out that really made the band into a big thing. While we were playing, we were primarily an underground band with some buzz around it. Back then there was more of a definite separation between punk and indie and mainstream so we were operating in a small world. For example, at our last show there were about six or seven hundred people there, and that was probably the biggest draw we had ever had. We did play a lot—I think the grand total was 130 shows (give or take) in two years, which is quite a few. The legend grew afterwards, much like bands like the Misfits or Minor Threat who became much bigger posthumously than they ever were while they were playing.

The Thing That Ate Floyd

LK 011 was Lookout! Records' most ambitious release up until that point and the most important for things to come. *The Thing That Ate Floyd* was thirty-four tracks on a double vinyl LP. The original release was billed as "34 California bands on two LPs . . . that's 83 minutes o' noise." This 1988 compilation was a grand cross section of the rich punk landscape of the day, with an illustration of the "snakey" by David Hayes. Hayes was the driving force behind the compilation, completed after briefly quitting the label and being coaxed back by Livermore. In the liner notes, he says, "Lots of bands should have been on here, but just imagine trying to organize this mess, and you might better understand why bands like MDC, Tally Hoe, Reason to Believe, Offspring, Jackson Saints, Crummy Musicians, all the great Santa Rosa bands and so on and so forth didn't quite fit," which also serves as a testament to how big the project became. The fourth full-length for the small label led to eighteen of the thirty-four bands eventually releasing individual records for Lookout! as well. Among the bands scattered across the epic compilation are various short-lived bands as well as others who moved on to longer, respected careers, such as No Use For A Name (featuring Stikky's Chris Dodge in its earliest lineup). *The Thing That Ate Floyd* is a time capsule of a very particular sound, place, and era and is best listened to in one sitting to truly appreciate the scene.

Neurosis

Blending into the East Bay and Gilman scene with a style unto their own, Neurosis was beginning to find their feet with the jarringly heavy attack they produced on the ten-minute *Aberration* 7-inch (**LK 012**), a release packed with intensity and rolling melodic bass lines in unison with crashing drums and throat-heavy vocals. The dark punk aesthetic on the band's 1987 debut LP *Pain of Mind* (Alchemy Records) was the stepping stone to a whole tapestry of groundbreaking music, pioneering a sound that incorporated various genre elements into a heavy musical soundscape.

Chad Salter (Neurosis): I didn't realize at the time that the band would or could hold strong and really make something out of it. We ended up doing the *Aberration* EP a few months before I was voted out of Neurosis, and Steve Von Till came in. There was a big style change along with a new outlook of what they wanted to achieve. I really didn't know what I was up against, just a young kid in the great Bay Area as a member of one of the most influential bands and pioneers of a sound that gave insight into what can be achieved.

Crimpshrine: Second Chances

Since being stranded mid-tour and recruiting Paul Curran to replace Pete Rypins, Crimpshrine had remained active, although without the extravagantly busy four-string work from the ex-bassman. With their next release, a four-track EP called *Quit Talkin' Claude* (**LK 015**), the band proved that they had not dumbed down or become irrelevant.

Paul Curran (Crimpshrine, Monsula, Go Sailor): Trying to fill the shoes of Pete Rypins was intimidating, to say the least. Besides being impossible to imitate, I also felt that his bass parts were his and not something that someone else should even try to play. So when you listen to the Crimpshrine stuff with me on it, it's pretty obvious that it's a different, and not nearly as good, bass player.

Recorded in January 1989, once again with Kevin Army engineering, the EP had a heavier emphasis on introspection. The opener, "Butterflies," an ode to simpler times, recalled the feeling of childhood with unison whistling, which distanced itself somewhat from the ramshackle early days of the band.

Paul Curran: I've always hated the whistling bit on "Butterflies." Jeff would do it along to the song when we practiced, but I always thought it should be this ethereal thing in the background. When it came out way up front and loud—with a lot of the out-of-tune-ness being on my part—I couldn't bear it. Still can't to this day.

Without the meandering bass lines and wandering musicianship, it stood to reason that they were a different band in their second incarnation. Jeff Ott's growing lead guitar breaks were evident, especially on "Inspiration." The lyrics were unguarded, with honest conviction and emotion. Ott was no stranger to emotional and heartbreaking conditions. From a young age, on and off, the frontman spent nearly a decade homeless.

Jeff Ott (Crimpshrine, Fifteen): I was raised in a family with an abundance of violence and sexual abuse where all the adults and some of the kids were addicts, so I tried my best to stay out of there. Those problems got in the way of the band in a lot of ways.

Paul Curran: We played a few local shows; we moved to the world's tiniest warehouse in Benicia, which was my hometown, and then the band kinda fell apart. I think there were some personal issues between Jeff and Aaron [Cometbus], and then there was an incident where Jeff took some money that belonged to the band, and that was the end of their friendship and the end of Crimpshrine. Jeff decided to play a final Crimpshrine show on his own with his friend playing drums, which, obviously, was an extremely fucked-up thing to do. For me, though, the breakup of the band was hard to process. We had gone through a lot together, and I felt a tight kinship with Jeff that was a little bit hard to let go of—maybe because we hadn't had enough time to learn each other's bad side.

Green Fever

Green Day: 1,000 Hours

Chris Appelgren: I first encountered Green Day when Lawrence brought a tape of their forthcoming EP to play on our radio show; they were still called Sweet Children at the time. My point of reference was that John ["Al Sobrante"] Kiffmeyer from Isocracy was the drummer. It was just great melodic and emotionally raw punk.

Green Day dates back to 1987 when two fifteen year olds, Billie Joe Armstrong and Michael "Mike Dirnt" Pritchard joined up with Kiffmeyer, who was three years older. An enthusiastic Livermore, whose well-documented "golden ears" for talent latched onto the band in its earliest days. With punk influences leaning towards the Midwestern melodic sounds of the Replacements and Hüsker Dü, the young band quickly carved out its own personal teen angst sound with masses of melody folded into a mix of youthful romance.

Even though they were young, the band struck a chord with the audience of 924 Gilman Street, under the guiding hand of Livermore.

Chris Appelgren: They were always a very well received live band—maybe some of the SF super punk *MRR* types didn't think it was punk enough—but Gilman kids really loved them and weren't hung up on how legit they were or weren't.

Robert Eggplant (Blatz): Early Green Day shows had appeal with punks and the outcast urban mutants. They had twice as much appeal with suburbanites; some of which are punks or misfits or mutants, but most seemed to be pretty normal people. Green Day were fucking naturals. Back then and I still see it now. Billie and Mike are a hot knife and butter.

During this time, Appelgren stepped up to work more closely on Lookout! releases while covering the label's weekend mail order. One of his first hands-on projects was the 1989 debut Green Day 7-inch EP, *1,000 Hours* (**LK 017**).

The art for *1,000 Hours* was handled by Hayes, without much enthusiasm, although one thing that stood out on his plain sleeve was the classic, original Green Day typeface. Some limited clear and green vinyl versions were pressed (along with subsequent vinyl colors) and several different colored sleeves—the available paper color often dictated the final artwork for a Lookout! release. The record was far from slick sounding, even with sugary sweet melodies and passionate vocals of Armstrong.

The Lookouts: Spy Rock Redux

After a three-year break between albums, Livermore and the Lookouts returned with album number two, *Spy Rock Road* (**LK 018**). To say the band had stepped up since *One Planet, One People* would be an understatement. Compared to their previous output, it showed many hours of solid practice.

With Kevin Army on board as a contributing musician and engineer, the eleven tracks on *Spy Rock Road* boasted wild upbeat execution, varying tempos and song lengths, and a fine smattering of improved musicianship from the still-teenaged Kain Kong and Tré Cool. Another guest on the album, playing guitar on the tracks "Living Behind Bars" and "Sonny Boy," was Operation Ivy's Tim Armstrong, featured alongside the shared vocals of all three members—each adding their own lyrical explanations on the very green foldout insert that came with the LP.

Livermore had added some interesting and sonically pleasing moments to the album, with Middle Eastern sounding guitar work on "Alienation" and engaging storytelling amid an upbeat, yet haunting piece of songwriting on "The Green Hills of England." The Lookouts had proved their knack for creating progressively more and more catchy writing—as showcased on the jaunty "Living Behind Bars"—and the future of the band looked increasingly more and more inviting.

Also adding to the green was the cover of *Spy Rock Road*, a scratchy yet detailed tribute to Livermore's Northern California stomping ground. In fact, it was probably Lookout!'s best looking album sleeve to date.

Hayes Departs

As 1989 rolled on, bringing the decade to a close, Hayes was increasingly unhappy at the label. Even with Livermore continuously persuading him to stay—the conversation had cropped up many times before his departure from Lookout!—Hayes officially bade farewell to Livermore and Lookout! Records in 1990, reputedly over a simple handshake—something that would not only haunt Hayes in the future but create fuel to throw at Lookout! later down the line, as their success escalated.

Robert Eggplant: The issue of *Lookout* zine where Larry announces David's departure is actually pretty graceful. Knowing how much David has maintained resentment to this day, yet Larry made the announcement with care and respect. There is a lot of heartbreak and disappointment to be found making a DIY project and pinning hope on small groups of young artists.

As 1990 rolled over, Livermore found himself the lone figurehead of Lookout! Records, with some apprehension about how to proceed. He even toyed with the idea of ending the label. During this time, Hayes had been putting together his own creative outlet, dubbed Very Small Records: a label that would not only preserve the connections with his projects for Lookout! but also live up to his desire to concentrate on the more diverse aspects of the underground, while still utilizing his own fantastic artwork and "out there" humor.

Chris Appelgren: When David split, Lawrence asked me to design an ad for *MRR*. I remember him saying he'd need more help with art stuff without David, and I was really enthusiastic about that. He also got some help from Aaron Cometbus, and I think John Yates did some ads too. I probably aped his style a little too much, thinking it was Lookout!'s style, because I was such a fan of his art. He didn't stay in touch. I mean, I'd see him at Gilman shows, but David could be snarky in *MRR* ads—which was sort of a language of their own at the time. But as far as walking out on a million dollar deal, maybe David did do that. If you look at the early releases, you can see which ones were Larry's and which were David's, and one of the last things David was supposed to do for Lookout! was the layout to the Corrupted Morals album—and it got delayed a few times because he just, for some reason, kept not finishing it.

Green Days

A record release show was organized at 924 Gilman for the next several Lookout! releases, featuring all the bands from **LK 021–024**. Each of these bands would go on to have their own impact on the music scene, creating success and longevity for Lookout!, splintering into other scenes, and having lasting influence.

Green Day, 1992 at 924 Gilman by Murray Bowles, Courtesy of Anna Brown

Chris Appelgren: I remember going to the record release show with Larry. It was the record release for Neurosis's *Word as Law*, *39/Smooth* by Green Day, Samiam's *I Am* EP, and the first Mr. T Experience 7-inch. Larry really wanted Green Day to play second to last, right before Neurosis, but Billie Joe was really nervous and uncertain about that. He felt that the Mr. T Experience was a much bigger and more established band, and Green Day should play before them, but Larry was insistent that because they had released an album, they should play after the Mr. T Experience. The show was huge and totally sold out. Neurosis played *Word as Law* in its entirety in order, plus their Joy Division cover. I sold merch for all the bands, and we sold so much stuff. I remember driving home in Larry's red Toyota truck pulling money out of all of my pockets to count. I counted over $3,000, which was more money than I'd ever seen—I couldn't believe I had it stuffed in all the pockets of my crummy pants. It was unbelievably exciting. I didn't know how successful the label or bands would be, but I knew that it was the most exciting and interesting thing to me in the whole world.

Robert Eggplant: An early sign of how big it was heading was when some kids painted themselves green and went to school. By then there was an air of fanaticism that was palpable. But it was hard to be lost in that fever. Billie Joe's non-show demeanor is so down-to-earth. And their brand of punk was spreading to other aspects of our scene, not just the bands—but our vision and lifestyle. *Revolution*. It did happen. What was unforeseen was the legions of Green Day imitation bands and songwriters.

Appelgren's first full-fledged foray into album art was the inlay for Green Day's debut album *39/Smooth* (**LK 022**). With plenty of "in-scene" touches—local band names on the instruments of the cartoon-style drawings of the band members, as well as a Puddle sticker in tribute to his own fanzine—the opportunity to be working not only for a record label but also on such an awaited release was a fantastic time for any music-loving teenager.

Mr. T and Samiam: Black and Blue and Other Colors Too

Also on board for new releases were the already-established Samiam with the *I Am* 7-inch (**LK 024**) and the Mr. T Experience with their *So Long, Sucker* 7-inch (**LK 023**). The Mr. T Experience (MTX) had just parted ways with their label, Rough Trade US, who had folded around the time of the band's last release, *Big Black Bugs Bleed Blue Blood* 10-inch (later to be reissued as **LK 145**). Without a label, MTX had entered the studio for a session that produced a seven-track demo to shop to labels—including a semi-interested Sub Pop Records. Two tracks from that session, "So Long, Sucker" and "Zero," became their aforementioned Lookout! debut single.

Samiam's connection with Lookout! was a no-brainer, even though the band was already signed to local label New Red Archives. Samiam took shape after the demise of Isocracy and consisted of former members, Martin Brohm and Jason Beebout, as well as guitarist James Brogan and

Sergie Loobko, the drummer of the seminal East Bay pop-punk band Sweet Baby Jesus but who moved to guitar for this project.

James Brogan (Samiam): After Social Unrest was finished playing together, I started looking around for people to form a band with. I had met Sasha Loobko—Sergie from Samiam's twin brother—and we liked a lot of the same bands and started jamming a bit. He's a very talented and great guy, but for whatever reason, we couldn't get the right personnel to join us. We actually jammed with Cinder from Tilt at one point. In 1988, I saw the early incarnation of Samiam play, and it was what I wanted to do, and I hit it off with all the guys. They were just losing Ryan, who played guitar, and it sort of fell into place. We all wanted the same thing—to tour a lot, record, and to basically stay busy—which we did.

On the original album artwork of Samiam's debut 7-inch with Lookout!, the word "Sam" fell off, and the band left its title as *I am*. Jason Beebout

Mr T Experience, December 8, 1989 at 924 Gilman by Murray Bowles, Courtesy of Anna Brown

found his unique voice as frontman. Following his time in Isocracy, he created an earthy, rich vocal style that would, over the next decade, influence many fledgling bands. Their rock-influenced sound plugged into speedy, tight, pop-punk melodies resonated throughout the 1990s, sparking its own scene.

While Samiam went on to enjoy a long and celebrated career away from Lookout!, the Mr. T Experience debut, *So Long, Sucker* was the foundation of a relationship that would stretch many years. The band was pivotal in pioneering the pop-punk sound that would spread globally. But as influential as they were during the upswing of 1990s punk culture, the Mr. T Experience never really got their due.

The main and ongoing voice of the band was Frank "Dr. Frank" Portman—a self-dubbed name left over from his former KALX radio show. Dr. Frank helped to solidify the first lineup of the Mr. T Experience before the East Bay pop-punk scene had begun to make waves, or even before Lookout! existed. He'd been playing with the Bent Nails—alongside future Mr. T Experience bass player Byron Stamatatos—before meeting guitarist Jon Von Zelowitz at the University of California. An introduction to drummer Alex Laipeneiks ignited the first lineup of the Mr. T Experience in 1985.

Frank "Dr. Frank" Portman (MTX, The Bomb Bassets): I knew Larry, slightly, long before there ever was a Lookout! or an MTX. I never had any interest in "the scene" per se. For me it was always mostly about figuring out a way to get the songs out there. "The scene" wasn't something I believed in anyway; it was just a bunch of bands. I liked punk rock, but it wasn't a lifestyle or an ethos or anything like that.

Through local airplay and live shows, MTX secured a following and debut album—at an impressively fast rate—with local label Disorder Records. Released a year after their initial formation, *Everybody's Entitled to Their Own Opinion* (later **LK 039**) was the first in a long line of memorable and clever songs coupled with Dr. Frank's humorous and quirky lyrics.

The New Lineup

College Dreaming

During the summer of 1990, Chris Appelgren felt the urge to distance himself from Livermore and Lookout!—trying to balance studying with the full-time weekend job at the label was weighing on him. While attending a summer college program in Arcata—where Livermore was also residing for the summer—Appelgren decided it was time to throw in the towel at Lookout!.

Chris Appelgren: I felt a little overwhelmed by Larry's expectation of me to make time to stuff 7-inches and do mail order when I was in this school program, and he could be very melodramatic. I basically told Larry I thought I needed a more conventional job.

Around this time, the label received a letter and package from another young follower, Patrick Hynes, a year or so older than Appelgren. The drawings and fanzine in the package impressed Appelgren and Livermore.

Chris Appelgren: I remember the package and how cool his art was. Pat [Hynes] was at college at Berkeley, and I was in my last year of high school.

Soon after, Hynes met Livermore during a meeting for volunteers at Berkeley's community station KLAX. While the older punk label owner was hitting it off with the young artist, Chris Appelgren was spending the next few months searching for gainful employment without much luck.

But with Livermore still actively working on new music in the Lookouts and Appelgren failing in his quest to find a "normal" job, it wasn't long before the two were collaborating again. A combination of having spent the summer months away from the label and Livermore's declaration that Appelgren was needed at Lookout! motivated Appelgren to jump back into the work. With Livermore now back at UC Berkeley finishing up a degree that he'd started in the early 1970s, Lookout! got a new Berkeley office in the form of a studio apartment that had come into Livermore's possession. Now, also on board, making the label a three-man operation, was Patrick Hynes, helping out on art tasks.

Chris Appelgren: I recall a number of conversations where I said that I wanted to go to college to figure out what I would do with my life, and Larry would always say that college was not a time to "figure yourself out," that I should just work to do what I really wanted to be doing. He meant this in a working class way—this is an opportunity, and don't miss it by figuring out if it's what you want to do. It was then around Christmas break 1990 that I met Pat. He came up with Larry to hang out when we did our radio show, and then the two of them stayed over at my house afterwards, and we worked on art for an *MRR* ad.

Appelgren and Hynes were fast friends. Easygoing and laid-back Appelgren found that the quiet, intelligent, and friendly Hynes aided the operation to no end. With the new Lookout! space in operation, the new dynamic of Livermore, Appelgren, and Hynes was the nerve center for the label over the next three years.

Larry Livermore: [A] profit sharing plan was instituted in 1991 [that] covered both [Chris Appelgren] and Patrick Hynes, who were Lookout!'s only employees at the time. There were two reasons for it: (1) Basic fairness—the workers who help create the wealth deserve to share in it; and (2) at the time I couldn't afford to pay them much more than minimum wage, so profit shares were an alternative form of compensation.

As a result, Hynes and Appelgren slowly began to own pieces of the rapidly growing company.

Chris Appelgren: We had a desk that was a door on two filing cabinets and another couple of doors on cinder blocks as a mail-order table. It was a tiny room with a bathroom behind a sliding accordion door. Long hours and lots of conversations—just Larry, Patrick, and me. Patrick and I spent a lot of time together, but often it was quiet working. Or, either Larry or myself—who I had maybe inherited some of his ability to talk at great lengths—would blather on. Patrick would often listen, and when asked to contribute his opinion on a subject, he would say something with a great economy of words. Pat was awesome, he was an inspiration to me personally. A very talented artist, a great musician, skateboarder, nice understated guy. . . . With three of us, it was kind of perfect for the work that needed to get done. Larry was the leader, Pat was the meticulous doer, and I was kind of the face to it all. As I learned how releases were scheduled and project managed, I was the one talking to our manufacturers, printers, and Ruth Schwartz at Mordam about scheduling. I felt challenged and inspired by Pat, but in the best possible way. He was way more of a teammate, collaborator, conspirator.

More Mix-and-Match Lineups

Fuel/Skinflutes/Monsula

Fuel played live shows on the Gilman stage at the beginning of 1990, supporting some touring bands such as No Means No and the Doughboys, and they shared studio time for their *Take Effect* 7-inch (**LK 026**) with the Skinflutes, who were recording their 7-inch, *Sawhorse* (**LK 029**).

At the time, Skinflutes drummer Scott Pelkey was sharing duties with another band, Monsula—a punk rock troupe with members from the mid-eighties band Poultry Magic. Paul Curran of Crimpshrine had been among the early members of Monsula.

Paul Curran (Crimpshrine, Monsula, Go Sailor): Monsula had already had a couple of different bassists before I joined. This band was very much in the right place at the right time. People were craving "East Bay" pop-punk—even though the band was from Benicia, which is technically not part of the East Bay. The band was pretty awesome live, mainly because Paul [Lee] was an excellent singer and had stage presence. I only played with the band a short while before I had to follow a vision quest to Dublin, Ireland. When I got back, the *Nickel* EP had just come out on Lookout!, and I was blown away at how awesome the side was with the new bassist, Bill Schneider.

Split into two sides of different sessions and members, the *Nickel* EP (**LK 027**) was Monsula's first solo release following their appearance on the Very Small *Coffee* compilation and the Absolutely Zippo compilation tape, *Time Capsule.*

Filth

Preempting other East Bay hardcore bands, and carving out its own style of hard-edged punk, Filth was another Lookout! band composed of members from other label bands and the local scene. After the breakup of Isocracy in 1988, Lenny Johnson had bumped up against Jake Sayles, a scenester and Crimpshrine accomplice. Filth took a much harder approach than that of its predecessors.

Lenny Johnson (Isocracy, Filth): I met Jake because of Isocracy, and we ended up getting our first house together—The Ashtray—in Oakland with Jesse Michaels. I'm foggy on exactly how we met Jim [Gray], but he moved here from Canada. We were the original three to put Filth together. I wanted to be in a band with a more aggressive sound, punch, or whatever. We just wrote stuff that we thought would sound good, and yeah, I took the sound more seriously.

Chris Appelgren: Filth was a force to be reckoned with, awesomely loud and brutal. They would get crazy fans from all over—kids were obsessed with Filth and for good reason.

On the band's debut in 1990, *Live the Chaos* (**LK 030**), Filth delivered a sharp shock that was not present in the aforementioned outfits. The 7-inch EP was noisily proud and lived up to its name. Housed in a cover penned by Operation Ivy's Jesse Michaels, the sound of the EP evokes mohawked, disgruntled kids in the pit.

Blatz

An export from Philadelphia, Jesse Townley found kinship in the walls of 924 Gilman Street after relocating to San Francisco in the summer of 1989 for the Anarchist Gathering and to join an art magazine. Attending Gilman to see MDC perform as part of the gathering, the young East Coast punk never left. Already well-versed in the punk world, having been involved in local shows since 1986, Townley changed the format of his *Philly Zine* to match his new location: *Berkeley Sucks*.

Jesse Townley (Blatz, The Criminals): Joey [Perales], Eggplant, and Marshall [Stax] were practicing in the side room at Gilman, and I walked in. They asked me if I wanted to sing for their band Blatz. I said sure, took out some lyrics from a three-month band I'd had during my three-month college career in 1988, and that was it. We decided to invite our friend Annie [Lalania] to join the band, but we all got confused and asked both Anna Joy Springer and Annie, and they fit in perfectly to our mismatched barrel of chaos, shrieks, and nudity.

Anna Joy Springer (Blatz): I knew Jesse a tiny bit. He was booking at Gilman, and I was starting to do that too. He wanted me to come join the band. The other members of Blatz wanted Annie. Annie and I knew each other from over the summer, and we loved each other so we told them we were both staying. Annie and I just told them what was going to happen—if they wanted one of us they had to take both.

Not unlike various other local bands of the time, Blatz had manic and chaotic live shows involving props and nakedness. As Isocracy had in the years prior, Blatz made it a priority to always entertain whoever showed up to watch them play.

Jesse Townley: I want a crowd to leave a show remembering our band—love us, hate us, whatever, I don't care—just don't shrug and say, "eh". One of Blatz's friends was this guy Kevin Dill. He would show up to our shows with inflatable sheep stuffed with rancid calamari or huge stuffed animals crammed with old fast-food garbage and hand it over to us to inflict on the crowd. Add in me getting naked, Anna and Annie growling and screeching respectively, and all the rest, and it was a pretty insane scene.

Working with Kevin Army, Blatz recorded five tracks released as the *Cheaper than the Beer* 7-inch (**LK 031**). The band captured the chaotic nature of their live set. With no less than eighteen "fucks" in the first three tracks, they were quick to shatter any hopeful views of the world, especially on the Lalania/Springer penned track, "Lullaby," a sobering adult take on the world to the children of tomorrow. The chaos surrounding the band also appeared to linger offstage, with the Kevin Army–manned sessions in the studio becoming more like babysitting sessions.

Jesse Townley: He was able to make us shut up and make decisions about our records. Blatz was six roommates who were always bickering. In a recording studio, that was a recipe for insanity and/or homicide. Kevin Army—like all good engineers—is also a master of the following:

When a band member asks, "Can we hear it with more [fill in the blank]?" and he knows it's a bad idea, he'll fake like he's moving the dial slightly, and then say, "How's that?" The band member invariably says, "Sounds much better!" I love that trick.

The environment surrounding Gilman was setting itself apart from the broader punk scene. As the 1990s came into view, the scene Lookout! was documenting was not only a quality network but a collection of unique talents.

Deepening Roots

Fifteen

With Crimpshrine in the grave, Jeff Ott put together a new band that he guided in the direction Crimpshrine had been taking since the *Quit Talkin' Claude* 7-inch. Fifteen wasn't actually meant to be a band at first, but on the way home from the Crimpshrine tour where Paul and Jack Curran had joined the band in Chicago, they spent many hours together in the back of a Pinto. Jack Curran had recently stopped drinking and using drugs, which captivated Ott as much as Ott's classic rock guitar riffs captivated Jack. Before long, they were trading sobriety lessons for guitar lessons and had informal plans to start a band together. By the time they got back to California, their new band, Fifteen, was born, despite neither member having a place to live.

Paul Curran (Crimpshrine, Monsula, Go Sailor): Most people just accepted that band as the next incarnation of Crimpshrine when Jeff and my brother started it immediately afterwards, which I found very annoying. Jeff changed the way he sang, there were a lot more songs about girls, and the Jimi Hendrix–style riffage. It sounded nothing like the rest of what Crimpshrine did.

Jeff Ott (Crimpshrine, Fifteen): A few things happened. First, there was no longer a person in the band maintaining overly-strict control of what was written, so it was kind of free to do whatever anyone wanted. Second, I gradually lost the ability to sing as I did in Crimpshrine. The amount of time I could sing before I would lose my voice got shorter and shorter until I couldn't do it at all. Third, I started hanging out with Jean Repetto and learning tons of stuff on guitar and that really changed my writing more than anything.

Ott would begin flourishing more on guitar with lead riffs and delicate intros as the band recorded their four-track self-titled 7-inch (**LK 034**). The four tracks highlighted a mid-paced band with extended songwriting, as opposed to the growling punk shrapnel produced by Crimpshrine. With Andy Ernst manning the studio desk, it was a nice composition with enough Crimpshrine-type grit in the production to not cast Fifteen as a new, slick answer to Crimpshrine's past.

Andy Ernst (Sound engineer): I remember when Jeff from Fifteen came into the studio, he hadn't bathed in a couple of weeks and didn't believe in wearing shoes.

Green Day

Local heroes Green Day had also been keeping in everyone's eyesight, and with *39/Smooth* their stock rose even more. Because of the general consensus among peers and fans—interestingly, a sound that was further "punked up" *after* mainstream stardom—it made sense to keep the material coming so they recorded a second 7-inch for Lookout!, the *Slappy* EP (**LK 035**), which provided further proof that the magic on their first full-length hadn't been a fluke. The EP featured a reworking in style and tempo of Operation Ivy's "Knowledge." The nod to the band's peers also continued on into the future, with the cover appearing in live shows throughout the years.

But then the original lineup hit a wall of differing priorities. Cofounder drummer Al Sobrante went out of town for college while Armstrong and Dirnt wanted to focus on the band full-time. Sobrante was also keeping himself busy with his own political agenda in the local punk scene. Reluctantly, they began considering new drummers to fill in during Sobrante's absence, with the plan for it to be a temporary arrangement.

John Quittner (Brent's T.V.): Everyone from Isocracy was in a new band that was doing well—Green Day, Samiam, and Filth—but Al had a real chip on his shoulder about Samiam not really being punk, being clearly ambitious, and so on. He used to picket their shows and fight with them. I always wondered if Al was a little insecure that people didn't think Green Day was "real punk" or whatever. He was literally holding a picket sign inside and outside Gilman; it would say things about how Samiam was selling out the scene and fucking Gilman over. According to him they had a five-hundred dollar guarantee, which at the time would get you called a sellout, obviously ironic considering Green Day's future . . . though I remember Martin eventually coming over and squabbling with him . . . "We don't have any guarantee when we play Gilman!" but arguing with Al was pointless.

Jason Beebout (Samiam): John [Al Sobrante] made T-shirts to sell outside our shows that said "greed" at the top over a little blurb about how people could find out more about our outrageous five-hundred dollar tour guarantees by calling our booking agent. I think it even had his phone number on there. At the bottom of the shirt he put our logo upside down. I don't know if that was for artistic reasons or if it was supposed to create some kind of inverted-cross vibe. The shirts were ten dollars. Pretty steep for a shitty band shirt in those days. I bought one though. What's ten dollars when you're raking in that kind of dough? I think I still have it. I'm pretty sure John bought a house with his Green Day earnings. Maybe he put tinfoil over the windows to punk it up a bit.

Late Night Laundry & Brent's T.V.

Halloween night 1988 marked the official live debut of a band in Arcata, a college town located in Humboldt County. The band in question had already been learning the ropes by playing in laundromats while piecing together their lineup, finally deciding on Brent's T.V. as the name. John Denery—the younger brother of Dallas Denery and the frontman for the Berkeley-based Sweet Baby Jesus—was the catalyst.

John Denery (Brent's T.V., Judy & The Loadies, Ne'er Do Wells, The Hi-Fives, The Bomb Bassets): Dallas always shared his music with me. He had a very organized collection of cassette tapes, hundreds of them, and when he went to college he kept feeding me tapes for the next few years—lots of early rock and roll, then lots of early blues, then punk rock stuff like the Ramones and Buzzcocks. The next phase of tapes was Berkeley bands like Soup, Crimpshrine, the Mr. T Experience, and, of course, Sweet Baby Jesus. Dallas would invite me to his shows, which was awesome. I had a nice brother who didn't mind hanging with his fifteen-year-old younger brother. I thought Sweet Baby Jesus was the best band I had ever heard or seen. During this time, we used to hang out with Virgil Shaw, who had the greatest voice, and we somehow got him to join us, found Brian Keeney and Jon Quittner, and that was Brent's T.V.

John Quittner: I believe they were one hundred percent unamplified at the time, two guitars, banjo, harmony singing, and Brian on low tom and spaghetti pot. The treble factor was off the charts, but it never occurred to me that they "needed" bass. I ran into John Denery in a burger joint and was minorly starstruck.

John Denery: Someone described us as the Kingston Trio trying to do Ramones songs. Acoustic guitars, a banjo, stand up drummer who used a kettle and a bike horn. We toured the West Coast only playing laundromats. We started in Arcata and played one laundromat in every town up to Crescent City.

John Quittner: I believe that the laundromat show tradition was an extension of Berkeley punk culture as absorbed through John [Denery] and Brian, but it translated well in Arcata. Sometimes the squares and older people kind of dug it—it was punk rock, but that band was a truly good time, not abrasive as such and owed enough to Jerry Lee Lewis and the Everly Brothers that it was understandable to a lot of people.

John Denery: It seemed like an obvious, best thing to do. Laundromats were always open, all ages could go, it had a wall socket and a built-in audience. Plus, clubs were too big for us, but we could fill a laundromat. The first one went well enough that we started doing them more often which inspired the song "Laundromat." Our friends would bring their laundry to our shows while we played.

John Quittner: We drove to Crescent City and played every rural laundromat we could find all the way back to Arcata. That tour included one non-laundromat attempt to play underneath the giant Paul Bunyan statue in Klamath—which is where the photos on the *Lumberjack Days* single were taken.

The seven-track 7-inch EP *Lumberjack Days* (**LK 036**) was the follow-up to a self-recorded tape of a live set at a party. The record introduced excitable, hip-swinging sounds unlike any other band on Lookout!, in a style reminiscent of rock and roll chipmunks. Brent's T.V. was lost on some people, especially *Maximum Rocknroll* staffers, who were unsure at what speed to even play the 7-inch.

John Quittner: We did one proper tour, in the winter of 1990/91, and Brian wouldn't come, which was a great shame because he embodied a lot of the spirit of that band. Six people in my 1978 Toyota Corolla liftback with a little fez on top that held what little equipment we could bring. Thank god Aaron Elliott came as our roadie. Green Day canceled but surprised us by showing up for the second half of the tour, screwing up most of the shows. In Vancouver, me and Virgil packed Green Day's car in ice and snow during their set. It froze overnight, and when they received a call at 6:00 a.m. insisting that they move it because it was in the hotel manager's parking spot, they received an impossible, frozen surprise.

CD Nation: MTX

After the Mr. T Experience christened their name on Lookout! vinyl, they went to work on their debut full-length, piecing together thirteen tracks culled from a couple of different sessions, titled *Making Things with Light* (**LK 037**)—the cover of which featured a cool retro-looking picture of the band on a Lite-Brite toy. It was the first Lookout! album to be released on CD.

Even though Lookout! had half-joked that they would never release a CD, once the format was out, the sales spoke for themselves. The punk-unfriendly compact disc soon outsold the vinyl releases, inspiring a massive reissuing of successful LP releases like Operation Ivy's—and Green Day's, which was already selling over 30,000 copies in its first year of release.

Aaron Rubin (MTX, Samiam): It was kind of controversial because at that time, CDs were still kind of suspect in the punk rock world. I think it's a pretty cool record, although obviously leaves much to be desired in terms of recording quality. It has a good spirit, though, and [Dr.] Frank's songs are good.

Still in the early days of the label, with the bands essentially relying on DIY promotion, the Mr. T Experience found themselves out on a tour in support of the album, pushing their wares with little promotion.

Aaron Rubin: There was no such thing as promo in those days for bands like us. This is before Lookout! was a real label. They just pressed the records, we sent out a few promo copies to college radio stations, and that was it. I remember we did a joint mailing with Mel [Cheplowitz] from Shredder [Records]. He had just released some Shredder compilation, and we did a joint mailing with him to save on postage costs.

The End of an Era

With all the admirably eclectic records that Lookout! had been putting out, one of the first stepping stones in the Lookout! history—the Lookouts—was drawing to a close. The Lookouts' final release was the *IV* EP (**LK 042**), with an early-style sleeve adorned with a hand-drawn California map, courtesy of the young resident label artists.

Trying to expand the Lookouts' sound, Livermore talked Billie Joe Armstrong into adding his skills to second guitar—the first time Armstrong and Tré Cool played together.

The hiatus was fuelled by Kain's move to Germany for an extended period. Although the band never officially ceased to exist, the next decision had an enduring effect, at least for Tré Cool. Encouraged by Livermore, he tried out for the now drummerless spot in Green Day. He clicked with the band, joined Green Day, and the Lookouts drifted away into the mists of punk folklore.

Crowd, March 28, 1987 at 924 Gilman by Murray Bowles, Courtesy of Anna Brown

8

Building Community

The Shit Split

In the tradition of the punk rock split record, the Filth and Blatz *The Shit Split* LP (**LK 043**) captured a great moment in local musical history in 1991—on what was surprisingly Lookout!'s first split release. The side labeled *A Touch of Blatz* was everything any fan of the band could hope for, a thorough stroll down a familiar punk shambles lane that highlighted the band's great chemistry.

Jesse Townley (Blatz, The Criminals): On one of the songs, "Cockroach Café," I think, there's a line by Eggplant that says "I'm a vegetarian." That's actually the tail end of a long joke or story about a vegetarian vampire he insisted be laid over that track. The rest of the band vetoed it, and I am so happy we cut that, thank goodness, but that was the kind of thing that we argued about in the studio during mixing.

Jesse Townley: Eggplant and I did our half of *The Shit Split* booklet in a rush. The cover was more Eggplant than me. We did our booklet overnight, I remember that much.

Robert Eggplant: We agreed to give Chrisser [Chris Appelgren] the duty of designing the cover of the Blatz side. There was a Kinko's on the western side of [the] UC Berkeley campus on Oxford Street, one of the first twenty-four-hour photocopy places where we printed the booklet. The Crimpshrine song "Sanctuary" relates to that spot. At the time, there were a couple of older punks who ran the show. They both wrote for zines and both died horribly within a few years. A couple years later, I picked the photo for the CD version and the Lookout! empire did the design. I understand Anna Joy held resentment with that cover since it doesn't have any of the women on it.

Filth marked their territory with an extended session of street war songs called *Destroy Everything*.

Lenny Johnson (Isocracy, Filth): As far as the release of the split was concerned, it was great, no hurdles or bullshit, just straight in-and-out recording. Lookout!'s concentration of the bands it was releasing was by design—I believe—to give a sense of community, and it did to a point. But the label was growing and bands were coming and going and heading in different directions. Lookout! until right around there was made up of relatively young bands.

Lenny Johnson: [Filth and Blatz] played together a lot, not just at Gilman but [at] other parties and such. The split when it came out didn't seem to really be such a big thing at home. I really noticed when we were on the road, some of the kids knew our stuff, and to that effect even more after we had broken up. Touring with Strychnine and floating from state to state there is some sort of Filth shit floating around every venue, small and large even all this time later, so I guess along the way it hit pretty good.

Chris Appelgren: I spent sixteen hours at a copy shop printing the booklets for the original pressing of *The Shit Split*. Jim [Gray] from Filth came by in his truck and hauled boxes of pages back to my house where we convened later that night to collate and staple them, [and] then send them off to the pressing plant. We stayed up all night—Joey [Perales], Jesse [Townley], Eggplant, Patrick [Hynes], and myself—drank Blatz beer and put the inserts together.

The Shit Split was the first of what would become an important part of the label's makeup, with the beloved split release—a staple of the punk genre.

Can of Pork

Directly following *The Shit Split* came another influential record: the *Can of Pork* compilation (**LK 044**) released in January of 1992. This unofficial sequel to *The Thing That Ate Floyd* was the first big project that Chris Appelgren and Patrick Hynes were given free reign to work on. *Can of Pork* evolved into a twenty-nine-band release, featuring many Lookout! artists of the day, along with many up-and-coming bands and other East Bay punk outfits. Bands such as Jüke, the Wynona Riders, Spitboy,

Pinhead Gunpowder, Rice, and Jack Acid made their Lookout! debut on *Can of Pork* before continuing to work with the label.

Chris Appelgren: NOFX were supposed to appear on *Can of Pork*, and Fat Mike proposed [we use] a song from a band he was working with called Section 8. He came to the Lookout! office—Larry's studio apartment—to deliver the recordings and said NOFX weren't quite done with their track but that he'd get it to us before the album was mastered. He also really wanted Section 8 to be at the beginning of one of the sides. Then, Section 8 changed their name to Lagwagon, and the NOFX track never materialized. Pat and I were in LA to master *Can of Pork* with John Golden. Fat Mike said to call him at the studio to get their contribution, and I never got through to him. It seemed like a bait and switch at the time, but who knows? It is, though, Lagwagons first appearance on record.

While assembling the compilation, Appelgren and Hynes collaborated on the artwork—a fantastic and typical Lookout! illustration in pink tones featuring a pig (who would also go on to grace the Gilman Street flyer for Lookout!'s tenth anniversary show) holding a can of "human." The name was inspired by an old, yet real, can of pork that had been dwelling in Chris Appelgren's residence, The Big House.

The original LP featured a large booklet packed with band information and drawings, par for the course in those days. Among non-Lookout bands featured on *Can of Pork* were the hugely underrated One Man Running, The Lizards (who would go on to work with Very Small Records), and the Minnesota band—the Porcelain Boys.

BFFs

Along with working together on the *Can of Pork* release, Appelgren and Hynes had also been collaborating musically in a new band by the name Bumblescrump. The band formed after meeting with Josh Indar (future member of Black Fork). Without any prior musical experience, the introverted Patrick Hynes picked up the bass guitar and played alongside the pair, accompanied by mutual friend Theo, also on bass, rounding out the band as a four-piece.

During a drunken evening following their first recording session, Applegren experienced his first and only emotional exchange from his quiet label and bandmate friend.

Chris Appelgren: We were exploring some weird creek tunnel in Emeryville in the dark—the whole band was hanging out basking in the glory of our achievement—and he stopped me and said something like "Chris, man. You know what? I fucking love you man!" I said, "I love you too Pat." He said, "No, wait a minute. I'm serious. I fucking love you." I started to get nervous as we were getting left behind by everyone else and said, "Pat, I get it and I mean it too, I love you too, but we should fucking hurry or we are going to be left in this weird underground tunnel in the dark."

Making Waves and Burning Buildings

Green Day: On the Verge

With a new lineup and ever-increasing following, Green Day was on their way to making their first major waves with their sophomore full-length *Kerplunk!* (**LK 046**) in December of 1991. Newly recruited Tré Cool on drums made for a slicker, tighter beast of a band.

Chris Appelgren: Tré was a much more accomplished drummer and really fit the culture of the band. He had the same kind of humor as the other guys. John [Al Sobrante] went to college at Humboldt State and tried to stay in the band, but as I understand it, it was kind of impossible for them to wait for him to come back for shows. Knowing Tré from before when he was in the Lookouts, he was just a really funny, charismatic guy.

The relationship was evident on *Kerplunk!*, an album that burst with up-tempo melodies, ("2000 Light Years Away," "Welcome to Paradise," "One of My Lies," "Words I Might Have Ate"), emotional angst ("Christie Road," "80"), and even a foray into humor ("Dominated Love Slave"). The band's production—assisted by Andy Ernst—was cleaned up from earlier releases, though it lost some of the romanticism of earlier tracks like "1,000 Hours" and "Disappearing Boy."

Andy Ernst: Green Day were some funny kids, and by funny I mean they were all comedians. Mainly Mike [Dirnt] at first, but when Tré joined the group the comedy was nonstop. They were easy to record, they were fast, they knew what they were doing, and most of Billie's vocals were first takes.

The new streamlined three-piece kicked off the album's release with immediate success, as was expected given the hype surrounding the band since *39/Smooth*, instantly selling out *Kerplunk!*'s initial run of 10,000

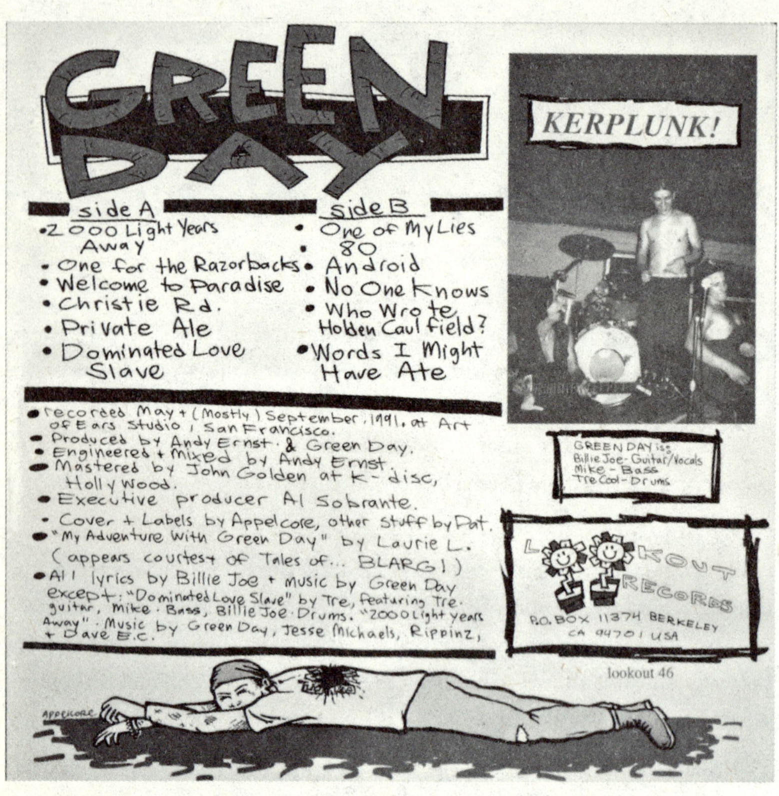

copies. As the band's profile increased, so did the attention of music press and industry types looking for a new face and sound.

Chris Appelgren: With *Kerplunk!*, Green Day was clearly the most successful band signed to Lookout! at the time. The band was loved locally, able to play all the time and draw a crowd without fail. Green Day came by the Lookout! "office" a lot, and I remember joking with Tré about how they would sign to a major label and would split the money with Lookout!—basically laughing about how ridiculous that was and how it might be funny to take advantage of a label's deep pockets.

Nuisance: Out of the Woods

Another outfit hailing from Humboldt County, Nuisance captured the sounds of their surroundings—the rural forested country in mountainous Northern California. The country locals were outsiders in the urban scene of Berkeley and Lookout!, but through live shows the band had picked up a local following, especially from playing frequently in Arcata.

Andy Asp (Nuisance, The Pattern): Well, it's very remote. . . . It's a very beautiful area naturally, but culturally it was, and I imagine still is, kind of a backwater. But because there was a university, bands did come through, and Arcata had a decent, small scene. It was a weird mix of weird goth girls that liked the Cure or Violent Femmes, some hardcore fans, but mostly a bunch of thrash metal dudes. Pretty standard for rural Northern California in the eighties and early nineties.

Jesse Wickman (Nuisance, Fifteen): Arcata was cool. I moved from there in 1989, but Nuisance played up there a lot since we all grew up in Humboldt. We were pretty popular up there since we knew so many people.

Andy Asp: We played Gilman quite a bit and with quite a few Lookout! bands—Green Day, Neurosis, the Wynona Riders, Fifteen. Monsula ended up becoming very good friends, and we did some touring with them. Gilman was a lot of fun—it was definitely a clubhouse in those years . . . a shithole, but it was our shithole. If Lookout! had any kind of "sound," we were definitely at the fringe—both musically as well as geographically.

With their Lookout! debut LP—1991's *Confusion Hill* (**LK 048**)—Nuisance put out thirteen tracks of top-notch rasping alternative punk, layered with accurate, busy drumming and powerful melodies. Challenging rhythmic bursts were coupled with backwater grit, creating an album ahead of its time for punk audiences preoccupied with Operation Ivy and MTX.

Andy Asp: Working with Lookout!, we were thrilled to say the least. I think we did okay. Being from the redwood forests up north, I think we had a different voice than the suburban angst of the time.

Five Years Strong

On Sunday, October 20, 1991, Lookout! celebrated its fifth anniversary by hosting an all-day musical matinee at 924 Gilman. The bands that performed gave their profits to the Gilman Street Project, raising a few thousand dollars for the club. Even so, attendance was thinner than expected due to an escalated grass fire that had spread from the Berkeley Hills into Oakland that day.

Chris Appelgren: It was crazy. There were burned pages of books, still readable but just cinders floating down from the sky. I had to leave the show early and miss Samiam because I had to go home to make sure my apartment wasn't burned down!

Also that year, an anti-Lookout! show was advertised. A bit of friendly punk heckling, it wasn't strongly attended. Two people who did attend, however, were Chris Appelgren and Patrick Hynes, who handed out fake recording contracts and candy to the audience who had turned up to see the headliner, 23 More Minutes.

Breakups: MTX

Although a fair amount of material had appeared by the Mr. T Experience over the years since the band's 1986 inception, there had also been a recent period of inactivity leading up to the band's fourth (second for Lookout!) album *Milk Milk Lemonade* (**LK 049**), with Kevin Army producing.

Frank "Dr. Frank" Portman (MTX, The Bomb Bassets): I will say there isn't another record like it for better or worse. Extremely ambitious considering our limited budgets and talents. It was a bit ramshackle, but each of those records has a distinct "mood" to it, and it was the result of a very conscious attempt to make that happen within our means.

The band's backseat approach, coupled with no touring in two years, had seemingly made MTX disappear. But with a new record, and inspired by Green Day's recent European tour, MTX headed out to Europe in 1992 to support the new album. Unfortunately, the tour stretched internal relationships further than could be sustained. They returned barely on speaking terms, which led to a breakup.

The Year of the Weasel

Aside from Green Day, one band was becoming synonymous with the world of Lookout! throughout the 1990s, influencing not only the world of punk, but also the way the label would operate and thrive: Screeching Weasel.

The first incarnation of the band came together in 1986, in a Chicago suburb called Prospect Heights. Coworkers Ben "Weasel" Foster and John "Jughead" Pierson paired up with drummer Steve "Cheese" Dubick, making a trio with Weasel on bass and vocals. But, lacking the ability to play bass and sing, Weasel handed bass duties to another local, Vince "Bovine" Vogel. This lineup recorded their self-titled debut with Chicago's Underdog Records.

John "Jughead" Pierson (Screeching Weasel, The Mopes, Even In Blackouts): In really early interviews with Screeching Weasel, I loved sharing my influences. Ben would say the Ramones, and I would say Queen and Jethro Tull. I liked that dichotomy. I liked the Ramones, too, and Circle Jerks and Angry Samoans and Adrenalin O.D., but I didn't want us to be pigeonholed. I love punk rock, but it made more sense to incorporate all my influences and to try to start over and do something different—which was Screeching Weasel's intention in the eighties.

The debut was a raw experiment, speedily recorded for around two-hundred dollars. There are traces of melodies that would become prominent in later works and played well locally. With most of the tracks barely hovering over the minute mark, it was an energetic attack of crude four-chord punk tunes. As they evolved as a band, Screeching Weasel attempted to disown their early output, with Ben Weasel citing this recording as being unrepresentative of the legacy created by future releases.

Warren "Fish" Fischer (from the Ozzfish Experience) quickly replaced Bovine after the self-titled debut, and they recorded a second album—which was, in the eyes of some, the band's first real album—*Boogadaboogadaboogada!*, originally released on Roadkill Records in 1988 and later re-released as **LK 062**. Shortly after that, the lineup changed again with Brian "Vermin" McQuaid replacing Steve Cheese, and then Dan "Vapid" Schafer replacing Fish. But Screeching Weasel was getting strong and finding its sound, even though the constant lineup changes made the band appear unstable.

Dan "Vapid" Schafer (Screeching Weasel, Sludgeworth, The Queers, Riverdales, The Mopes): I was asked to audition as a singer in a local hardcore band called Generation Waste. Screeching Weasel and Generation Waste did a show together in 1987, and I caught a ride back to Chicago in Ben's car because he, John [Jughead], and I all lived close by in neighboring suburbs. On the ride home, Ben had played some new demos that Screeching Weasel had, and I was really into them. I remember really liking the song "American Suicide," and thought it was better than anything that the other local bands were doing at the time. That is where I became a big fan of Screeching Weasel and knew they were on to something. Soon after that, Generation Waste was in the studio trying to make a record, and it was just a disaster. Not too long after, the band was done, then Warren [Fish] left [Screeching Weasel], and Ben needed a new bass player. Ben and I were like-minded about the kind of music that we wanted to play, and we were from the same area. I was just learning bass, but he let me in anyway.

With the new and improved lineup, the band headed back into the studio to record the first release with what became its classic nucleus. The six-track 7-inch EP *Punkhouse* was released 1989 on Limited Potential Records (and later re-pressed by Ben Weasel, and again by Selfless Records)—and showcased a pop edge emerging for the band.

Dan "Vapid" Schafer: When I joined Screeching Weasel in 1989, the band had done just one tour prior. We played locally a few times at a place called McGregor's, but my first actual tour with the band was in Ben's car, and we had no equipment. We just packed our guitars and some merch and left for the West Coast. Our first show of the tour was in Corvallis,

Oregon and it took about forty hours to drive there. Our next show was at Gilman. On the way there we blew a tire. We brought the tattered tire on stage that night. Jesse from Operation Ivy and Jake from Filth had spiked their hair and were in the pit. The next show, we traveled up to somewhere in Northern California and played a show with Green Day. Screeching Weasel and Green Day stayed at Larry Livermore's house that night. He lived way the hell up in the mountains, and there was snow everywhere. I thought we were going to slide off the road and die that night.

After the tour, Screeching Weasel broke up. Vermin and Vapid kept busy with Sludgeworth—later coming out with **LK 131** *Losers of the Year*. Ben Weasel and Jughead went on to form Gore Gore Girls, and Weasel played guitar for the Vindictives. Screeching Weasel appeared to be history.

But two years later, in 1991, a one-off Screeching Weasel reunion was organized with profits going towards debts incurred by the band. With a successful return under their belts, the conversation turned to putting the band back together. Everyone was in agreement except Vermin.

Brian "Vermin" McQuaid (Screeching Weasel, Sludgeworth): I declined because Sludgeworth was moving along nicely, and I had a lot of input on what Sludgeworth did. In Screeching Weasel you just rode in the backseat while Ben drove. Also, Screeching Weasel was going a very Ramones route, and truth be told . . . I hated the Ramones. You have to take into consideration my age at the time. I did my first tour with Weasel when I was sixteen! So at age eighteen, I ruled the universe in my little brain. I got a taste of self-induced success—as far as Chicago punk goes—and didn't want to just ride along.

They recruited Dan "Panic" Sullivan on drums. Ben Weasel moved full-time to vocals, with Dave "Naked" Lally on bass and Vapid on second guitar.

The songs on Screeching Weasel's third album, *My Brain Hurts* (**LK 050**), were written in sessions between Weasel and Vapid.

When Livermore offered a record deal for the new release, Ben Weasel wanted to drop the Screeching Weasel legacy into the ocean and start afresh with a new name, but Livermore was insistent they keep it.

The new contract also stipulated that the older track "I Wanna Be a Homosexual" be included on the record.

John "Jughead" Pierson: I remember Lawrence taking Ben and [me] out for pizza, the decision to keep the name the same seemed to become a bigger deal with hindsight. The wheels were in motion for the record to be released by Lookout! under the name Screeching Weasel prior to the recording. We promised the song "I Wanna Be a Homosexual" to Bruce LaBruce; it wasn't left off as has been claimed: we chose to give it exclusively to Bruce. We knew it was a good song. Lawrence almost canceled the deal based on this, but it went through.

Dan "Vapid" Schafer: I remember thinking in a small way that the band had made it—Screeching Weasel was the first band outside the East Bay to have signed to Lookout! Records. We had stopped in San Francisco in the summer of 1991 while on tour to record *My Brain Hurts* with

Andy Ernst at Art of Ears Studio. I thought it was cool to record in a city other than Chicago, where all these bands from the East Bay and other Lookout! bands were recording.

John "Jughead" Pierson: I often talk about how we were struggling on a tour, and then one day we had a show in Philadelphia in some dingy bar called The Flame. I thought, oh my god no monitors, no audience, just another day, and then hundreds of people showed up and were singing our songs. All because of the release of *My Brain Hurts* on Lookout!.

Following *My Brain Hurts*, the band replaced Dave Naked with a new bass player named Scott "Gub" Conway. Conway continued with the band for the following two tours, prior to his leaving before they went on to work on their next full-length, *Wiggle*.

Scott "Gub" Conway (Screeching Weasel, Even in Blackouts): Dan Panic and I were roommates and previous bandmates in a band called Ivy League. I was going to roadie and drive them for a tour. Well, things worked out that I would just play bass as well. Every day we were having a good time, in my book. I always got along with everyone. There was always someone who wanted to try and argue with Ben. They would try but they always would make themselves look like an ass. I think for everyone at that time things were not so P.C. You were not so concerned about saying the right thing to not offend someone. There were no publicity machines pushing shows and records for punk rock. You had *MRR* and a dozen local fanzines as your PR. Your local promoter was contacted on a payphone. Better bring a map, there was no GPS and definitely no big label advances. We were all doing this on our own, with our own finances. Building networks from friends. The world we lived in was falling into destruction, and we were all pissed off. With that in mind, there was a real sense of humor invoked as well, just to keep our sanity.

Crowd, June 14, 1987 at 924 Gilman by Murray Bowles, Courtesy of Anna Brown

Love Is in the Air

Jüke & the Wynona Riders

Taking a break from learning the business side of the label, Chris Appelgren attended a Bratmobile and Tiger Trap show in Sacramento. Molly Neuman, the drummer of Bratmobile, met Chris after the show, and they hit it off at a local donut shop.

Chris Appelgren: We hung out, and I got to be friends with Molly. We were then penpals for a few months, I'd write letters to her that would arrive before she'd get to towns on the tour she was on. Our relationship grew from there. We moved in together in 1993 and got married in 1996.

While the future spouses were dating, more and more bands were turning up with the classic Lookout! logo on the back of their records. The next two releases were from Jüke and the Wynona Riders, bands that had made their Lookout! debuts on the *Can of Pork* LP. The Wynona Riders formed back in 1987 but weren't immediately active in the live scene.

In the early years, the band—originally called Miss Conduct—changed its lineup so many times that all of the original members were gone, and Ron "Skip" Greer became the only consistent member. Greer had put together a live show for Miss Conduct, and chatting with Jesse Townley of Blatz, he mentioned that he wanted to be in a band called the Wynona Riders. Townley promptly changed the band's name on the flyer to the Wynona Riders without telling them. The name stuck.

Jüke was cut from the same punk cloth as the Wynona Riders, with Richie Bucher performing in both bands. The groups were some of Chris Appelgren's early hands-on projects for the label.

Chris Appelgren: Jüke had the craziest shows at Gilman—barbecuing chicken outside the club, their singer, Nick, wearing a full-body nude suit and using a wireless microphone, having a pig's head on a stick inside Gilman that I think they also blew up. Nick would always go around the sparse audience and sing right into the faces of each of the people there.

Their two releases came as two 7-inch EPs in 1992—the Wynona Riders' *Some Enchanted Evening* (**LK 052**) and Jüke's *Don't Hate Us Because We're Beautiful* (**LK 053**). Both were examples of the early nineties East Bay punk sound—melodic, gritty, and energetic with plenty of tongue-in-cheek undertones.

Chris Appelgren: Skip, Richie Bucher, and I drove down to LA to master the Wynona Riders' and Jüke's EPs. We ran out of gas on the way home in the middle of the night and had to push Skip's car to the next gas station.

Ron "Skip" Greer (The Wynona Riders): We were driving back from mastering, espousing the scene and how we were going [to] define it, and we got so caught up in deep philosophical discussions about how we were going to change the world that we forgot to get gas and found ourselves stuck in the desert . . . which about sums up my entire experience with Lookout!.

Skip was known to have some harebrained ideas, with one instance in 1993 that included the singer asking Appelgren to design a campaign brochure for his run for Mayor of Alameda.

Chris Appelgren: He was quite serious, but then, quite frankly, it's hard to tell with Skip. It could have been some elaborate sort of performance art. There was a huge sense of irony in everything he was involved in. I never knew if it was intentional or not.

Ron "Skip" Greer: I ran for mayor of Alameda, California, in 1994. I came in third with 738 votes—which was 700 more than I expected to get.

A few years later, in 1996, Skip took an interest in the rising popularity of the internet. Although unskilled in this area, he proceeded to form a web company with another friend. One of the early projects was what then became the first Lookout! Records website.

Rancid: Keeping It in the Family

With Operation Ivy off the scene, several bands popped up in the wake of the ska punk pioneers—the Dancehall Crashers, Downfall, Big Rig, and a short-term band, Generator, formed by Operation Ivy guitarist Tim "Lint" Armstrong. As Generator was winding down, Armstrong spoke to Appelgren about a new band, Rancid, that he was putting together with Matt Freeman of Operation Ivy.

Chris Appelgren: The East Bay scene was still sort of its own bubble at the time. Things hadn't gotten too crazy, so it was natural for us to talk to Rancid about doing a record. I don't know if any other labels talked to them at the time, but it seemed like it was really important for Tim to avoid as much of the hassle and bullshit that went along with the personal politics of being in a band. I don't know what his experiences were, but it seemed like he wanted to focus on working with people he could trust rather than scene veterans. We had these cool plans for them to go in and record a bunch of EPs over time and then to release a CD album collecting all the tracks, hence the title, *Single #1*.

Armstrong and Freeman inducted drummer Brett Reed into the ranks initially, creating a power punk trio along the lines of the scrappy upbeat music played by Crimpshrine or Grimple. Rancid turned out some quality local live performances attended by Appelgren prior to the release of what would be a self-titled 7-inch EP (**LK 059**) in 1992.

Chris Appelgren: The band went into the studio and cut ten songs for a five-song EP and even fitting that many songs onto the record sacrificed the sound quality a great deal. I remember going back and forth with Tim [Armstrong] about that, but ultimately he decided it was a better deal to get more songs and shittier sound than better sound and fewer tracks.

Andy Ernst: Years after the fact, Tim told me that he was nervous the first time he recorded with me, but I never noticed it. I did notice that their bass player, Matt Freeman, was awesome. Rancid knew what they were doing too, so everything moved quickly. All of the earliest Lookout! recordings were on a tight budget so everything had to move fast.

Rancid became a more streamlined and polished punk machine following the release of the EP, with the decision to move to Epitaph Records for their debut full-length.

Chris Appelgren: The guys came in and told us that they were going to sign with Epitaph, that they felt like the label really believed in Rancid and were enthusiastic about the band. They liked the idea of working with such a great label and roster.

Full Tilt

But Lookout! had other projects to worry about, including another East Bay band about to launch its debut—with a vocalist from Nebraska named Cindy Morgan, later known as Cinder Block.

Cinder Block (Tilt): I had moved to San Francisco in the mid-1980s with a band I started called the Spam Grenades. That band blew up in a drug haze, and I ended up in the East Bay living in a huge punk/hippie/artist warehouse called Phoenix Ironworks, where I met Jeffery Bischoff. There was a lot going on at the time. Green Day was still living in a warehouse down the street from Phoenix Ironworks, and we heard rumblings about them, but I hadn't seen them yet, and Operation Ivy had been the big thing at Gilman, but they had just broken up. Tim Yohannan had been sued over some kid breaking his leg in the pit, and Gilman had to close for a while. Since Honey and the other Gilman bookers suddenly had no venue, we started hosting shows in the back room of Phoenix Ironworks.

It wasn't long before Bischoff and Morgan became partners in business and in romance. They got married and cofounded Cinder Block, a T-shirt screen printer, and opened a stand on Berkeley's Telegraph Avenue.

Cinder Block: I started rising from the ashes to stretch my voice and seek a band once more and had been in an East Bay project with the twin brother of Sergie from Samiam. Jeffery finally decided to pick up an electric guitar again after having forsaken his punk roots in favor of jug band acoustic for a while. Then we met Pete Rypins of Crimpshrine and Vince Camacho—who had been in Operation Ivy precursor Basic Radio—through the burgeoning "Gilman crowd," and we started jamming. When the guys from my other project saw Tilt at a band practice, they just bailed in the realization we had something good going. We started playing shows at Gilman and around the greater Bay Area.

Caught in a whirlwind of early energy, Tilt recorded a demo at Palo Alto's House of Faith, producing brilliant, upbeat, gritty short bursts that would resurface later in songs like "Crying Jag" and "White Homes." Not long after the band's first studio foray, Samiam guitarist Sergie Loobkoff recommended the screen printing services of Cinder Block for the label's merchandise.

Cinder Block: Jeffery and I were trying to be productive members of society by starting the T-shirt company and working on Tilt. Lookout! was our first major account, and we were pretty stoked to be printing shirts for the bands we'd enjoyed on their label. I'm not really sure how Larry's interest got piqued about the band, but we definitely started an association with Lookout! bands as well as being a part of the Gilman scene. I remember Larry coming to a Tilt practice and saying how he thought we were too slick, but he signed us anyway.

Tilt, March 29, 1992, by Murray Bowles, Courtesy of Anna Brown

Chris Appelgren: Lookout! began using Cinder Block for printing purposes around the time that we started working with Tilt, and I just remember that they were really committed to the band and worked very hard—even coming to our warehouse space and helping me stuff 7-inches.

Four of the House of Faith session tracks made it onto Tilt's debut vinyl release in 1992, a self-titled 7-inch EP (**LK 061**) with powerful vocals and a weaving, catchy backing band. Accomplished musicians already, the band was aided by Rypins's bass work, on-the-mark drumming from Vince Camacho, and Jefferey Bischoff's guitar.

Cinder Block: Everyone had already cut their teeth on the punk scene, and it gelled in a way we didn't expect. You have to understand that right before pop-punk took hold of the Gilman scene, the East Bay was coming out of a period where speed metal and thrash metal ruled, and that's how we ended up recording at Bart Thurber's House of Faith—we had heard of this recording studio where a lot of these hair-jockeys recorded. I had recorded at friends' houses up to that point, so I was pretty stoked to be able to use a real microphone to lay down vocal tracks. I just remember looking at the many pornographic Meat Shits album covers on the walls as I sang.

Tilt, November 7, 1992 at 924 Gilman by Murray Bowles, Courtesy of Anna Brown

Follow-ups

Another Year of the Weasel

Following the success of *My Brain Hurts*, Lookout! reissued their out-of-print second album, *Boogadaboogadaboogada!* (**LK 062**) with Lookout!. With the original release on Roadkill Records, a UK licensed pressing on Wetspots Records, and a very different sleeve image, the album was available on CD and cassette for the first time. The original Roadkill release was only pressed once and many of the records were destroyed while the band was driving in Florida.

John "Jughead" Pierson (Screeching Weasel, The Mopes, Even In Blackouts): We toured in a mailbus and had a big white carrier thing we attached to the roof. We had hundreds of copies of the record up there, and they all melted. In Pensacola, we did a free show where we gave away hundreds of unplayable records.

For the Lookout! release, Appelgren adjusted the cover from pink to green, featuring the now iconic smoking Weasel, and added the band's logo and album title.

Chris Appelgren: The album was always a big seller, and Ben always thought it was just because of the fact that their logo was huge on the cover, hence other albums featuring the weasel head prominently. The cover art for *Boogadaboogadaboogada!* suggested that it was *the* definitive Screeching Weasel album.

Although the destroyed records incident made that version of the album a lot more collectible, the most prized possession remains the Screeching Weasel / Ozzfish split 7-inch from the earliest days of the band. Originally advertised on a show flyer for the record-release event, the band received the original test press of the 7-inch, which was going to be a press run of five hundred. Although the sleeves were printed—all five hundred—the pressing plant burned down following the test press, and the record was never pressed. The test still exists, in Jughead Pierson's possession, comfortably hidden away alongside the five hundred unused sleeves.

During Screeching Weasel's early days, pre-*Boogadaboogadaboogada!*, the band struck up a friendship with Massimiliano "Mass" Giorgini, a Lafayette, Indiana, punk who played in Rattail Grenadier and owned the all-ages punk club, Spud Zero, which he'd opened with his college savings.

John "Jughead" Pierson: Mass was there from close to the beginning. I had sent him a demo before we had a record out. He called me up one day, and I remember being in the bathroom, and my roommate handed me the phone. It was Mass, calling from Lafayette, and he said he loved our demo and wanted to book a show with us in Lafayette at a place called Spud Zero. He had a contract with one of my favorite punk bands at the time, Toxic Reasons, so I said yes. He introduced us to the singer's brother Dave Best, who lived in Chicago, and then he contacted us to start a label—Roadkill—where me and Ben [Weasel] would offer up bands, and then Dave would offer up bands. We put out *Boogadaboogadaboogada!*, and he offered up Rattail Grenadier's first record. So we started playing some shows together, and we hit it off with all of them.

Mass Giorgini (Rattail Grenadier, Squirtgun, The Mopes, Screeching Weasel, Common Rider): The first involvement I had was with helping the bands get bookings in the Midwest. Larry and I started communicating via snail mail late 1987. I first heard of Screeching Weasel in 1987, too. Future Squirtgun singer Matt Hart—who was one of my best friends and in several bands that played my club, Spud Zero—went to an acting camp in the summer of 1987 and met Portia Graham, who later became Ben's first wife. Portia and Ben were already dating, and she took a cassette of a couple of Screeching Weasel demos to camp with her. She played them for Matt, who said he thought I might want to put on a show or two for them. So she gave him her copy of the tape, and he mailed it to me. I listened to it and loved it. The Rattail Grenadier singer, Steve Best's older brother Dave, talked to me about wanting to start a label—he had the money, but not the time or desire to run it. I knew Ben and John wanted to do a label, but didn't have the money, so I connected them and Roadkill was born.

The Giorgini name became known in the local scene through the Spud Zero club, Rattail Grenadier—with Mass's brother Flav, and through the face of their father, celebrated Italian artist Aldo Giorgini. Mass Giorgini soon discovered studio engineering as a way to record and support local bands, which would flourish to become Sonic Iguana Studios.

The first studio work Mass did for Lookout! was Screeching Weasel's follow-up album to *My Brain Hurts*, 1993's *Wiggle* (**LK 063**). The writing process for *Wiggle* was a collaborative effort, but with the added pressure of the success of *My Brain Hurts*.

John "Jughead" Pierson: Johnny thought what worked on *Wiggle* was that Dan [Vapid] and Ben [Weasel] got along well. Ben also would leave rehearsal early, and then the rest of the band would jam for hours. We liked playing together, but that record was our first pain in the ass. [It was] the moment I felt like an actual band—loaded with pressure. *My Brain Hurts* was literally an overnight success. Ben and I then let Lawrence reissue *Boogadaboogadaboogada!*, which easily topped *My Brain Hurts*—so the pressure was on to create a good record.

Much like the transition from *Boogadaboogadaboogada!* to *My Brain Hurts*, the songwriting continued to evolve, with the pop sheen sanded down and a tougher, edgier sound added. The melodies remained firmly in place, as is evident on pop-punk tunes "Like a Parasite" (cowritten with Joe King), "One Step Beyond," and the cover of "Ain't Got No Sense" from Canada's Teenage Head—a band cited as a major influence by Ben Weasel.

Nuisance: A Common Aesthetic

After studio clashes over their debut album *Confusion Hill*, Nuisance returned to the fold with their sophomore album, *Sunny Side Down* (**LK 064**), this time with the better-suited studio pairing of Andy Ernst. The jarring, country-tinged, rambling punk-folk group managed to capture some magic with the sessions, adding some points of departure from their debut record with a nice measure of punk angst and alternative rock.

Andy Ernst: By the time I recorded Nuisance, it was clear to me that there was no particular Lookout! sound. It was a wide variety of styles. Every member of Nuisance was very good, but Andy [Asp's] voice was special, unique and unforgettable.

Andy Asp (Nuisance, The Pattern): While folks might remember Lookout! for a certain sound, I think Larry was always looking for some common aesthetic, rather than a sound. It was definitely a changing of the guard—these were the new kids coming to offer an alternative to the pretty violent punk scene still lingering from the hardcore years.

Fifteen: Gas Money

Fifteen's second full-length expanded on their first, *Swain's First Bike Ride* (**LK 040**), to greater effect. With a new lineup, Jeff Ott had created a tighter and more technical album, even experimenting with some double kick drum rhythms on *The Choice of a New Generation* (**LK 065**). The 1992 album was predominantly upbeat and left little room for the older influences of Crimpshrine and earlier Fifteen. Drummer Mark Moreno was a rock sticksman complete with a huge kit, but after a big tour he'd been asked to leave the band. Jesse Wickman of Nuisance was asked to jump aboard, and with only two rehearsals was quickly thrown into a twenty-eight show, thirty-day tour.

Jesse Wickman (Nuisance, Fifteen): The tour was great! Jeff nor Jack [Curran] had their driver's license, and when I joined, they got a big check from Grass Records and had me buy a van and register it in my name so we could go on tour. They also gave us enough money for some new gear. Jack got a nice bass rig, Jeff got some new guitar stuff, and I got a bunch [of] new drum stuff, which I still have to this day. Kids really loved Fifteen on that tour, we had a lot of really great shows.

The check was an advance for Fifteen to do their next two albums with Grass Records. The band released both, *Buzz* (1994, later rereleased in 1996) and *Surprise* (1996), following the 1994 *Ain't Life a Drag* 7-inch on Iteration Records. To clarify matters to their fans, they spelled out their decisions in the song "The Deal."

Jeff Ott (Crimpshrine, Fifteen): In between *The Choice of a New Generation* and *Buzz*, the van died, and doing *Buzz* on Grass was the only option that involved enough of an advance to buy another van. It also got me the first decent amp I ever owned, which was a really good thing. This is the only reason why *Buzz* and *Surprise* were not on Lookout!. It had nothing to do with the label. The label was great until Larry left much later.

Chris Appelgren: Fifteen was a great band musically but, back then, did not seem very organized. Still, it was disappointing to lose them, but I recall us feeling like it might make things easier and that Grass was going to have their hands full.

Simultaneously and unknown to Appelgren, both Jack Curran and Jeff Ott had kicked hard drugs and were much more equipped to handle the band's business in their new states. The band booked some well-attended shows and incorporated a stage act of getting naked in front of

the audience. With Curran now only on black coffee, Wickman found it difficult at times, leading to some inter-band issues.

Jesse Wickman: Jack and I butted heads here and there. When we got back from that tour, we were going to record an album, but we had no songs to record—which ended up being *Buzz*. Jack wanted to write these songs in a week and record them before we went to Europe. I suggested we go to Europe, play a month's worth of shows with the new songs that we could write before we went to Europe, and then record there. Jack did not like that idea, he wanted to record before we went. He said he wanted the money from Grass ASAP, and that's why he wanted to record *now*! At that point, I hadn't heard from them in a couple of weeks, and we were supposed to go to Europe in about five or six weeks. They wouldn't return my calls or anything. Finally, I got a hold of Jack, and he told me they had found a new drummer—which was the dude on *Buzz* and [*Extra Medium*] *Kick Ball Star*. The funny thing is, I had the van and all the gear up in Santa Rosa, and they had to find someone with a license to come get it.

The Queers and Queercore

The Queers

Walk into any punk event in the 1990s and you were sure to see at least one person wearing a T-shirt for the Queers.

The original lineup of the Queers was created in Portsmouth, New Hampshire. Much like Screeching Weasel, the Queers evolved through various lineups and changes behind one front man, Joe "Queer" King. Bonded through their mutual love of the Ramones, Black Flag, booze, and drugs in the mid-eighties, the original lineup didn't last long before imploding due to arguments and personal issues. But first they recorded some material that was not released until many years later. The second version of the Queers was Joe King, Hugh O'Neill, Kevin Kecy, and JJ Rassler. This lineup lasted a bit longer, gigging in Boston dive bars. One of these bars was immortalized on the track "I Met Her at the Rat." Playing alongside punk legends like the Dickies and the Ramones, the band was a party outlet for its members, and they became accustomed to receiving abuse as part of their performances.

After another period of inactivity, King and O'Neill recruited teenager Chris "B-Face" Barnard, who clicked with their three-chord punk chaos. Around the same time, King heard Screeching Weasel, and he got in touch with Ben Weasel.

Joe King (The Queers): When we first met each other, Screeching Weasel wasn't really together and didn't have a record label. Then, a bit later, Ben told me Lookout! was putting out *My Brain Hurts*. I knew Operation Ivy and Green Day but didn't really know much about the label at that point. Then, about the time that *My Brain Hurts* came out, Ben had me send a cassette tape to Larry with demos on it—songs that ended up on *Grow Up* and *Love Songs for the Retarded* later. Larry called the café I used to own—I remember it was a Friday evening. My cook Don answered the phone and said it was Larry Livermore. I, of course, knew what that meant—though I'd never spoken to him—and he asked if we wanted to do a record with them because he liked our songs.

The record in question was The Queers' debut Lookout! LP, *Love Songs for the Retarded* (**LK 066**) consisting of sixteen tracks of painfully heterosexual, insulting, juvenile, vulgar, confrontational, yet catchy, punk. By Joe King's own admission, the band never set out to play anything other than three-chord "classic" punk, but with that in mind, the Queers were always able to bring out an element of melody that stuck with you. Weasel and King's punk sneers complemented each other, and the bands would become associated with each other. Lyrically and sonically, they were similar, with Screeching Weasel's "Cindy's on Methadone" and "Teenage Freakshow" running parallels with the Queers' blasts of snot punk like "Noodlebrain" and "Teenage Bonehead." As soon as *Love Songs for the Retarded* surfaced, the Queers hit the ground running. For several years after, not only did the release schedule kick into action, but the punk party lifestyle also went full tilt.

Chris "B-Face" Barnard (The Queers, Groovie Ghoulies, The Mopes): We partied like crazy. It's all I knew—I had no idea there were other punk bands that weren't like us. Where we come from, if you're into punk or rock and roll, you live it, although it's not necessarily a wise way to go about things. Lord knows Joe and Hugh did. I sort of just followed along, and it fit me perfectly because I was already into just going out and getting nuts. Those guys, though . . . wow. They took it to the next level and kept going. I learned a lot in my early years with the band—mostly what not to do. I generally just stuck to booze, although I got my first taste of hard drugs from those guys. But some of the best times of my life were with Joe and Hugh, and among those times are many parties and general idiocy. The early rehearsals, when we wrote most of *Love Songs for the Retarded*, will always be among my favorite memories. The craziest times should and will remain locked away in our brains, hopefully never to see the light of day. Hugh had been around the Boston rock scene for years, and saw all these guys like the Real Kids and even Aerosmith—he was dating Joe Perry's wife's sister—and various other bands just living the "rock and roll life." He had never been in a band that quite reached the level of success where they could tour as much as the Queers did, so when he was with us he took advantage of the situation and made up for lost time. That dude was fun, period. I was younger than Joe and Hugh, and I just wanted to have a good time, and I couldn't believe I was—eventually—getting paid to do so. Not much, mind you, and it was hard fucking work, but we definitely took time to live it up. Of course, there's a downside to living like that. It will catch up to you, sooner as well as later.

Joe King: For *Love Songs for the Retarded*, B-Face, me, and my roommate Harlan rented a cargo van and drove out to Chicago. I drove all the way out and back. I was a madman back then. Larry was there, as was Vapid and Ben. We went to Lafayette to record at the original Sonic Iguana. Hugh had to fly out, but he missed his flight and finally made it to the studio around 3:00 p.m. on Saturday. We busted out all the songs, and the next day he flew out around 2:00 p.m. I did vocals, and we banged

it out quick. It was fun, though all of us in the Queers knew we could have done better at home. Still, if Lookout! was paying for it, we were honored to go do it. Ben was a real inspiration, as even then I highly respected his songwriting.

Pansy Division & Queercore

While queercore traces to Olympia, Washington, in the early 1990s, it was Pansy Division that brought the genre to the mainstream. The Bay Area band centered around two musicians, Jon Ginoli and Christopher Freeman. Guitarist and singer Ginoli had been a longtime member of the Outnumbered, an indie punk band from the mid-1980s. Having played over two hundred shows and released three full-lengths, Ginoli's experience proved vital to Pansy Division's business dealings.

Jon Ginoli (Pansy Division): It wasn't really my first label experience that was instructive, but rather watching other bands in the eighties indie scene make mistakes. Bands trapped into bad contracts, their records never coming out (or taking forever to), never getting paid royalties they were owed, or records going out-of-print with no way of getting them back into circulation. Those were things we weighed in selecting the kind of label we wanted to be on.

After the Outnumbered folded, Ginoli dreamed of an openly gay band that could rock out against preconceived stereotypes. In 1991, Ginoli brought bassist Christopher Freeman on board, and they began writing tunes. The early songs and live shows were more performance art than band, with Freeman and Ginoli singing over a drum track tape while multiple dancers created a spectacle involving props and silly string. At this early stage, the band had already contacted Larry Livermore with the concept of Pansy Division.

Christopher Freeman (Pansy Division): We did want to get better as a band. That was the deciding factor for Larry. We had sent him the tape, and he heard it and liked it, but we really weren't a band yet, so we had something to prove to him. Then we did get a drummer—Jay Paget—but he often had scheduling conflicts with his other band, Thinking Fellers Union Local 282. Later we picked up another drummer, David Ward—a bi guy who looked great with his shirt off—although he wasn't really a good match musically. We went with it because he had such a great attitude and was adorable as a person. Once we had a drummer in place that we knew we could potentially tour with, we got tight as a band by playing lots of shows. That's when Larry signed us.

The signing of Pansy Division took place in Livermore's apartment, with the band, Livermore, and Appelgren present.

Chris Appelgren: Jon [Ginoli] seemed to like our easygoing attitude about "signing" them, and they had the album completed, so it was pretty easy. The debut EP and *Undressed* were sort of a package, meaning we did the 7-inch to introduce the band but knew we were going to do the album.

Jon Ginoli: To me, being independent meant doing as much of it yourself as reasonably possible. Doing our own label would have been too much work, so we wanted to find an honest label with good enough distribution so that the records could find their way into the good indie stores. One reason we were so concerned about control was our subject matter. If someone else owns your songs and recordings, they can control what's done with them. We were afraid they might be used against us, made fun of by people who thought we were a joke, so we held tightly to our own control. This was our strategy to get our music out there, to give it the chance to catch on. In hindsight, it worked out about as well as it could have, for almost a decade. So much of a band's fate is up to luck, so we got really lucky, too. Our band materialized at the right time—being on Lookout! at that time. If we hadn't been on Lookout!, the Green Day tours probably wouldn't have happened, and who knows how differently things might have gone.

Christopher Freeman: I remember meeting Larry and Chrisser in Larry's dumpy little Berkeley apartment and thinking, WTF?! But they were passionate and had done so much with so little.

Pansy Division's 1992 *Fem in A Black Leather Jacket* 7-inch EP (**LK 069**) was a three-track affair that perfectly captured the sound of the band—melodic, hilarious, and catchy pop-punk. The band was openly gay—and played it up in an endearing way. One listen to "Homo Christmas" would set the record straight on the band's intentions. But they also felt like outsiders in the predominantly heterosexual punk world.

Christopher Freeman: We felt a kind of kinship to a lot of other bands on the label—and those on Mint Records—but we were always the odd sister out. We played a few showcases for the label, like CMJ in NYC, and while I felt the bands on the bill fit together somewhat—primarily in ideals, influences, and a spirit of fun—there was a certain feeling of not being totally accepted. It wasn't necessarily a conscious thing on the other bands' parts, just that most straight musicians didn't know how to relate to us. Except that we rocked, which we knew we had to do in order to get across. And we didn't ever try to change our sound or tone things down to fit in, either. In fact, we later did an about-face to keep from sounding too much like every other band on the label. For instance, while certain people at the label were trying to get us to use Mass Giorgini or Kevin Army, we opted for Steve Albini to sound completely opposite. There was one person in particular that was especially uncool to us: Ben Weasel. For some reason, he just hated us. And he nearly disowned Danny Panic for playing that Green Day tour with us.

Chris Appelgren: The songs themselves were provocatively playful with their overt sexual content, but that was also what made them interesting. I feel like all of the bands at times expressed this idea that they were outsiders. Maybe it was a stretch to be on a label with a band called the Queers that wasn't gay, but I thought it was pretty fucking brilliant myself and subversive.

Their follow-up full-length, *Undressed* (**LK 070**), arrived soon after. It was indie-pop friendly, with flashes of punk urgency and full of great compositions and off-the-wall humor. Keeping in spirit with the debut EP, the album featured a "reworked" cover (this was a continuing theme for the band throughout their career)—a version of the Ramones' "Rock 'N' Roll High School," which became "Rock 'N' Roll Queer Bar."

Sea Changes

Punk Goes to Campus

Through 1993 and 1994, the punk underground was undergoing change and upheaval. Profiles were raised for bands associated with the newly "discovered" Nirvana. Punks dug deeper into underground punk, much to Lookout!'s benefit. Major labels began to catch on after having a taste of how profitable the underground could be with a little retooling—they began sniffing around Green Day since they were an established phenomenon in the underground punk scene. Everyone in their proximity felt they were primed to go on to bigger things.

Chris Appelgren: Looking back, the signs were there. I did think it was telling that when my high school friends went to college, they all seemed to buy the two Green Day albums and Operation Ivy's *Energy*, when they hadn't been interested in them so much when we were in school together. With being involved with Lookout!, it was a vindication since no one in my small school was much into what I was. I mostly bonded with my friends around skateboarding, but punk was something that was sort of my own in the small rural area I lived in. Plus, I guess I wasn't paying attention so much to the world at large and wouldn't know how to contextualize it anyway.

Tilt

But Green Day was not the only band to leave Lookout! in 1993. Having built a healthy following through hard work and live shows, Tilt followed up their debut 7-inch EP by recording their first full-length, *Play Cell* (**LK 071**). The album featured fourteen tracks of their infectious, melody-heavy punk. Cinder Block's vocals sounded even more confident and powerful, especially on tracks like "Locust," "Yellow Bellies," and "Crying Jag"—a track that was featured on the soundtrack for the movie *Glory*

Daze. *Play Cell* was recorded at Sound and Vision in San Francisco and captures the grassroots essence of the band.

Pete Rypins (Crimpshrine, Tilt): I think the songs on *Play Cell* are good, but the sound quality is substandard. So I'm happy with the writing, but unhappy with the way it sounds.

Cinder Block (Tilt): Lookout!—at that time—was a small label and didn't have much money to spend on recording. The guy we found didn't really know how to capture punk rock, he had been recording a cappella gospel groups for a living. I was actually happier with the production of our demo at House of Faith. However, I think people responded to the passion of the songwriting, and I know people listened to *Play Cell* because now all of a sudden people were singing the words along with me at shows.

But, the punk rock landscape was changing during the "punk explosion" of the 1990s, and with it the attitude of bands and venues began changing, especially from the early 924 Gilman Street bands. Having seen interest and attendance blossom, many were ambivalent about the shift.

Pete Rypins: We played a lot with MTX, Green Day, Jawbreaker, Rancid, Citizen Fish, and Nuisance. There was a definite surge amongst all these bands in the scene that was weird, because it was such a commercial and very rapid ascent. We were playing these rock clubs that previously turned a blind eye to pop-punk music. Touring was no longer the exception, but the rule. There was pressure from the label to tour a lot. There was a cultural divide I could sense coming on. Believe me, I like to earn money—but the touring circuit that paid the bills was a much more "rocker" social scene than the one I grew up with.

With wider interest, Tilt decided to shop around labels, potentially looking to release the next record onto a larger playing field. Fat Wreck Chords had shown interest in the band already, and although there had been talk of a second LP with Lookout!, the band had not made any concrete plans and had been open about the plans for the future. Following a tour stint with Green Day, Chris Appelgren approached the band.

Chris Appelgren: I spoke with Jeffrey [Bischoff] and naively felt that Lookout! had been wronged by the band exploring their options. We arranged a meeting at a burrito place near the Lookout! office, and I let them know that we did not want to do the next album. It was a prickly conversation and I feel fortunate that the band took it so well, because things changed so much in the local music scene soon after that. Tilt had done well, due in large part to their hard work and dedication, and I don't think they expected that from us. We remained friends and supporters of the band and worked with Jeffrey and Cinder's merchandise company, Cinder Block, for many years.

Cinder Block: It didn't feel very good when they dropped us. But five minutes after we got home, Fat Mike was on the phone inviting us over to Fat Wreck Chords, and I'm proud of the work we did with Fat, so it all worked out for the best. It's also important to mention that despite the scene being supposedly "antiauthoritarian" and "nondiscriminatory," there were few female singers fronting punk bands. I was the only woman on Fat Wreck Chords for over ten years. I never admitted to myself sexism existed, and that's how I powered past it, but subtle sexism was and is still part of the hurdles female musicians must overcome. It doesn't usually come in the form of overt discrimination but is evident in the form of disregard. Some people don't even see you standing there unless you're selling your sex—promoting yourself with sexuality. I didn't wear push-

Tilt, March 8, 1992 at Your Place Too by Murray Bowles, Courtesy of Anna Brown

up bras or dominatrix boots in Tilt. It was a ripped T-shirt with lyrics scrawled over it, a boyish haircut, and converse sneakers, though I did wear miniskirts, but that was to beat the heat onstage. I have to say it was a trip when girls started showing up to Tilt shows looking like me. I wasn't totally original though. It was kind of a Gilman riot grrrl thing to wear short pink hair with plastic barrettes and popper bead chokers, but Tilt's touring spread the style in a small way. I liked candy necklaces too, but they melted on your neck in a club's humidity. Pop-punk was actually cutting edge for a little while. I've been through various incarnations of rock and roll in my life. The pop-punk scene seemed to value the feminine perspective more. That's why I felt at home there. Women didn't have a place in the thrash metal scene that thrived in the time between the seventies punk and pop-punk to grunge times.

Following Tilt's move to Fat Wreck Chords, and prior to stepping into the studio to record *'Til It Kills*, Rypins decided that his life in the increasingly popular band was finished.

Pete Rypins: I just wasn't comfortable moving on and building a career with Tilt. Heading into that second album, there were too many instances where I thought I was dumbing down parts in order to fit in with the other players' abilities. The less talented players definitely made up for the lack of aptitude by embracing commerce and networking into the rockish side of the punk scene, hence the rapid ascent.

Cinder Block: I really didn't care much who played what as long as they had fun onstage. The moment someone starts pooping their pants I get really bored. Life's too short to mope around.

The Splits

LK 073 was an odd pairing: a split Screeching Weasel / Born Against EP. Already New York hardcore heavyweights, Born Against had played some well-publicized live shows at 924 Gilman Street, with front man Sam McPheeters having already built relationships with the Bay Area scene. Through working on his own label, Vermiform Records, and through his *Maximum Rocknroll* columns, McPheeters was high profile in the Bay Area.

Sam McPheeters (Born Against): We met Screeching Weasel in Chicago on July 28, 1991. Sometime in late '91, Larry Livermore wrote an *MRR* column about Born Against, and we became correspondents. Larry told me once that Green Day had introduced him to Born Against.

For those accustomed to the Californian punk output of Lookout!, the EP seemed a little strange, but it made sense once placed on the turntable. Both bands penned lyrics for each other's tracks, which resulted in four tracks (the CD release featured two bonus tracks) of harsh, straight-ahead punk riffs. The cover was also role-reversed with Born Against taking the more off-the-wall model cover, while Screeching Weasel showed off a much more bleak Erika Grove–designed art piece.

The combination of this split-record pairing resulted in Born Against adding the Ben Weasel-written song "Janelle" to their discography, a song that floated north to Olympia, Washington, where it reached the ears of riot grrrl band Bratmobile (a future Lookout! band at **LK 252**). The song was about Janelle "Blarg" Hessig, the popular East Bay punk comic zinester of *Tales of Blarg*, who happened to be a roadie for Bratmobile when the song came out. Bratmobile responded with 1994's *The Real Janelle* EP, whose title track pokes at Ben Weasel. Four years later, Bennie Weasel (as he's named in the Bratmobile song) included "The Last Janelle" on Screeching Weasel's *Major Label Debut* EP. The song references "ugly riot grrrls," and its title implies a "last word" on the call-and-response, cementing this song feud in airwave history.

Janelle Hessig: In 1993, Jolt Cola flowed freely at the corner store, vegetarian bean burritos were 59 cents at Taco Bell, and my friend Richard the Roadie was on tour with one of my favorite pop punk bands, Screeching Weasel. Their other roadie was Ben Hamper, a middle-aged agoraphobic author who wrote the blue collar comedic-tragedy cult memoir, *Rivethead*, about maintaining humanity while working at the GM auto plant in Flint, Michigan. I had read *Rivethead* three times and was a huge fan of Hamper's and asked Richard to introduce me to him. However, Richard got his wires crossed somehow, and he told Ben Weasel I wanted to hang out instead, lol, lol, enter *America's Funniest Home Videos* sound effects here. But it was the early nineties, and I was a fan of Screeching Weasel too, so I just rolled with it and met up with Ben Weasel before their show at Gilman Street. We had a little adventure walking around town. We crept through the Albany Landfill at night, back when it was still sketchy and feral, before the City ruined it by turning it into a legitimate park. I was in high school and punk and raggedy and excited. Ben was an older chain-smoking Chicago smart ass. I think our night out was beyond his usual comfort zone, and we made a connection and became friends and pen pals, and he went back to Chicago and wrote a song about me. This year was also a big one for riot grrrl. After hearing their demo tape and reading their fanzine, I had booked a backyard show for Bikini Kill with Nation of Ulysses and Blatz at my (older) ex-boyfriend's house while he was out of town (moral of the story: don't date teenagers). A connection between Olympia and the East Bay was forged on multiple fronts, and later that summer, I roadied for Bratmobile for a few shows. The Born Against/Screeching Weasel split had just come out and Allison Wolfe was like, "Why are guys the ones that write songs about cool girls? Girls should be writing songs about other girls," and she wrote "The Real Janelle," an answer song in the spirit of the early NYC rap feud between Roxanne Shante and UTFO. There were a bunch of songs about me in the ensuing years, by bands like the Rickets, Scared of Chaka, All You Can Eat, etc., but the Bratmobile song is the one that people always remember and still bring up to this damn day. It has been inescapable for decades. If "The Real Janelle" is on my tombstone, I'm going to haunt the shit out of all of you. I think that "Last Janelle" song by Screeching Weasel was a reference to people riding a bandwagon and the dawn of internet gossip and turning someone (in this case, me) into an anecdote rather than respecting their humanity. But I honestly don't think I ever even listened to that song more than once because it wasn't kind and didn't really have anything to do with me, and my musical tastes were veering away from this brand of pop punk by 1998.

With the release of the 7-inch split, Born Against was being courted by Lookout! with plans to release more material.

Sam McPheeters: Born Against did have an oral agreement with Larry to release our back catalog on CD through Lookout!. This was made sometime in '93 and was entirely a result of my own total lack of business foresight. After Vermiform joined Mordam [Records] in late 1993, Ruth Schwartz was flabbergasted by this decision and correctly pointed out that I would be giving away tens of thousands of dollars by not releasing those CDs myself. I had an awkward conversation with Larry sometime in early '94 that more or less ended our friendship, and Vermiform wound up releasing the CDs.

Screeching Weasel released a compendium of new material on overdrive, including *You Broke My Fucking Heart* 7-inch (**LK 075**), and the classic *Anthem for a New Tomorrow* LP (**LK 076**). *You Broke My Fucking Heart* is unanimously one of Screeching Weasel's strongest EPs. The band was at a creative peak, with some excellent shorter compositions and collaborations between Dan Vapid and Ben Weasel.

John "Jughead" Pierson (Screeching Weasel, The Mopes, Even In Blackouts): *Anthem [for a New Tomorrow]* is where we were more of a strong touring unit, so we played together well, but Dan and Ben were not writing together anymore so it's also sort of bittersweet. The album feels streamlined because Ben would write songs and bring them in, and we would play our parts. It was great at the time, because playing-wise it really felt like we were a tight unit. So I don't think Panic, Vapid, or I cared that the writing was all coming from Ben. But during that time, it seemed the only thing I was doing was recording, practicing, touring, and looking at contracts.

Dan "Vapid" Schafer (Screeching Weasel, Sludgeworth, The Queers, Riverdales, The Mopes): Ben had some new songs he wanted to show me. At the time, I was his roommate. He made a pot of coffee, we picked up our instruments, and I started playing along. Sometimes singing along for fun—most of the time I was encouraged to do so. He probably showed me half the record in an afternoon.

As the band was hitting its stride and gaining ground on the live front, Ben Weasel was spending more time with Chris Appelgren and attending to a lot more Screeching Weasel–related business. The pair collaborated, with Weasel staying over at Appelgren's house, working on Screeching Weasel artwork and other band affairs. The artwork for *Anthem for a New Tomorrow*—a Devo-type collage of pink and subtle blue pop art featuring the stars and stripes waving behind a 3D-glasses-wearing figurehead—

was overseen by Appelgren and Weasel after initial work by Samiam's Sergie Loobkoff. Similar cut-and-paste art was used through the inserts, with the iconic weasel head only getting a small spot.

Moving Up

After the huge success of *Kerplunk!*, the possibilities for Green Day continued to grow. With bigger and bigger shows forthcoming, and more record sales for the label, the band shopped around for a manager to help them move up the food chain.

Chris Appelgren: We met the managers and knew they were going to shop around for a major. They were selling lots of records; we had to keep pressing them on all formats, especially CD, which was also taking off as a new format. We were also super nervous not knowing if their new label would take their albums—with Green Day's new managers being lawyers. So Larry thought it would be a smart tactical move to hire one of them to represent Lookout!, thinking that he could not give us misleading advice and thus would be able to come up with a written agreement between the label and band that would confirm our rights to the first two albums. But basically, it just was the same Lookout! agreement with a few minor changes. Green Day's lawyers told them—Tré told me this later—that the records were theirs to take whenever they wanted. The lawyer we hired hadn't protected the label's interests because of the fact that he was representing both sides, which was sort of Larry's theory—the band later let these lawyers go. We were nervous for them, there had been no other bands like them that had not been chewed up and spit out by major labels, so all-around it was uncertain—but when they did get signed, it just felt like things went very well for them, from the recording onwards. It felt like something important was going to happen, and then it pretty much exploded way beyond what we could have expected. At the time Green Day left Lookout! and signed to Reprise, I felt like my special band had been taken away. We just thought that the world would miss the point as it usually seemed to do, and we were sort of wrong and sort of right.

Green Day fondly parted with Lookout!, and the rest is documented history. Some backlash was expected, mainly from the elitist punk community not centered around the Gilman or *MRR* scenes that actually knew the band, but mainly from the surrounding outer Bay Area.

Chris Appelgren: When they did sign, I remember they played a show in a nearby town, Petaluma, where some punk types actually picketed. I didn't go but the story is interesting as the show was with Nuisance—their last actually—and that was overshadowed by the demonstration against Green Day. The Gilman Street punks were mostly friends with the band, and while they might not have liked the decision, none of the band's friends gave them a hard time. It also seemed like the majority of the *MRR* types in San Francisco hadn't ever really taken Green Day seriously anyway. I know that the band was sensitive about this idea of them selling out.

Changes at Lookout!

The events laid the groundwork for the next phase of the label. With the stresses and the unknown future of the Green Day titles and Lookout!'s growing income, Livermore began to feel the pains of helming the ship.

Chris Appelgren: We handled it, but that was when we had to get credit for the first time. It seemed to haunt Larry—who used to have kind of severe depressive bouts. He would get worried and depressed. There were days when Patrick and I would get to the Lookout! "office" and he'd lament "Oh, the day is already over!" and it was only nine in the morning. It was just his nature. After our friend Utrillo Kushner had come on board helping out with mail order, we realized that a big source of anxiety for Larry was that the office was his apartment—he couldn't get away from Lookout!. When we started making more money and hired Molly [Neuman] to do promotions stuff, she took on the idea of getting us moved into an office space, and we found a great spot just around the corner. It was nearby, first and foremost, had room to grow, and the landlords would rent to us. Other places had reservations about a record company, thinking we would be too wild. We did it mostly without a vehicle—although we did use Larry's truck and Molly's car for a little of it. I moved boxes on my skateboard. There wasn't too much stuff—two computers, a refrigerator we used to store master tapes, a big portfolio box for art archives and a table with all the stuff for mail order, plus some cool colored vinyl that Larry was stashing in the closet. When we moved, we had to buy furniture.

Over the coming months, with the advent of the punk explosion and the release of Green Day's Warner Bros. debut *Dookie*, Lookout! began to see the sudden growth in terms of income and staff. After leaving the apartment office in 1995, life became all business for the grassroots punk label.

Chris Appelgren: It was Larry, Patrick, Molly, Utrillo, and myself. Soon after, we hired Cathy Bauer and Tristin Laughter. Soon after, even more came on board—Chris Imlay to do art, Alexis to be the receptionist, Rop and Tim to help with mail order, Xandy to do the bookkeeping. It was exciting that the work we had done was sort of paying off, that it all was becoming more real-seeming in a conventional sense, plus it was great to be able to involve people we liked and respected in running this business. It was around this time, I was given the title "President," but really we were all doing a little bit of everything. In fact, the workload got a little more reasonable because there were more of us, but we also really kicked up our release schedule a great deal. I don't know if we took it that seriously, but for a time Larry had an idea that I would be the good-natured business face to the label, Pat would be the CFO type, Molly would be the sort to say no, and Larry could kind of phase out of the day-to-day business. Larry was always trying to back off and had been since '91, but it wasn't feasible. He was sort of grooming Pat and me to take over the biz and have him remain an owner, but he wanted to make recommendations, talk to bands, do the more fun stuff and not really get too bogged down in the bummer hard work after all the years he'd done the bulk of it.

Punk Goes Mainstream

The world of punk rock continued moving into mainstream consciousness, beginning with the success of Nirvana and the Mighty Mighty Bosstones. After Green Day signed to Warner/Reprise Records in 1993, the floodgates opened for another punk stalwart jumping ship—Bad Religion. Bad Religion's cofounding guitarist, Brett Gurewitz, also owned Epitaph Records, causing some of Epitaph's bands to be discovered in the same surge of interest. The Offspring, Rancid, and NOFX hit record sales, and when the Offspring released their aptly titled third album *Smash*, everyone took notice, including MTV and mainstream shows like *Saturday Night Live*, which featured Rancid performing live in 1995.

Joe King (The Queers): Oh yeah, you could feel it. I mean, the bands around were really fucking good. The Muffs, Green Day, Mighty Mighty Bosstones, and of course Screeching Weasel and MTX. All bands I really respected, and having them around made me try to write better. And yes, when Green Day hit it big we all got caught up in the groundswell, and Lookout! bands really caught on.

Almost everyone involved in the world of punk and alternative began to feel the massive effects the mainstream was having. Many fans began to feel betrayed, and cries of "sellout" became a regular occurrence. Sales exploded on all fronts, and suddenly it seemed like being in a punk band could be a lucrative move. Along with the successes the larger punk family was feeling, the ripples, turning into waves, of success traveled through Lookout!'s world, its bands, and on to its future signings.

Mel Bergman (The Phantom Surfers, The Go Nutz): Our first release sold double our previous independent, and that was due to a "rising tide lifts all boats" phenomena.

Jon Ginoli (Pansy Division): Sales tripled or quadrupled. Our first CD had sold about five thousand when it came out. The second one sold over twenty thousand. There is nothing so wonderful as being in the right place at the right time. And it is *totally* out of your control.

Christopher Freeman (Pansy Division): It opened the doors for many more hybrids to appear, and our own idea of using powerpop as a music medium was then legitimized.

Grant Lawrence (The Smugglers): There was a time when Lookout! was *the* label to be on in the *world*, and we were on it at that time, and it was magic! We would play a show in Madrid or Minneapolis—and if you stood at the back of the venue, all you could see was the Lookout! Records logo on the back of every T-shirt.

Joel Reader (MTX, The Bomb Bassets, The Avengers): All Lookout! artists enjoyed a career highpoint in those first post-*Dookie* years, and MTX was certainly no exception.

Chris "B-Face" Barnard (The Queers, Groovie Ghoulies, The Mopes): The shows got larger and larger, then we started seeing kids that might have been at their first punk show or just people you wouldn't expect in the early days. Like jocks, nerds, or just normal-looking people. Being on Lookout! surely helped us. The label grew along with the bands, and when they were more successful, it affected us positively, just like they were affected positively when their bands were doing well. It was a pretty exciting time to be in a punk band.

But the newfound success at Lookout! was proving to be a double-edged sword. More money pouring through the doors meant more responsibility. The former bedroom business had turned into unbelievable dollar amounts, and past agreements and contracts now had to be scrutinized. Lookout! had often worked on a handshake agreement. This was now no longer viable, especially with new bands and higher expectations coming in through the door. Another issue raised was the lack of security for the label if a band wanted to take back its releases. This point was made all the more real with the amount of income generated from the Green Day back catalog. The label was funding current releases and staff solely from the sales of the two Green Day LPs.

Chris Appelgren: It made me feel more vulnerable. Often Larry would make the point that our biggest bands could pretty easily take their records, and the label would be in very bad shape. He reacted out of fear and concern for this. At the time, I thought that was silly and sad. We just had to move forward and do what we thought was best by signing new bands and not being preoccupied by how a certain band felt about the direction of the label. Maybe I was wrong as some of the artistic—if you can call it that—or directional choices I made for Lookout! did go beyond the pop-punk sound, but I guess I am proud of being brave. Even if it was not always the best idea business-wise, I think that, ultimately, Lookout! wasn't really equipped to be as big as it became. Our agreements were pretty much meaningless—two pages written by Larry that didn't even assert ownership of the masters. Very punk and progressive, but not very smart business. Larry also always talked about how he could sell the label for millions of dollars, but those contracts—no label would have paid anything for them, it was all just based on friendship and goodwill.

Frank "Dr. Frank" Portman (MTX, The Bomb Bassets): When the label was suddenly successful, it was like Larry's plan paid off, but the paradox was that it was not sustainable as a label. They couldn't keep spending nothing at all on records and hope for another Green Day, especially because this theoretical Green Day would have lots of other options and wouldn't want to record an album for eight-hundred dollars and live in a van, so they had to start acting more like a real label, and that was a hard business to be in.

Artsy Additions: Imlay & Grove

Two of the employees who made their mark over the coming years were Chris Imlay and Erika Grove, who were also roommates at one time. With Imlay being a musician himself in the Brent's T.V. and Hi-Fives family, he came together with Chris Appelgren in the mid-1990s to work on art projects for the label. The pair often shared an office space, collaborated, and played the video games Quake and Marathon when not challenging each other's creative sides. Erika Grove (who had already given her artistic touch to the Screeching Weasel / Born Against EP) was from Rockford, Illinois, and neighbor to Rick Neilsen of Cheap Trick, who was also a family friend. After she moved to Minneapolis, Appelgren crossed paths with Grove while playing in Bumblescrump in a basement with the Voodoo Glow Skulls. As well as having roots in the Midwest DIY scene, Grove was also a penpal with Livermore and had already made several East Bay visits in the early 1990s. The visits from Minnesota to California ultimately ended with a permanent move to Oakland and into shared accommodation with local musician and scenester, Richie Bucher. With a new move to the East Bay, Grove became one of the long-lasting and memorable figures to come into the Lookout! world.

he Mr. T Experience

ight Shift At The Thrill Factor

OKOUT

AVAILABLE ON VINYL LP AND CD

Follow-ups and Rereleases

Mr. T

The Mr. T Experience had returned in 1992 for **LK 068**, the *Gun Crazy* EP—following their European EP *Strum Und Bang, Live!?* on Spain's Munster Records. After their previous breakup, founding member Jon Von Zelowitz left the band and didn't rejoin when they re-formed for *Gun Crazy*.

Aaron Rubin (MTX, Samiam): There had always been some tension in the relationship between Jon and the rest of the band, and it just sort of festered for years until he finally quit. I don't recall what the specific event was, or even if it was anything specific. It was all just the kind of stupid kid stuff that seems to matter so much when you are young but really doesn't.

The next LP with the three-piece lineup was *Our Bodies, Our Selves* (**LK 080**) circa 1993. The band had begun to develop a studio slickness and tight musicianship that sat well with audiences. Doubtlessly lending to this was the band's having been ahead of its time for the past eight years.

Frank "Dr. Frank" Portman (MTX, The Bomb Bassets): *Our Bodies* [*Our Selves*] to me has a kind of sonic "darkness." We did it in a very different way than the others, and there was an uncertainty about what we were going to do from there on that I think is reflected in the mood, but I had never worked so hard to make lyrics that were balanced and integrated with each other—to have the lyrics be like a book where you could read them from beginning to end and they would—not exactly tell a story—but be comprehensible.

For followers of MTX, the album was a treat, stacked with cleverly humorous tales from the mind of Dr. Frank; and their head-on, catchy punk formula lost no momentum without Zelowitz's second guitar. Again, with tracks like "Even Hitler Had a Girlfriend" and "Are You

There, God? It's Me, Margaret," Dr. Frank proved his place as a punk wordsmith.

Frank "Dr. Frank" Portman: People weren't paying attention to any great degree—we were doing it for ourselves mostly. I never felt like it was lost or wasted because I knew it would still be there, but I wondered, what do you have to do to get people to notice what you're doing? I was pretty frustrated and bitter about it, but on the other hand, what can you do?

Aaron Rubin: Back then, every time an MTX album came out, people said they liked the older albums better. Then, after a while, the new album would become one of those older albums, and people would say they liked it better than whatever the newer new album was! I'm sure that was the case with *Our Bodies, Our Selves* as well. Alex [Laipeneiks] was on the verge of quitting, and then I went to law school soon after it was released, so that sort of marked the end of that era of MTX to me.

Laipeneiks left the band shortly after the release, leaving the drum stool empty for Jim "Jym" Pittman.

Aaron Rubin: I do think that when Jon [Von Zelowitz] left was the point where MTX really became Frank's band and gave Frank freedom to do what he wanted in terms of songwriting and direction. Frank was always the main creative force, but Jon was a founding member and also a songwriter and singer, so it was a change when he left. Plus, Jon's style and skills were much more in the Ramones bar-chord tradition, whereas Frank was starting to expand beyond that, so Jon's leaving let Frank move the band more in the direction that he wanted to go.

The Queers

The Queers' follow-up to their popular Lookout! debut found them borrowing some members from Screeching Weasel during a dark period for Hugh O'Neill. The addition of Dan Vapid and Dan Panic expanded the band to a four-piece for the 1994 album *Beat Off* (**LK 081**) and its subsequent tour.

Joe King (The Queers): Hugh was strung out and couldn't do the tour, so Panic and Vapid jumped in. We had to do an album in the middle of the tour and just used Panic 'cause he was there. He was a bit busy on drums but kept a steady beat. Weird fucker to tour with. Vapid, me, and B-Face were like a gang, and then there was Panic. We used to laugh at him because he was so strange. I did like him a lot though, and I know he drove Ben crazy, and I could see why, but I always liked Panic.

Dan "Vapid" Schafer (Screeching Weasel, Sludgeworth, The Queers, Riverdales, The Mopes): In the early nineties, I toured with the Queers a lot. We had a lot of great moments, but the pivotal one was opening for the Ramones. Joe King called me less than a week before the show and asked if I wanted to trek down to New Hampshire to play with them. It was just a one-off show, but it was something that I couldn't pass up. I asked my friend Pete Mittler if he felt like taking a road trip in his van. He liked the idea of a Ramones road trip, and we began our seventeen-hour drive from Chicago to Hampton Beach, New Hampshire. It was a little surreal for me to see Johnny and Joey Ramone walking around the club before their soundcheck. The Queers played well that night, and the Ramones were amazing. When I got home from that show, I ended up writing a song, "Hampton Beach," about the experience, which was later used for the Riverdales debut record.

Featuring a live audience photo on the sleeve—with a fine cross section of middle finger flicking—*Beat Off* was a twelve-track trip once more into the Queers' brand of fuck-you punk. Recorded in Chicago and produced by Ben Weasel, the record kicked off with the ultrafast, instrumental "Steak Bomb," and included some favorite live tracks and anthems such as "Drop the Attitude Fucker" and the tribute, "Ben Weasel" with the lyrics, "Ben Weasel—he's an asshole, Ben Weasel—he's a jerk, Ben Weasel—you just hate him 'cause he don't hafta work."

The LP artwork was a great looking Patrick Hynes/Chris Appelgren effort, with some tweaking of the Lookout! logo—a practice that had become commonplace throughout the 1990s. Also making his debut was the Queers' Felix the Cat–inspired mascot by Appelgren.

The newly bolstered lineup on the record, however, would prove to be misleading not only to the audience but also to the actual players on the album. Although pictured on the sleeve as a member of the band, as well as laying down guitar tracks in the studio, Dan Vapid found himself confused upon royalty check time. A statement showed that Dan Panic had received a payment from Lookout! for the record, while no payment was forthcoming to Vapid.

Dan "Vapid" Schafer: Of course I thought this was a mistake at first, so I called Lookout! Records to find out what was going on. They had no idea why I wasn't paid, so I called Ben Weasel to see what the problem was, and that was when I got the truth. Ben Weasel, who produced the record, had taken all of my tracks off the recording. I guess he had told Joe [King] that he needed to let me know that I was not on the record and would not be paid for my work. However, Joe never let me know that I was taken off the record—neither did Larry Livermore, who was at the recording session and was aware of the situation. Joe, B-Face, Dan Panic, and Larry all later called me to apologize for the situation. They all seemed to point an accusatory finger at Ben, saying that they wanted my tracks on the record, but Ben adamantly insisted that my tracks should

not be used and that I should not be paid. The *Beat Off* record does not have rosey memories for me.

Avail

By 1991, Avail had been around for four years, rocking their southern-influenced, blue-collar brand of hardcore out of Richmond, Virginia, when they were introduced to Chris Appelgren through a mutual friend.

Back in 1987, guitarist Joe Banks put a lineup of the band together in the Virginia suburb of Reston, later bringing in local Tim Barry to initially sit on the drum stool. Honing the band's anthemic sound and stance, they moved to Richmond and began the process of creating a solid lineup. They converted many local scenesters into believers with their storytelling and blazing folk-punk style. One of the new members was Beau "Beau Beau" Butler, a roadie working for five dollars per show.

Beau "Beau Beau" Butler (Avail): Since they weren't making any money they told me I was in the band, and I lost my pay! Bastards!!!!

Butler was the official band "cheerleader," entertaining the audience with stage moves and backing vocals. Rounding out the early lineup were Erik Larson and Charles McCauley—McCauley was a high school friend of Tim Barry's and already a big fan of the band. **Charles McCauley (Avail):** The rest of the guys were already living there and generously offered me a place to live. We all shared a big apartment that had as many as twelve people living in it. Beau had been roadie for the band for a couple of years by then. Around February or March of '91, the band's singer left, along with the bassist. At that point, Tim decided he was tired of playing the drums and said he was going to sing. Joe agreed. Of course, there were no questions about his vocal abilities; in all things musical Tim just sort of has a knack.

Having built its live reputation from constant gigging in the D.C. and Richmond areas, the new lineup plowed ahead. Feeling well-received in the Richmond scene by audiences and supportive venues, the band ably gelled with local bands.

Charles McCauley: The first song we wrote together was "Pinned Up." It was an eye-opener as far as what the direction of the band was going to be from that point on. Joe decided he was ready to drain his savings account to finance another demo, then, not long after that was decided, I got a call from Adam Thompson. He was starting a new label and wanted to know if we wanted to release its first LP. Things seemed to be lining up well for us, and we jumped at the chance. We decided to call the album *Satiate*, as from the chorus of "Pinned Up."

Chris Appelgren: I became aware of them when I went to New York for the first time. I went to see the band Heroin from San Diego play at Born Against drummer John Hiltz's house in New Jersey, where we saw [the original release of] *Satiate*. I was making fun of the fact that the back cover had a cartoon drawing of all the band members. We went with Heroin to WFMU, where they were doing a live session, and spent the whole time making a list of bands that had cartoon caricatures of themselves on their records. John had helped get the album released and had given some money and had told me the drawing is silly but the record is really good.

Livermore's attention was brought to Avail because of an invitation from Butler to check out the band. Avail had previously forwarded material to Lookout! that was seemingly ignored.

Beau "Beau Beau" Butler: He was there, saw us, and said he didn't listen to our stuff we sent—he thought we were too rough and aggressive for Lookout! at the time. Then he went back and listened to the stuff we sent and said they would re-press it and see how it did. Lookout! was the only label I wanted to be on.

Charles McCauley: After we played, Larry came up to Tim outside the club and asked him to take a walk. As they did, Larry said to Tim that he had heard good things about us and was considering signing us. After seeing us, he decided we were "too heavy" for his label. He wished us luck, and we were off. Legend has it, when he returned to his Bay Area office he found a copy of *Satiate* sitting on his desk. After one listen he decided he wanted to release it.

Satiate was rereleased by Lookout! in 1994 and became **LK 082**, in CD-only form with two bonus tracks from the *Attempt to Regress* 7-inch, recorded post-*Satiate*. What would come to be an expected ferocity from the band was only hinted at on the debut, with a keenly upbeat and anthemic sound, calling for an us-against-them mentality. Their ultra-tight musicianship and catchy songwriting was, however, in full force with the marching beat intro of—aptly named—"March." Although not overtly chunky and powerful, the tracks on *Satiate* had a big sound down to the impassioned sing-along structures and honest, fist-pumping choruses. Tracks like "Bob's Crew" and "Stride," fused exciting hooks and hopeful lyrics.

Charles McCauley: I think we made a pretty decent album. The addition of Jena Patterson's vocals at the end of "March" still sounds like a mission statement to me. One of my favorite moments is of Erik, Beau, and I doing the backing vocals for "All About It": "Push it!"—and Beau doing his best to crack us up. I'm pretty sure it was Tim's idea for us all to be recorded just talking and joking around for the middle section of "Upward Grind." All of us crammed ourselves into a closet and just let loose. It really captured a great moment.

PANSY DIVISION
FOR THOSE ABOUT TO SUCK COCK
PANSY DIVISION
DIVISION
presents
RATED
X
OUTPUNK
Attack Of The Pansies
PANSY DIVISION
with
Jackson
Laurel

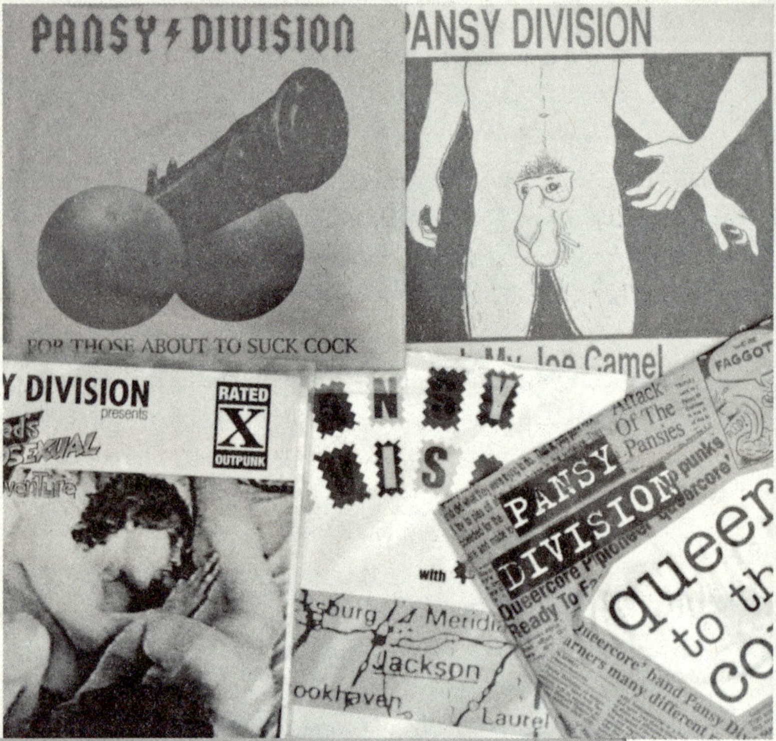

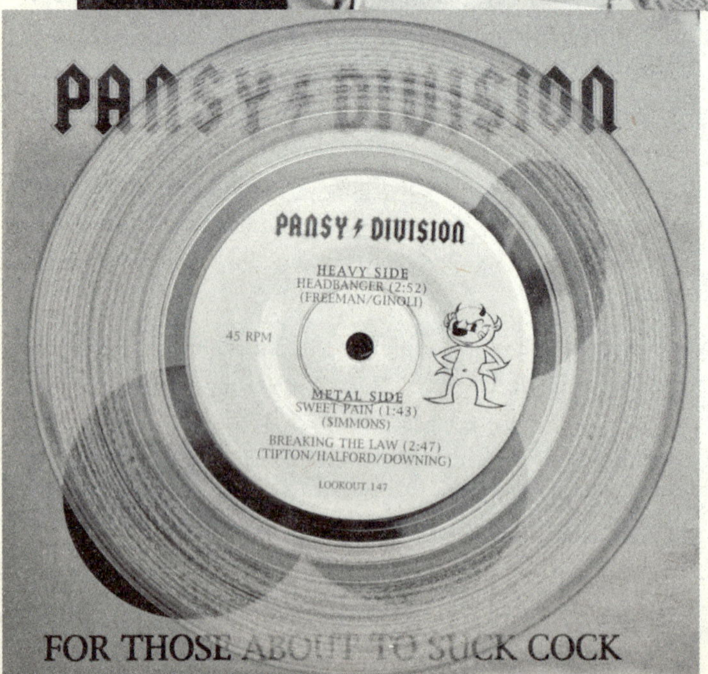

PANSY DIVISION
PANSY DIVISION
HEAVY SIDE
HEADBANGER (2:52)
(FREEMAN/GINOLI)
45 RPM
METAL SIDE
SWEET PAIN (1:43)
(SIMMONS)
BREAKING THE LAW (2:47)
(TIPTON/HALFORD/DOWNING)
LOOKOUT 147
FOR THOSE ABOUT TO SUCK COCK

Stadiums & Scenes

Pansy Division

After their successful first album release, Pansy Division was excited to be returning once more for a second full-length for Lookout!. Following the band's first US tour in 1993, they self-financed and recorded *Deflowered* (**LK 087**) and some extra tracks. With *Deflowered* on the shelves, the band was asked to appear on the summer leg of the exploding Green Day stadium tour for *Dookie*.

Jon Ginoli (Pansy Division): It was scary, because we didn't know how we'd go over. It was hard at first, partly because the way you win over a large number of people is different than with a smaller crowd who can see you eye to eye. But we learned, and by the end of the arena tour, we were winning crowds over most of the time. It was a mind-blowing experience, and Green Day were never anything but nice to us.

Pansy Division had the fortunate position of being on a prime stage, during an unrepeatable time for punk rock—quadrupling sales of their Lookout! releases. With smart business sense, Ginoli and Freeman also noticed an opportunity for making some extra cash.

Jon Ginoli: During the first tour we did with Green Day—they weren't playing larger venues yet—we were averaging about seven hundred to a thousand people per night at that point, though all sold out. I noticed from day one that they were not selling the Lookout! LPs or CDs at their show, and they also weren't in many stores outside the usual indie suspects, and certainly not in chain stores yet. Since we were vending our own stuff before and after we played, I asked Billie Joe if he minded if we sold the Green Day Lookout! releases. So we bought copies of their stuff from Lookout! and sold it along our merch, and we made extra money that way. When we did the arena tour with them, they had wised up and brought the other titles along because we had done very well selling them, so they had noticed. But we had been selling them right next to Green Day's merch guy, Gordon, and when it got busy we'd help him sell Green Day shirts too. It is amazing how lightly staffed the band was; even on the arena tour they lacked more than the minimum to do the basic tasks of putting on a show. I guess that changed later, but it proved you didn't need a ton of people tagging along with you to do a rock show.

Pansy Division continued to tour in support of *Deflowered*, jumping back on board with Green Day later in the year following their own set of dates. With over a hundred live shows clocked up for 1994, the band had experienced an all-around busy and exciting year.

The Vindictives

After entering the label's consciousness on the 1994 Ben Weasel *Punk USA* compilation (**LK 077**), the Vindictives, brainchild of Chicago native Joey "Vindictive" Volino, joined the ranks with the *Rocks in My Head* 7-inch (**LK 089**).

Joey "Vindictive" Volino (The Vindictives): I met my first punk friends while shopping for records. They told me about La Mere Vipere, and we would meet up and hang out in front of the club, sneaking glimpses through the doors and listening to muted songs through the walls, as we were too young to get into the bar. The things that went on in La Mere Vipere could never live up to what was going on in my imagination. These experiences—tracking down records like a detective and then getting so close to the source but being restricted from entering the venue—turned punk into something deeply mysterious for me, so I'm perhaps a little thankful I wasn't able to get in.

Viktimzofsociety was young Joey Vindictive's first scrape with the punk scene, a band he put together in 1980. They recorded *Wicked Rock Music Is Killing Our Children* in 1984, released by Brain-Box Records in 1986 after the band had broken up.

Joey "Vindictive" Volino: I was through with punk. I was much more into bands like the Butthole Surfers, Einstürzende Neubauten, the Residents, Throbbing Gristle, and the Birthday Party. When I was introduced to punk there was this infinite variety of styles and attitudes that fell under the "punk" banner—and by the mid-eighties it was all about metalish hardcore, which I had very little interest in.

At a going away party thrown by a local punk radio DJ, Vindictive met another young upstart who was already aware of his work in Viktimzofsociety: Ben Weasel. The two quickly struck up a friendship, trading tapes and exposing Vindictive to the new wave of local bands from the suburbs.

Joey "Vindictive" Volino: I was more into my home recording projects of avant-garde and experimental music. I did begin to videotape the new scene, though, and started to notice a melodic thread that a few of the new bands had going on—particularly Screeching Weasel—that I really liked. I was in college, running a support group, a dental professional running my own dental lab, and busy raising my daughter. So, being anything more than a "fan" hadn't yet occurred to me. But I would always fiddle around on my guitar back then, and bits and pieces of songs started

to come out. I think at first I was trying to ignore them. I wasn't sure if I wanted to go through that again.

Vindictive had suffered from some depression following the breakup of his band. Spending time with Weasel and witnessing the growth of a new fertile local scene of musicians gave Vindictive the motivation to jump back on the music bandwagon. In October 1990, Robert "Dr. Bob" Nielson found Volino through an ad he had placed in a local Guitar Center. Via cassette recording, the two would hash out new songs on Nielson's back porch. Weasel jumped in on bass, Gore Gore Girls drummer Erik Elsewhere was signed up next, and the Vindictives were born. Over the course of the next few years they released several 7-inch EPs on their own homegrown label, VML Records.

After some early recording sessions, the Vindictives' lineup solidified in 1992 with Patrick "P.J. Parti" Buckley replacing Erik Elsewhere on drums and Ben Weasel dropping out to concentrate on Screeching Weasel, replaced by Billy Blastoff. Patrick Buckley's relationship with the members of the band went back to the mid-1980s. The Chicago faction of punks were all close and spent many hours partying together in the early 1990s. Patrick Buckley was particularly close to Vapid's then-current punk outfit (and future Vindictives' labelmate) Sludgeworth.

Patrick "P.J. Parti" Buckley (The Vindictives): I used to have crazy parties back then. The Queers left one party really quick because it was so out of hand. That was around the time they stayed at my apartment for a week or two while they recorded *Love Songs for the Retarded*. The Sludgeworth guys would show up, and we would party. The Queers were really cool guys, but our Chicago scene was too much for some people. The Queers and I preferred to hang out, listen to tunes, while Joe King would cook for us. Once in a while, we'd head out for a couple of beers. My buddy Greg used to brew "Weasel Brau," their own beer! The other Vindictives didn't party. I was from the city; they were all suburban. I've always known Joey to keep to himself, and he is a very smart man. But all the partying was myself and the Sludgeworth guys.

Joey "Vindictive" Volino: I was pretty zonked out on psych meds the entire time [and] "partying" was the last thing on my mind—I was using the Vindictives to keep me sane. None of us were really big scenesters.

Our whole world was strictly the Vindictives. P.J. had a group of pals and a bunch of other local musicians that all were really their own thing—all-night-long, beer-soaked parties, thus the name P.J. Parti. I was never really close with P.J., and it wasn't due to a dislike or anything; on the contrary, we had a lot in common, both being record collectors and music trivia buffs. In hindsight, I think we were looked at as unfriendly by many in the Chicago scene, but there was a whole private world of Vindictives inner drama that we dealt with. I had The Dummy Room record store to manage—a wife and two kids.

Now a label talent scout for Lookout!, Weasel brought the Vindictives on board. Weasel and Vindictive shared an easy relationship, living in the same building for half a decade. The 1994 *Rocks in My Head* EP was recorded prior to a contract with Lookout! and was a perfect snapshot of the insanity-flavored feast of punk the Vindictives were cooking up. Vindictive was a huge part of the band's sound, his vocal style conjuring images of a babbling psychopath spewing paranoid visions at full speed. The band had always sounded tight and was a bit faster than the mid-paced pop-punk sound of the era—almost as though the members were racing each other.

The Queers

With muddy production and charming punk anthems, the Queers' debut album *Grow Up* (**LK 090**) was reissued by Lookout!. Recorded and released in 1990 on Shakin' Street Records, the album featured twelve blasts of the Queers' basic rhythms coupled with sing-along choruses, and occasional killer melodies. Ben Weasel remixed the reissue, but the basic production made it difficult to make the tracks sound much brighter. Fortunately, part of the appeal of *Grow Up* is the rough edges that rattle around compositions such as "Love Love Love" and "I Met Her at the Rat." As an explanation for some of the juvenile lyrics contained on the full-length—strangely never an issue on any other future Queers' releases—the reissue featured a disclaimer in the liner notes: "We know some of these lyrics are pretty insensitive, but we didn't write these songs to hurt anybody's feelings. We were a lot younger then and even if we aren't any smarter now, we're not as dumb either." With the inclusion of the track "Gay Boy," it was an understandable, if not understated, move.

Weasel vs. Vapid

The lean and tight touring version of Screeching Weasel had finished its live run with the *Anthem for a New Tomorrow* LP, and the band fell into another period of disarray. Vapid, Jughead, Panic, and Weasel reconvened to begin work on a follow-up album, choosing to record in the basement of Jughead and Vapid's residence. Weasel was experiencing worsening panic attacks, and the basement provided a filter from the outside world. During the process, Vapid and Weasel had a falling out, resulting in the bassist and songwriter leaving Screeching Weasel.

John "Jughead" Pierson (Screeching Weasel, The Mopes, Even In Blackouts): I told Ben early on that letting Vapid go was going to be devastating. He didn't think so at the time, but years later he told me I was right.

Dan "Vapid" Schafer (Screeching Weasel, Sludgeworth, The Queers, Riverdales, The Mopes): I was touring with the Queers, and we were drinking a lot on the road. When I got home, Ben caught wind that we were drinking a lot and wanted a band meeting. Ben felt like I'd had "more than my fair share" as he put it, of alcohol, implying that I had a drinking problem. I was given the ultimatum that I either stop drinking or be replaced in the band. So I quit. I didn't believe that I had a problem with alcohol. To this day that decision is backed by Jughead and, to a lesser extent, Dan Panic. It never made a drop of sense to me or those around me. My girlfriend at the time, my parents, my brother, and all my friends weren't concerned at all. Soon after, Ben got Mike Dirnt from Green Day to fill my shoes in the band. I feel like that is when I knew what all the "drinking problem" malarkey was all about.

John "Jughead" Pierson: I just remember taking Mike to get bass strings and not knowing how popular Green Day were then because I didn't listen to the radio. We walked into a music store, and he was recognized, so he picked up a bass and started playing a Green Day song. I thought that that was funny. He was pulling a sort of Ringo Starr and saying to himself, I'm just happy to be here. I think he was probably the most loveable in the band. Just a goofy guy that knew how to play bass.

How to Make Enemies and Irritate People (**LK 097**) divides the Weasel fan camps. The recording was slick and solid thanks to the Mass Giorgini and

Ben Weasel production, topped off with some impressively tight rhythm tracks—case in point was the opener, "Planet of the Apes" (or "Planet of the Dupes" on the reverse jacket tracklist where every track was retitled). As a classic-era Weasel release, the overall full-length was a winner, with little, if any, filler found on either side. Mike Dirnt shone with his bass work and backing vocals, and the songwriting was solid. However, the short, sharp punk attacks of *Anthem for a New Tomorrow* were absent, leading to an all-around mid-paced affair without any standout tracks.

Not surprisingly, after so many ups and downs, Screeching Weasel bade farewell after the *How to Make Enemies and Irritate People* release. Ben Weasel broke up Screeching Weasel with the intention of this LP being the band's last, though the next year saw *Kill the Musicians* (**LK 095**), a collection of demos, B-sides, and unreleased and out-of-print tracks. Foretold in the liner notes for *Kill the Musicians*, Ben Weasel, Vapid, and Panic were already working on a new band.

Lookout Christmas Card, 1994

Upstarts & Downfalls

The Potatomen originally formed in 1992 around the nucleus of Larry Livermore, Chris Appelgren, and Patrick Hynes. Once the concept and lineup were in effect, Livermore promptly departed on a trip to London. Upon his return, he was armed with a set of songs for the proposed new trio. Practice sessions began at the Lookout! office with Hynes on bass using a rehearsal amp, Livermore on acoustic guitar, and Appelgren making use of a random yet convenient box. The songs came together in short order, with the new set Livermore brought back from London comprising 1994's *On the Avenue* EP (**LK 098**) and 1995's *Now* LP (**LK 101**).

Chris Appelgren: We actually started playing pretty quickly, after the first or second time we practiced. We went and set up outside a donut shop in Albany, one that the punks would all hang out at on Wednesday nights. By "the punks" I mean our group of friends from Gilman basically. Afterwards, we started playing shows outside of Gilman between bands, and then finally played in the Gilman "store"—the area where they sell sodas and water. When we finally booked a real show, we played next to the stage, as opposed to on it.

The basic acoustic folk-punk ditties that the Potatomen were producing in the Lookout! office had their charm, but many people didn't really "get" the band.

Chris Appelgren: It was really more of Larry's project, meaning that he wanted to put the records out. But the sales were not that impressive, even though the Potatomen were certainly part of the family of bands. Plus, frankly, the band wasn't as active as they should have been. More touring would have made a big difference.

With Livermore becoming the voice and motivator for the band, Appelgren's interest began to wane. The simple structure of the three friends getting together and making music changed once the band had started recording. Livermore wanted more sophisticated leads and songwriting for the band, and Appelgren was losing motivation.

Chris Appelgren: We recorded the tracks with Andy Ernst, and in the process of making it, I got a little disillusioned as it became a more fleshed out band in the studio.

Probably the bigger issue was the amount of time the three Lookout! coworkers were spending together. Livermore would often spend time by himself away from the others, but with the Potatomen playing a short West Coast stint with the Queers, awkward tension sometimes arose.

Chris Appelgren: Larry would write on his old Apple PowerBook and get very moody and intense. Pat [Hynes] would be driving, and I was in the backseat with our friend Utrillo [Kushner], who was working at Lookout! and also our "roadie." While we were in the back, playing [a] Sega Game Gear, laughing and listening to [the] radio and singing along, Larry would shoot us these very disappointed looks from the front seat. Then, on the way back home from that tour, we got a hotel room south of Seattle and went to see the movie *The Chase*. Larry was being mopey, and for some reason said he would sleep in the rented minivan outside. We didn't know why, but as we were relaxing in the room he was in the car, seemingly unhappy. As he was parked right outside the window, we would peek out to look at him from time to time, and he'd pretend not to notice us. Although we all understood that this was just sort of how Larry was at the time, it was really weird. Pat was more tolerant of him in ways that I wasn't, but once on that trip he almost kicked Larry out of the van. He could just be very frustrating for no clear reason. I just basically said I didn't want to be in the band anymore, and suggested Utrillo take my place. He was more of a real drummer than I was. He was in the band for a while but then bailed as well.

Downfall

Once Operation Ivy broke up, the members (minus Jesse Michaels) reconvened to form Downfall. Tim Armstrong moved over to vocals, and Jason Hammon of the Dance Hall Crashers was brought on board as guitarist. Drummer David Mello enlisted his brother, Pat Mello, for guitar duties. After a handful of live shows at backyard parties, 924

Gilman Street, and Berkeley Square, the band abruptly ended—but not before recording an album's worth of tracks, first scheduled for release by David Hayes's Very Small Records in 1989 and next by Lookout! in 1994. The album was never released. The only existing recordings of Downfall were split into two sessions.

Jason Hammon (Downfall, The Dance Hall Crashers): One session was all punk stuff recorded in a home studio, and the other session was the ska stuff with Kevin Army. It seemed like Lawrence Livermore was interested in putting something out from the get-go, but I wasn't really involved in the business stuff. I knew him from shows with my previous bands Rabid Lassie and Breakaway. I wish the whole album had been released. I think there's some great stuff on it.

With the band still in its infancy, it had been surprising that they suddenly broke up without much explanation.

Jason Hammon: Honestly it came out of nowhere. Matt [Freeman] let me know that we needed to take a break. I think that's how it was conveyed. I was bummed. I learned a lot during my brief time playing with them. That being said, the Dance Hall Crashers were working on songs for an album at the time, and I just put more focus there.

Once Rancid formed and had moved on to record for Epitaph, Lookout! still wanted to release a Rancid / Avail split 7-inch EP (**LK 083**) and scheduled it to come out close to the already recorded Downfall CD (**LK 099**), but both records were canceled prior to release. Vinyl labels were already printed for the split, however, and were given away free with mail orders.

Chris Appelgren: We really worked on [the Downfall CD]. We found the original tapes, baked them, and then took them to LA to remix with Lars [Frederiksen], Tim, and Mr. Brett [Brett Reed]. The recordings that are available online are the original mixes, but because Tim had used some of the lyrics for Rancid, he cut some new vocal parts with different lyrics and also found a song that Matt sang. It was kind of a rock and roll song, like the Rolling Stones or something—really cool. We also worked on a Downfall dub track, and Jesse Michaels had already drawn some cover art. It was geared for a release right around the time of the Rancid / Avail split EP. Then I had a meeting with Tim and Matt and, basically, I think that Rancid was starting to get really big and came to understand that they couldn't keep recording for various small labels, doing splits and comp cuts, so they felt they needed to focus on Rancid. They told us the split was canceled, and the Downfall release would come out—but not until after the next Rancid album when they could work on it again. They never really found the time to finish the work, and it sort of languished, close to being released ever since.

A Slice of Lemon & the Peechees

What could have been an epic moment marking Lookout!'s hundredth release in 1995 turned into an underwhelming affair bogged down with average material. Slim Moon's underground label Kill Rock Stars had been putting out challenging and varied music since 1991—an important documentation of music circulating in the 1990s punk and indie scene. However, the collaboration with Lookout! for **LK 100**, *A Slice of Lemon* double album, was lackluster. The point of *A Slice of Lemon* was to juxtapose Lookout!'s style of bright punk and Kill Rock Stars' eclectic roster of indie punk noise and underground bands, but the template didn't seem to gel.

Chris Appelgren: Some people thought it was not enough *Can of Pork* and too much Kill Rock Stars-ish stuff and didn't feature enough established Lookout! bands. We tried to get more Lookout! mainstays, but they didn't come together.

The artwork didn't help, particularly compared to eye-catching artwork of *Can of Pork* or *Punk USA*. The angular and stylized artwork was absent, replaced by an inexplicable and sterile photo of a lemon. The comp did include Pansy Division, the Mr. T Experience, the Potatomen, the Tourettes, the Frumpies, and many bands that would go on to release with Lookout!, such as Black Fork, the Crumbs, Go Sailor, the Bomb Bassets, Cub, and a new group, the Peechees.

Rop Vasquez of Rice had jumped on board to work at Lookout! HQ. Since the demise of Rice in 1992, the singer had moved to Oakland, spending even more time with Chris Appelgren and Molly Neuman. The three, along with Rice's Carlos Cañedo, became the Peechees.

Rop Vasquez (Rice, The Peechees): I moved to Oakland around 1994 from San Diego to make the Peechees a full-time thing. I started stuffing records for Kill Rock Stars first, then sometimes some work for Lookout!. A couple months after Green Day made the jump, mail order for Lookout! was getting bigger and bigger, so Chris asked if I wanted to work full time. I started doing mail order at Lookout! with Utrillo. With Molly on board starting to manage things, and Utrillo and I on mail order, then Pat and Chris, and sometimes Larry, it was crowded. We were still working out of Larry's old apartment in Berkeley; I remember stuffing boxes with records in his bathroom. Mail order was getting out of control at this time, so it was moved inside Mordam Records, in a little corner nook near the returned merchandise area of the warehouse. This made more sense since all our records were there, and we didn't have to wait for them to send a box to Larry's apartment to fill orders. We'd get over fifty letters a day, with forty of those only for Green Day merchandise and records. The following year, Lookout! decided to rent an office in Berkeley to finally put us in one area since Larry's house couldn't hold everyone anymore. We had so much fun from then on, I mean, we were punk kids now playing "office" and doing what we loved doing.

Sweet Baby

Dallas Denery (vocals) and Matt Buenrostro (guitar and vocals) founded Sweet Baby (originally Sweet Baby Jesus) in 1986. Along with Dr. Frank of the Mr. T Experience, the band created its own style of upbeat punk and roll that fit perfectly into the scene building around the Bay Area. This lineup was short-lived but soon became stable with Richie Bucher on bass and Sergie Loobkoff on drums.

Dallas Denery (Sweet Baby, The Bomb Bassetts): Matt and I hardly felt like pioneers, more like reactionaries than anything else. The punk scene had devolved into tuneless hardcore yelling. Every song had some "powerful" message expressed in painful cliches. Skinheads were overrunning shows. It was all pretty dreadful. One day Dr. Frank, who had started MTX with Jon Von [Zelowitz] about a year earlier, asked if we would play at his girlfriend's eviction party. He volunteered to play drums—a stand-up snare, a garbage can, a cardboard box or whatever else was handy—and another friend, Crispy Jim, volunteered to play bass.

The party was great and the response was great. Everyone loved it except for a few guys, no doubt artistically offended by our unwavering devotion to melody and speed (well, that and our overwhelming sloppiness) who started chanting "You suck"—in time and in tune I should add—during "Gotta Get a Girl." That was great because it told us we were on to something; we had unwittingly come up with a style guaranteed to annoy the people we couldn't stand. And this kept happening, we would play with hardcore bands, and they would laugh at us. There was this awful political hardcore band who had a song in which the singer kept screaming, "It's just a state of mind! It's just a state of mind!" Just miserable stuff. So, [afterwards] Matt had pretty much written "She's from Salinas" on his own and had played it for me the first time, we just stuck that line, "It's just a state of mind!" on at the end. It had nothing to do with the song, it just seemed so ridiculous when this other guy sang that we had to include it. A few weeks go by, we play with the god-awful band again, they play that song, then we play ours, and later the singer starts threatening us for making fun of him.

One of Sweet Baby's sonic standouts was the influence of outside genres, immersing itself in the pop sounds of other styles. Incorporating these influences, it is easy to see why Sweet Baby were pioneers, adding punk to the tunes of yesteryear—similar to the way the Ramones had already blended two-minute tunes and bubblegum pop.

Dallas Denery: When we began writing songs, never with any thought of performing, we simply wrote what came naturally—short, simple love songs, hopefully catchy. This was all done in a sort of vacuum. Our originality was really more about time and place, rather than really doing something new. Even at Gilman Street for that entire first year, we were pretty much the odd band out. There was no "pop-punk scene" at Gilman during those early years. There were great bands—Isocracy, Operation Ivy, Crimpshrine, Sewer Trout. None of them were pop bands. They were punk and they were melodic, but they all had different visions, styles, and ideas. The Mr. T Experience was slowly coming around, but Frank was years away from his "This is a song about a girl" routine. In fact, that was a line I used at our second show, at some art opening at UC Berkeley, to distance us from all the other art bands on the bill that night. "This is a song about a girl, so deal with it" was our attitude. We were awful that night. Our instruments were literally falling apart, screws coming loose, strings breaking. To hear it, it must not have sounded like they were songs about anything at all. We improved with Richie and Sergie. But let's put it this way, there is a reason why we were not one of Lookout! Records' first releases, and that had everything to do with us being too poppy, too melodic, not punk enough, not hard enough, and not political enough. Larry Livermore was always a real supporter, but David Hayes wanted nothing to do with us. That's fine, it was his label, and we didn't much care one way or the other, but it says a lot about what people wanted in their music even at Gilman Street.

Although Sweet Baby broke up in 1989, the recordings on the 1996 split *Hello Again* CD-only release (**LK 102**) are from their original demo—the majority of which had been recorded as the band's debut album for Slash Records (later **LK 157**)—as well as later recordings with a new lineup, in preparation for the band's planned second album, *Submarine Races*, which never came to fruition. Brent's T.V., provided the second half on the split—tracks 21–40, over half of which were live, with the rest culled from band demos. The split release showed that both bands were close relatives musically as well as in reality (Dallas and Brent's T.V.'s John Denery are brothers). It was packed—quite literally—with beat-tastic pop-punk tunes. Sarah "Ivy" Clift, who had broken up her own band—Kamala & The Karnivores—to join Sweet Baby, played on the later recordings that were collected on the *Hello Again* release.

Ivy Clift (Kamala & The Karnivores, Sweet Baby): Dallas and I were hanging out a lot trying to write pop songs because both of us were bored and underemployed. Sweet Baby was my favorite band, and I used to see them every chance I got. In fact, it was seeing them the first time that made me decide I needed to start my own band. When Sergie and Richie quit after the first half of their national tour, [the band] asked me to join. Kevin Army was not thrilled because I lacked actual playing skills. But Matt Freeman coached me, as well as Kevin, Matt, and Dallas and I was able to get passably through the tour and recording the tragically lost second album.

Sweet Baby, although disbanded for seven years at the time of the *Hello Again* release, was far from forgotten. The band found a new younger audience over the next few years, courtesy of Lookout!.

18

In the Studio

Avail's New Record

With only a rerelease on Lookout!, Avail still felt they had a lot to prove, even after a year. Constantly writing new material for a second proper album after the reissue of *Satiate*, Avail was also seeing the groundswell effect of being on Lookout!, especially on the live circuit.

Charles McCauley (Avail): Being on Lookout! had its perks, and it certainly opened doors when it came to booking shows. I remember the first time we got to a show and saw "Lookout! Records" under our name on the flyer. To consider ourselves part of that great musical legacy was quite an honor.

Straight after a three-week tour, Avail landed back in the studio in June 1994 to begin working on *Dixie* (**LK 103**). With the backing of Lookout!, the band handpicked Uncle Punchy Studios in Silver Spring, Maryland, to do the job. Taking more time initially to get the sound that they wanted, the band also chose to put emphasis on the album's mixing. With the elements in place, laying down the basic tracks of drums and bass took only a few trailblazing hours, all played live with no overdubs.

The Wynona Riders

The Wynona Riders' 1995 debut full-length was the *J.D. Salinger* LP (**LK 104**) which was recorded twice and fully mixed twice in the second session, proving to be far more expensive than anticipated.

Ron "Skip" Greer (The Wynona Riders): I thought I'd convince them to put out the best demo recordings that were supposed to be *J.D. Salinger*, and they agreed. Then Dave [Hayes] convinced them to let us rerecord, and again they agreed, but then we needed to find a new guitarist. East Bay Ray—of Dead Kennedys—rehearsed with us twice and was in the running, but then Dave convinced Eric Matson to return. So Eric recorded with us but left again, and rather than dissolve, we got my friend Joe Selby to play guitar and tour with us. For the most part I wrote all the lyrics—and I wrote many of them while raking leaves in the Alameda Public Park system.

Joe Selby (The Wynona Riders): When Skip first thought of doing a professional recording of the Wynona Riders' stuff for Lookout!, his original idea was to have a bunch of guest guitar players, and he'd asked me if I'd be interested, which I was. But that never materialized and the next thing I heard, *J.D. Salinger* had been recorded with Eric, and they were going out on tour. Then I ran into Skip at a party, and he told me Eric had quit and wanted me to audition. I was actually specifically brought into the band to tour to support *J.D. Salinger*. I hadn't heard any of their demos or any of their earlier recordings and had never actually seen them play, so I was utterly and completely unfamiliar with the music.

J.D. Salinger is a top-notch, sprawling collection of songs the band had worked on over the years. The original vinyl was packaged as a 12-inch with a five-song 7-inch, while the CD version with the same tracklist felt quite epic for a punk band. The full-length is a massively underrated release of East Bay punk gems with sharp corners and ultra-catchy guitar hooks—one of the highpoints is undoubtedly Skip's vocals that run the spectrum of genuine passion over some of the best guitar work that Lookout! had seen.

Andy Ernst: One of the best Lookout! recordings I did was the Wynona Riders' *J.D. Salinger*. It was the first time I ever had a punk band sign a production contract, but Skip wanted a lot of input from me. They took over a week to record, and we only mixed two or three songs a day. It was slightly over the top, but it was meant to be.

The Mr. T Experience

Meanwhile, the Mr. T Experience was going through another of their near-trademarked patches of member ups and downs. With Jym Pittman on drums and Aaron Rubin freshly back from law school in Los Angeles, the band recorded a selection of new tunes.

Aaron Rubin (MTX, Samiam): When I moved back, I got in touch with [Dr.] Frank, and we started talking about doing some MTX stuff again.

We found Jym through a flyer at a record store, and he joined us for the recording of the *...And the Women Who Love Them* EP.

Frank "Dr. Frank" Portman (MTX, The Bomb Bassets): Jym particularly made a difference, in that the way he played suited my songs, and it wasn't so much of a struggle—then the scene was set and we jumped into it, and while it worked, it worked pretty great.

The **LK 106** 7-inch was released as the *Tapin' Up My Heart* vinyl, while the **LK 106** CD version became *...And the Women Who Love Them*—a seven-track EP featuring the 7-inch along with five extra tracks. The recording had originally been pitched to Chris Appelgren by Aaron Rubin at a time the band appeared to be disintegrating. The outcome of the session was a leaner, rawer version of MTX. The leads and solos appeared to have been elbowed out once and for all, while the total catchiness of Dr. Frank's songwriting stood proudly atop the shoulders of the new version of the powerpop trio. Kevin Army once again helmed the recording, the recording that would, upon completion, see the real and final departure of Aaron Rubin.

Aaron Rubin: To me, it's really the *...And the Women Who Love Them* EP that marks the turning point for MTX. That is my favorite record from the time that I was in the band, and I think [it] is where Frank started to zero in on the formula that would lead to more success with *Love Is Dead* and the later records. Kevin produced almost every record I did with MTX. I think, starting out, it was a learning experience for all of us, and some of the earlier records show that. Plus, the studios we used in those pre-digital days were not great. But overall, I think Kevin did a good job and definitely got better as time went on. I do remember that Kevin had a bit of that Berkeley political correctness in him, and he would sometimes cringe at some of Frank's more irreverent lyrics. Then Samiam got busy so I didn't have time to do MTX anymore.

The Queers

With Screeching Weasel's Dan Vapid still on board, the Queers returned with an EP release of a Ben Weasel cowritten song, "Surf Goddess." The 1995 *Surf Goddess* EP (**LK 108**) didn't add any new surprises to the track and was joined with two covers, as well as the track "Quit Talkin'." A solid stopgap on the way to the band's next album, it featured another cool Chris Appelgren cover illustration featuring his Felix the Cat–inspired Queers mascot riding a surfboard.

Chris Appelgren: I had done the *Beat Off* artwork with some logo illustrations by Patrick Hynes, and the band seemed to like the Queers cats I was making. I had borrowed some old Felix comics for the art for the *Love Songs for the Retarded* album and was continuing the theme. It wasn't requested by them—I sort of foisted it on them. By *Move Back Home*, they were pretty tired of it I think.

Released shortly after the *Surf Goddess* EP, *Move Back Home* (**LK 114**) was the band's filler album. With the punk-by-numbers compositions, the Queers had lost some of the flair of the two previous albums, giving the impression of rushed new songs. While not bad by any means, they had been building up to something on another level with the fantastic *Love Songs for the Retarded* and *Beat Off*, which is probably why *Move Back Home* felt disappointing.

Chris Appelgren: The art was uninspired—they wanted a live photo and threw out my idea of a Queers cat standing head down in front of a cartoon front door, looking dejected. The recording wasn't that strong, and while there are some great songs, it's got some weak tracks. It still did pretty well but didn't feel like a step forward as the previous releases all did. I always appreciated records that felt like they were progressions from where the band had been before, and *Move Back Home* felt like a lateral record. It didn't advance the notion of the Queers.

Pansy Division

In addition to their 1995 *James Bondage* (**LK 109**) 7-inch EP, Pansy

Division also released a collection of singles, compilation tracks, and B-sides called *Pile Up* (**LK 110**) as CD-only in the same year. Gathered from previous releases on labels like Lookout!, Outpunk, and Empty Records (along with other rarities), this collection is telling in its depiction of the creative core of Christopher Freeman and Jon Ginoli. No less than four drummers are credited on the recordings that span only a few years, with only Ginoli and Freeman pictured on the inlay. Also pictured is Freeman's infamous "dick" shirt—a white T-shirt with a full-size photo image of a giant penis. Bought at a street fair, Freeman took great pride in wearing the shirt at as many shows as possible while touring with Green Day and beyond.

Christopher Freeman (Pansy Division): For the second leg of the tour, we used my shirt as the model and made our own tour shirts with the Pansy Division triangle logo on the back. It was one of the bestselling shirts we've ever had. Then, at the end of the tour when we were in NYC with Green Day at *Saturday Night Live*, Mike [Dirnt] asked me if we had any more Pansy Division logo shirts, and we didn't. I was wearing the last of the "dick" tour shirts with the logo on the back, so between tapings I took it off, cut out the logo from the back and safety-pinned it to Mike's shirt. You can see it if you look at the footage.

The shirt would again get some attention when the band had played a show, upon Green Day's insistence, at Madison Square Garden during the 1994 *Dookie* tour.

Christopher Freeman: We played with a huge lineup: Hole, Weezer, Toad the Wet Sprocket, Melissa Etheridge, Indigo Girls, Sheryl Crow and . . . *Bon FUCKING Jovi!* He was such a dick. They made us all clear the backstage when it was time for their set. I waited until they passed our door and followed Jon Bon Jovi out to where he was doing air-punches like Rocky while being filmed for his big return to [Madison Square Garden]. I was wearing the dick shirt, and I made sure I got within his sightlines. He saw me and paused for a minute, totally distracted, then shook it off and went back to being the big fucking poser that he is.

The Lookouts, March 27, 1987 at 924 Gilman by Murray Bowles, Courtesy of Anna Brown

And New in the Lineup . . .

Cathy from St. Louis

Having discovered punk in the mid-1980s in St. Louis, Cathy Bauer built a network of like-minded people through tape trading with pen pals, becoming well-versed in the punk scene.

Cathy Bauer: I remember the first copy of *Flipside* that someone lent to me, and I combed over every page, squinted at every photo, and read every single advertisement. It was a new world, and I wanted in. My friends and I started going to shows before I could drive, and there was a guy booking shows who joined the service, so my best friend and I decided that we should give it a go and take over the all-important role he was leaving vacant. Over the next three years or so, we booked bands into town, from Ignition (our first show) to Shudder to Think, SNFU, Operation Ivy, and, as a send-off before college, Fugazi. This was how I got to meet a few of the early Lookout! bands that came through town like Crimpshrine, Neurosis, and Operation Ivy. I befriended Kamala [Parks], who was booking these tours, and David Hayes when he stepped into the Boilermaker's Hall along with the guys in Operation Ivy. These tours were 1987/88. On a trip to D.C., I bought a copy of the double 7-inch comp *Turn It Around!* that *MRR* put out. It was revolutionary to me, and just like *Flipside*, I read and studied every inch of it.

Bauer moved to Santa Cruz for college in the fall of 1989 with the hopes of getting into the fertile East Bay scene. With rumors circulating already that 924 Gilman Street was coming to an end, and with local bands breaking up, including Operation Ivy, it seemed as though she might have already missed the boat.

Cathy Bauer: About a month after I got to campus, there was a tremendous earthquake and everything shut down. I hitched a ride with my roommate to Oakland and spent that week with Matt Freeman and

Kamala—and we watched footage of my new hometown on the news as people were able to get cameras and help down there. Everything was a mess, but they made me feel right at home. I went along with Matt to band practice, and his new band played their first show that weekend. At Berkeley Square, I saw Samiam play their first show along with Downfall. In the ashes of Isocracy and Operation Ivy, these bands provided the sound of a whole new East Bay to me.

Over the course of the early 1990s, Bauer became a fixture of the East Bay scene, befriending, among many others, Chris Appelgren and Molly Neuman.

Chris Appelgren: I knew Cathy from the local scene, having seen her with Matt Freeman. I finally talked to her during a Rancid show, at the Punks with Presses warehouse. She was a photographer and saw the Peechees a bunch of times.

For Appelgren, Bauer's help easing the workload was a chance to focus his energy on other areas of the label. Bauer took over production work, learning hands-on.

Cathy Bauer: When they decided to go on tour, they asked me to come into Lookout! and answer the phones and keep an eye on things. I stayed on after they got home, just doing whatever needed to be done in the office. That summer of 1995, Lookout! had just moved from Larry's house to an office on University Avenue. There seemed to be tons of space, and it was so nice compared to Larry's house where you had to yell up to the second floor to let someone know you were outside. I never worked at the house, but visited there a few times. [Larry and I] went out for coffee, and he said that there was a job for me, he just didn't know what it would be. If I decided to work there, we'd figure it out. I said yes and started by taking over production from Chris, who was completely [in] over his head. I had a thousand questions for Chris since at that time we were up to over a hundred releases and certainly had some trial by fire as Green Day was blowing up and our distributor was struggling to keep up with the demand. I was struggling to keep up with all of it. In 1995/96 there were a ton of new releases too, and every record outsold what it would have done before Green Day. So I was working on everything—

Queers, MTX, Hi-Fives, Riverdales, and more. Posters, band merch, 7-inches, new LPs (and tapes), and ordering Green Day by the pallet-full.

MTX: Reader Moves to Berkeley

Joel Reader spent the early nineties with a variety of his elder sister's punk LPs and tapes after she went to college in Berkeley. During Reader's senior year, he visited his sister Nicole, taking advantage of the trip to preview the local life along with the University of California, where he planned to attend. After spending the night in student housing and touring campus, Joel spotted another potential music opening.

Joel Reader (MTX, The Bomb Bassets, The Avengers): I'd taken a flyer from a telephone pole which read: "Pop-punk band seeks bass player. We sound rather like the Mr. T Experience." I figured it might be a good idea to connect with some musicians who shared my musical tastes for when I started college and wanted to join a group, so I pocketed the number. I also knew that no trip would be complete without checking out Gilman Street. So there I am at Gilman, watching the bands and taking in the scene, when I spot Dr. Frank in the crowd. I work up the courage to approach him and tell him what a big fan I am, and also to ask if they're still together since I hadn't heard about them being up to anything in a little while. He answered that they were sort of still together, but that they were having trouble finding a bass player and by the way, he asked half-jokingly, he didn't suppose that I played. That's when the lightbulb went [on] over my head. It turned out that the flyer I had in my pocket was for the Mr. T Experience, only they weren't getting any responses so they changed the wording to mislead applicants into thinking they'd be joining a new band. At this point, I was feeling my destiny calling me, but once I'd admitted to Frank that I was only in high school I don't think he took me very seriously—I was thirteen years his junior, after all. However, I was diligent and called the number to set up an audition. I had already taught myself almost the entire back catalog.

Chris Appelgren: I remember that it really seemed with the departure of Jon Von and then Aaron Rubin that the Mr. T Experience may be ending. I heard from someone that Frank had met a kid that was a huge MTX fan and that he was going to be the new bass player. It was around this time that I started working with Frank more, and though I don't know if I saw them immediately after Joel joined, I did start to see them playing out a lot more—and with a lot more great energy. The shows felt more energetic, lively, and somehow less adult. Joel was really enthusiastic and lively onstage and had sort of a punk pinup appeal.

With the revitalizing injection of youth, Dr. Frank dubbed this lineup the "MTX Starship"—an in-jokev on *Star Trek: The Next Generation*, as well as a play on the shortened title of Jefferson Starship to plain old Starship.

Chris Appelgren: Before the Starship lineup, MTX was playing to, locally, more of a college type circuit, over-21 shows, and seemed to gig with other, older and more established Bay Area bands. Although that may have been my own skewed perception from the time, I was barely an adult myself.

Joel Reader: It felt very natural while it was happening. We did away with any guitar solos or extended instrumental sections and simply played the songs with efficiency and with as much energy as we could muster. Plus, I really do think that Dr. Frank was reaching another level with his songwriting, and the new material seemed to flow effortlessly and endlessly out of him.

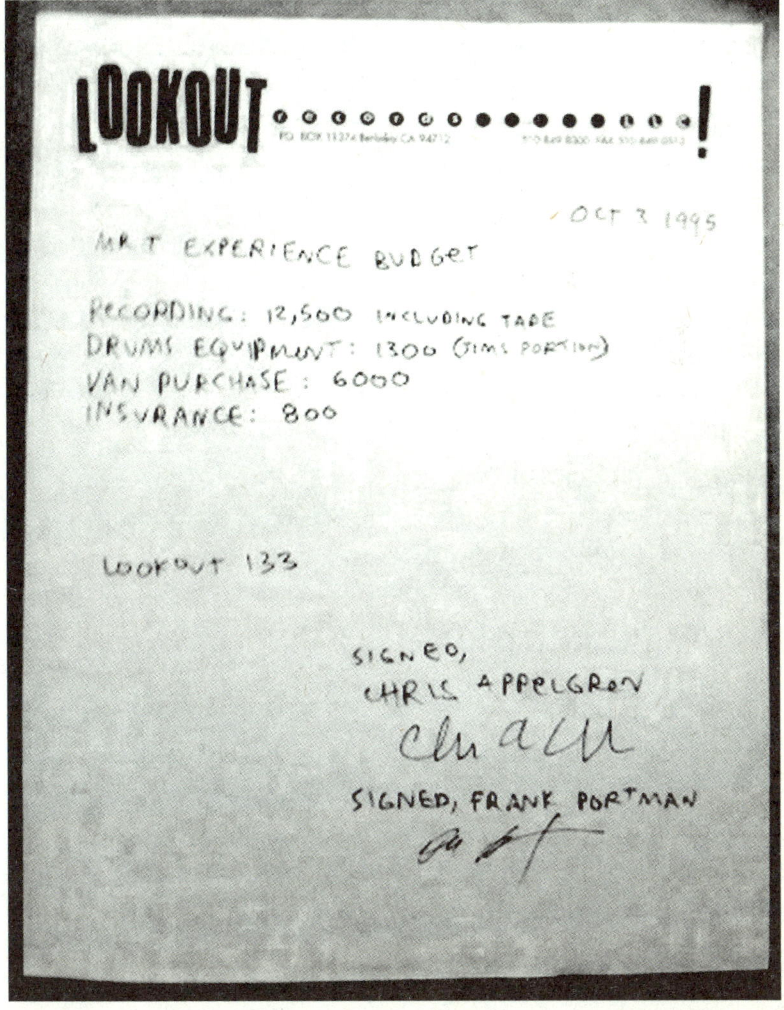

LOOKOUT!

OCT 3 1995

MR T EXPERIENCE BUDGET

RECORDING: 12,500 INCLUDING TAPE
DRUMS EQUIPMENT: 1300 (JIMS PORTION)
VAN PURCHASE: 6000
INSURANCE: 800

LOOKOUT 133

SIGNED,
CHRIS APPELGREN

SIGNED, FRANK PORTMAN

The contract and budget for the Mr. T Experience's 1996 album, Love is Dead. *They had watched recording budgets skyrocket over their time with Lookout!.*

Excitement was running high at Lookout! with hopes that the interest in the band—spurred on by the successful releases *...And the Women Who Love Them* and *Alternative Is Here to Stay*—would make the new album more of an event all around. Stepping into the studio, once again with Kevin Army, the Mr. T Experience laid down the tracks for the album *Love Is Dead* (**LK 134**). Enjoying the biggest recording budget from Lookout! up until that point, the Mr. T Experience recorded a collection of tunes that would be regarded as the band's finest hour.

Chris Appelgren: Frank seemed particularly inspired. As I recall, he was out of a relationship and full of the kind of awesome bitterness that produced the album title and songs like "Dumb Little Band."

Joel Reader: We did tons and tons of touring behind that album. We toured with the Smugglers, Groovie Ghoulies, the Hi-Fives, and Squirtgun. It was new to me, of course, so I didn't know any different, but I have to believe in hindsight that I came along during a chaotic and transitional time in Lookout! Records' history. Chris was involved by the time I came on the scene . . . and I can only imagine that the explosion of their catalog and subsequent influx of income must have been like trying to drink from a fire hose for such a small, DIY label.

Flying high, the MTX Starship found it the perfect time to reissue some out-of-print material. As was a Lookout! business move with other artists, the label rereleased MTX's work from other labels for **LK 144**—*Night Shift at the Thrill Factory* and **LK 145**—*Big Black Bugs Bleed Blue Blood*, both originally released by Rough Trade.

WaterWorks

Squirtgun

Having appeared on the *Punk USA* compilation in the band Rattail Grenadier, siblings Massimiliano (Mass) and Flaviano Giorgini piqued Lookout!'s interest with their new project, Squirtgun. Mass and Livermore had known each other since 1987, and the band's joyful sugary pop-punk styling made them an obvious fit for the label. Livermore had also traveled and spent some time with the brothers and their father. Mass's close friend Matt Hart rounded out Squirtgun on vocals and Dan Lumley played drums.

Matt Hart (Squirtgun): The Giorgini brothers and Lumley grew up in Lafayette, Indiana, and I lived in Evansville. I was in a band called the Indoor Plants. We ended up playing a show together in Evansville in 1987 and really hit it off. That one show made us great friends. After that, my band—which always seemed to be changing—would go to Lafayette and play. Rattail Grenadier would make its appearances in Evansville, and then later in Muncie at Ball State where I went to college. My band during those days was F.O.N.—Freaks of Nature. After college, I went to grad school for philosophy at Ohio University. One day I got a call from Mass asking me to drive over to Lafayette and do some vocal tracks for a new project that he and Flav were working on. One thing led to another, and that new project turned out to be Squirtgun.

Mass Giorgini (Rattail Grenadier, Squirtgun, The Mopes, Screeching Weasel, Common Rider): Squirtgun was definitely born directly out of Rattail Grenadier. Rattail Grenadier was a very scattered band, stylistically speaking. We ranged from Ramones-style three-chord pop-punk to very metallic hardcore. With Squirtgun, we focused our energy [on] one of the many styles of the band. When I mentioned the name to Larry, he said he didn't like [it] and added, "It sounds like a coy reference to a cock."

The *Shenanigans* 7-inch EP (**LK 118**) took hold on the first listen with its catchy, bouncing pop-punk, and showed how much of a good time the band must have been having. Listening to this record was a good time, so much so that the first track, "Social," found its way into the opening titles of the 1995 Kevin Smith movie, *Mallrats*, as well as onto the film's soundtrack.

Matt Hart: I think one of the first songs we recorded of mine was "Social," and according to Mass—I don't remember this—the vocals were done in one take. I remember I played the guitar solo on this skronky, beat-to-shit Telecaster I had—it was crazy with a stupid skull painted on it and a volume knob that was so loose you can hear it rattling through the amp on the track. Right before the solo starts, you can hear the volume as I turn it up, this moment of metal knocking against wood. It sounds noisy and sort of dissonant, and wrong—which is why I love it. The fact

that so many people have seen *Mallrats*, and know the band because of it, is great. Even when people don't know the band, a lot of them have seen that movie, and they remember that opening sequence. Most bands don't even get one song that hangs around in the ether the way "Social" has, so I'm grateful for that. It's so funny to think that I wrote that song in a dorm room at Ball State when I was eighteen. I probably still have the journal I wrote it in somewhere.

The Riverdales

After Screeching Weasel had broken up and released their departing gift for Lookout!, *Kill the Musicians*, Ben Weasel and Dan Vapid had already begun work on their next project. The new band, the Riverdales, was highly influenced by the Ramones and fifties chart hits. Dan Panic was on drums, rounding out the trio. Although the band had initially been a new musical outlet for Ben Weasel outside of Screeching Weasel, it didn't sit well with Jughead.

John "Jughead" Pierson (Screeching Weasel, The Mopes, Even In Blackouts): Well, obviously it was too emotional for me to even listen to. It was everyone but me. So I could never get past that, when he peopled it with everyone but me. But my feeling is that even though at times they may have enjoyed my voice being gone, the voice of a mother, I think Dan [Vapid] and Dan [Panic] had a hard time with Ben. I think, ultimately, Screeching Weasel was more a place of experimentation for Ben. Riverdales were all about being the Ramones.

Dan "Vapid" Schafer (Screeching Weasel, Sludgeworth, The Queers, Riverdales, The Mopes): Ben asked if I wanted to join his new band the Riverdales. I thought about it and told him that I wanted to sing the songs that I was writing. He said, what if I sang my songs and you sing yours? I agreed.

LK 115 and **LK 117** marked the 1995 vinyl debuts for the newly formed Riverdales. The two singles were A-sides picked up directly from the forthcoming Lookout! debut LP, with exclusive B-side tracks. Both 7-inches had a similar vibe and featured cover art designed like Arturo Vega's classic Ramones designs, with black-and-white, leather-and-jeans photos against brick wall backdrops. Screeching Weasel is still detectable throughout, though the intentional direction shines through and gives the band a smoother edge.

Not long after, the Riverdales released a debut album. Working alongside Mass Giorgini at Sonic Iguana and with Billie Joe Armstrong on board to help with the mix, the Riverdales' self-titled, twelve-track LP (**LK 120**) distinguished them from Screeching Weasel. Dan Vapid, rather than Ben Weasel, was featured singing lead on the black-and-white action shot on the sleeve, with Weasel supporting, head bowed. As previously agreed between Vapid and Weasel, the dual songwriters performed the vocals for their own compositions.

Dan "Vapid" Schafer: Even though this record is probably my least favorite record I've ever played on, it sold great—it was the perfect time to be in a pop-punk band on Lookout! Records. We were pretty much doing the right thing at the right time. If I could go back in time and do it over again, I would have opted or hoped for Billie Joe Armstrong to have been there for the recording process and not just the mix. Working with Billie was my favorite part about making the record as he had some great ideas. I think if he was involved from the start I would have really liked that record. But he wasn't, and we made some rookie mistakes.

Although the Riverdales were immediately embraced by pop-punk listeners, the first album was a bumpy start. The songwriting was a little flat, and the recording may have been slightly premature. Given Vapid's obvious skill at honing a hook—as evidenced in the broken-up Sludgeworth—the potential for an astounding album was there, but it never really stepped up.

Chris Appelgren: The Riverdales were in many ways an extension of Screeching Weasel—leaner and more refined but still corresponding to Ben's ideas about punk sound and look. At the same time, all of the members—especially Ben—had done a ton of small-scale and mostly unprofitable touring. It was the beginning of the [Lookout!] staff feeling taxed to provide results for Ben and his bands but never feeling very appreciated. We had done a ton of work to get them on a Green Day tour, to help get Billie Joe to remix the album, and yes, it was frustrating that Ben didn't seem to appreciate it. I think our sour attitude contributed

tracks

- *Fun Tonight*
- *Judy Go Home*
- *Wanna Be Alright*
- *Back to You*
- *Not Over Me*
- *She's Gonna Break Your Heart*
- *I Think About You During Commercials*
- *Rehabilitated*
- *Plan 13*
- *Outta Sight*
- *In Your Dreams*
- *Hampton Beach*

From Chicago come ***THE RIVERDALES*** *who, with every beat and every riff, extol the virtues of punk straight outta the textbooks of RocknRoll High School. Lookout Records swears that you can trust Ben, Vapid and Panic to deliver the goods; their time served in SCREECHING WEASEL stands as their testimony. Oh yeah, the LP comes with a deluxe giant* ***RIVERDALES*** *poster.*

prospective release date June 23, 1995
UPC # 7-633610-0120-4-3 (-2-9)
exportable to all territories

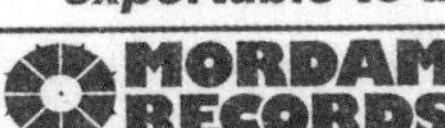

PO Box 420988, San Francisco, CA 94142
FREIGHT: 2180 Folsom St., SF, CA 94110
(415) 575-1970 FAX (415) 575-1977

to the breakdown between the label and Screeching Weasel when they later re-formed.

When the Riverdales scored an opening slot on Green Day's *Insomniac* tour, Weasel's distaste of touring ended the opportunity abruptly, and the Hi-Fives filled in. Also, by his request, a PR company had been hired to push the band and tour, to underwhelming results. Trying to move the Riverdales to the next level was proving to be a hard sell, and with Foster's cooperation not forthcoming, Appelgren's tolerance was thinning.

Chris Appelgren: I remember how we worked hard, thinking it would be a big release. It just seemed that the idea of the band was too narrow for the kind of success they hoped to achieve. Screeching Weasel's peers were Green Day, Jawbreaker, Samiam, Offspring, and Rancid, and it seemed to make sense that if they put the energy and work into a new band, they could create a large-scale success but hopefully without signing to a major. They shot a video with Bruce LaBruce, but they hated it, and we shelved it after spending thousands of dollars. I went down to LA for two shows of the tour to try to smooth things over with Green Day's tour manager, who had been really frustrated by the Riverdales. It was all expensive, and we gave them tour support—something Lookout! had never done before—but still it was a slog and not very fun or triumphant. Being an opening band on a big tour doesn't pay well and requires a certain kind of attitude—super positive and hungry. It was just frustrating, and there was a palpable feeling that Lookout! had done so much to help make the band successful, and they didn't seem to appreciate the effort or didn't want to follow our advice.

It was not a surprise when Weasel broke up this band as well. Livermore had previously promised him a role in Lookout! itself, but began to distance himself as the label's other successes grew. After bringing bands like the Vindictives and the Queers to the table, Weasel began to feel unappreciated—even cheated.

Crossing Borders

Leading into 1996, Lookout! began a host of one-off appearances and EPs from various bands from all over the globe as the release frenzy from the label's golden financial period blossomed.

Some of the bands seemed to come from left field, but others showed Lookout!'s affection for the growing garage punk and rock roster taking shape outside of the powerpop punk scene. The label teamed up with a couple of Canadian bands as well as with a label partner to the north, Vancouver-based Mint Records.

Cub & Cuddlecore

Cub was the creation of singer and songwriter Lisa Marr, a former member of the Evaporators; with Robynn Iwata, Marr's college radio comrade in British Columbia; and Valerina Fellini, a fellow musician and friend of Marr's from the Ridge Theater—a single screen movie house where Mint Records cofounder (and Lisa Marr's then boyfriend) Bill Baker worked.

Lisa Marr (Cub): The first Cub practice was in my basement on May 15, 1992; our first show was at a summer solstice party at my house in June. We thought it was going to be a goofy, once-in-a-while kind of thing, but it just sort of snowballed. Valeria left the band in 1994, and then Lisa G. [Nielsen] joined.

Between 1992 and 1994, Cub released several EPs and a debut album, *Betti Cola*, on Mint.

Lisa Marr: Valeria had absolutely no interest in touring. It was Robynn, me, and Dave Carswell of the Smugglers on drums. Grant Lawrence of the Smugglers came along as tour manager. We played a show with the Ne'er Do Wells at Manila Hall, just outside Arcata, California, and Larry was there. We hung out again at our show in San Francisco and went to a Potatomen show at Gilman Street the next night. We got along terrifically right from the start.

Following Cub's second full-length for Mint, *Come Out Come Out*, the band collaborated with Livermore's Potatomen, recording a split 7-inch EP/CD (**LK 124**) after various shows and short tours together.

The four-track split (six on the CD with an additional cover version by each band) was the first of several co-releases between Mint Records and Lookout!. Bill Baker and cofounder Randy Iwata (Robynn Iwata's brother) had similar values and ideas to what Lookout! had been doing, so Mint was a good fit. The split was a perfect taster for new listeners unaware of the north-of-the-border songstresses and self-styled "cuddlecore" pioneers. The bands fit well together, and it was a successful release in a series of great split EPs between the two.

The Smugglers & the Hi-Fives

The Summer Games EP, a 1996 Hi-Fives / Smugglers split 7-inch/CD (**LK 129**) introduced another band that bonded with Lookout!. Having formed in 1988 in West Vancouver, British Columbia, the Smugglers had already spent half a decade cranking out their high-energy and visually impressive rock and roll. By the early 1990s, they were working with Seattle's PopLlama Records.

Grant Lawrence (The Smugglers): We were tired of the Seattle PopLlama scene; grunge was dying out—although we were always way more pop rock and roll than grunge—and I just loved all those Lookout! records. I got into local show promotion, and we put on a gig for the Queers, and one of the opening acts was the Potatomen. We put on a great all-ages show, which the Smugglers played, and everybody from the Queers and the Potatomen liked us a lot. Chris and Larry said "You're just like this band we know called the Ne'er Do Wells!" which we would hear a lot for the next few years. I stayed in touch with Larry, and he visited Vancouver often, visiting Mint Records where I worked. I put on another show for the Potatomen and the Smugglers, and this time Mass Giorgini was playing bass with them, and he offered to produce us. I took him up on it, and that's how *Selling the Sizzle* got recorded in Lafayette, Indiana. We weren't signed to Lookout! yet, but Larry was very interested and even flew out to the recording sessions so we knew it was pretty much going to happen. Then we arrived in San Francisco after recording the album, as we had a gig at the Bottom of the Hill club, and Chris and Molly [Neuman] met us at our van as we pulled up and said "We've heard your record, and we want to put it out." We all freaked out. Mint put out the record in Canada, Lookout! the rest of the world.

The split between the Hi-Fives and the Smugglers prompted a tour to promote the release between the kindreds. The bands each recorded another Lookout! release: the Hi-Fives' *And a Whole Lotta You!* (**LK 135**) and the Smugglers' *Selling the Sizzle* (**LK 136**). The two bands formed a bond over being constantly compared, making them valuable touring and partying partners.

Jess Hillard (The Ne'er Do Wells, Judy & The Loadies, The Hi-Fives): The Smugglers and their friends were always pretty awesome to be around—great senses of humor, and of course they always sounded great—[they were] one of the bands we'd played with that I actually enjoyed seeing and hearing.

Chris Appelgren: I think as guys they were very similar—both liked sixties garage and pop and were fans of each other.

Grant Lawrence: We were very close friends with the Hi-Fives. Larry and Chris were right to compare us, but we couldn't really tour that much together because we were too similar.

The band hit the ground running after the *Selling the Sizzle* full-length was released. The album's first track "To Serve, Protect and Entertain" hit the speakers with its rolling garage intro and Grant Lawrence's trademark nasal punk vocal tirades, proving the Smugglers fit right into the new wave of Lookout! bands.

Grant Lawrence: It was a really amazing time in music and punk rock and somehow, some way, our band had actually become a part of Lookout! Records, and it was a dream come true, like winning the rock and roll lottery. Before Lookout!, when we were on PopLlama Records of Seattle, the artists were a lot older than us. On Lookout!—besides Larry—they were all our age so we instantly got along with the staff and the bands. It turned out I knew Molly from her riot grrrl days in Bratmobile. It was a great time.

Pansy Division Goes Down Under

After spending 1994 treading the boards with Green Day, Pansy Division found itself embarking on the Flowerslave tour in January and February of 1995, before heading to Australia and New Zealand for a string of gigs.

Christopher Freeman (Pansy Division): I do remember that we played in Canberra at some upscale bar that was clearly an inappropriate venue for a rock band—but I did meet a guy who must have been the model for Crocodile Dundee. We had great shows in Melbourne with the Mavis's, a band I fell in love with and still do love. Regurgitator was on some of the shows as well. Evan Dando came to see us in Sydney, and Jon [Ginoli] was truly smitten. We reminded him that we'd met before at Madison Square Garden a few months earlier. One of the things I liked most was that we were treated like we were stars. It felt really good to have that kind of attention on us, and I think we delivered to those who were at the shows. We were taken around to different radio stations for interviews and meeting local celebs, and it was all a pleasant surprise since that had never happened to us before that. The worst part was a show with Boom Crash Opera. They were nice, and I totally didn't mind them, but somehow the promoter thought having this double-bill play on a stage that folded out from a semi parked in the lot of a YMCA by the pool was a good idea. It wasn't. As soon as those families with little kids heard "Fem in a Black Leather Jacket," it was over. I remember gritting my teeth through most of the set, and Jon just not singing most of the lyrics. He looked over at me as we started "Bunnies," shook his head and mouthed, "No way." By that point, most of the crowd had left the pool area, parents giving us dirty looks as they whisked their kids away from those "bad people."

Pansy Division was also busying themselves with a new EP—the 1995 *Valentine's Day* 7-inch (**LK 127**)—that was, while still lighthearted, not as filled with sexual humor, balancing the scales between explicit and introspective.

Follow-ups

Squirtgun

Squirtgun returned to the scene with a self-titled full-length, **LK 128**, jumping in where the *Shenanigans* EP left off with another upbeat pop-punk album kicking from song to song at full throttle. If, at the time, the album got lost in the shuffle at Lookout!, that wasn't the only hiccup.

Matt Hart (Squirtgun): In the early days it was rough. I didn't know what I was doing, and I think on some level—as silly as it sounds—we all wanted to be rock stars, which added pressure to the whole thing. To put it another way, we all felt like—or at least I felt like—this was our big chance to get to a point where we could play music for a living, the thing we loved to do. On the other hand, I was also pretty young then and not really totally invested. I was being pulled in every direction back then. I was in two other bands—and at one point three—all more noisy, dissonant, indie rock kind of outfits, and I was already really into poetry too, which is what I do now, teaching creative writing and literature at the Art Academy of Cincinnati. So for me, it all spun out of control pretty quickly. I couldn't do everything, and I wasn't willing to tour nine months a year, or more, which is what we probably needed to do.

Squirtgun did, however, make it out on tour, playing alongside pre-fame Blink-182 in Florida during a cold April.

Matt Hart: We got interviewed for the release video during that tour, and there's some ridiculous footage of me reading John Berryman's "Dream Songs" during the entire interview—what a moody bastard I was. We were all sort of miserable. I also remember at the end of the first tour playing a hardcore festival in Cleveland, thinking we were going to get our asses kicked. Of course, we didn't. Everyone stood politely with their arms crossed while we played. So, I quit the band after the first tour . . . but then stayed in . . . and everybody was angry. It was ugly. I was disappointed a lot of the time, but I shouldn't have been.

Sludgeworth

Dan Vapid and Brian Vermin's 1989 band Sludgeworth remained one of the most underrated punk bands from the early nineties.

Dan "Vapid" Schafer (Screeching Weasel, Sludgeworth, The Queers, Riverdales, The Mopes): There were two bands in the eighties that made me want to be in a punk band. One was the Ramones, and the other was Naked Raygun. The latter were my hometown heroes from Chicago. My favorite memory from Sludgeworth was a random band practice where our drummer Brian received a call asking if Sludgeworth wanted to open for Naked Raygun.

Brian "Vermin" McQuaid (Screeching Weasel, Sludgeworth): The pivotal show for me was opening for Naked Raygun. I remember we were rehearsing in my mom's basement, and she told me Naked Raygun was on the phone. It was Jeff Pezzati, and he was like "Would you be interested in opening for us at the Riv?" It was so exciting. Then after we played the show, he came up to us and said he was blown away.

Dan "Vapid" Schafer: I was excited and very nervous that we were getting the chance to play with one of my favorite bands. The show was at the Riviera, and there were approximately 2,300 people there that night. It was nerve-racking, but we just went out there and did our thing, and it went over really great. After our set, Jeff Pezzati asked if we could sign our 7-inch record for him. My mom happened to be at the show that night too. When the show was over, she came backstage, and I could tell she was proud. I was really touched by that—the combination of making an impression on both my mother and Naked Raygun in the same day was more than I could have ever asked for.

The early shows swayed local opinion to their corner, and Sludgeworth gained momentum on their home turf, releasing a 7-inch EP for Roadkill Records. Having two members of Screeching Weasel in the ranks didn't hurt. It looked as though Sludgeworth had a bright future. During 1991, up-and-coming Johann's Face Records released the band's debut album, *What's This?* The record blistered with the band's melodic and heartfelt punk anthems like "Waste It Away," "Two Feet on the Ground," and "Another Day." Vapid had stepped out from behind the bass and was solely handling the vocals, literally finding his voice—one that created a dedicated fan base in various guises over the years.

Sludgeworth self-released the *Brightside* 7-inch the next year, with two upbeat anthems that made you feel like you were discovering music for the first time, and then disbanded, leaving the door open for a Screeching Weasel reunion.

A few years of inactivity from Sludgeworth and a surge in popularity promoted a conversation between Chris Appelgren, Ben Weasel, and Dan Vapid about the out-of-print productions from Sludgeworth. The talk turned into a retrospective CD release. The reissue of the vast majority of their discography—minus funk tracks—arrived in the form of *Losers of the Year* (**LK 131**). The CD-only release also featured *What's This?*, tracks recorded for an aborted second album, unreleased tracks, and the *Brightside* EP tracks, making a fifteen-song compilation.

Brian "Vermin" McQuaid: The funk stuff was good for live shows. Recorded—not so much. As far as the funk stuff being omitted from the Lookout! release, it was a good idea to not put it on. For live shows, it was quirky and fun and a nice vacation from the crowd hearing about Dan's hopes and dreams—I'm joking Dan!

Dan "Vapid" Schafer: Sludgeworth was the most fun I ever had in a band. Despite everything, we suffered from the Chicago "local syndrome"—drawing great crowds in Chicago but virtually unknown everywhere else.

The Queers

Following *Move Back Home*, the Queers set out to dig in and put together an album that would rise above their past couple of releases. With higher expectations, they determined to step it up, knowing that they were capable of writing a classic Queers album that would capture everything the band stood for—big melodies, punk attitude, and great songwriting. What was captured was quite possibly the Queers' greatest achievement to date: the 1996 full-length *Don't Back Down* (**LK 140**).

Chris Appelgren: The Queers made an album that was not a misstep in any way. *Move Back Home* was a slight flop—filler songs, uninspired production. For *Don't Back Down*, we just all agreed not to fuck around. Loving the Beach Boys as I do, it just really spoke to me. I loved the photos and the simple art we did, and the response was great. Joe [King] is always talking about different cool projects, and sometimes they come together, sometimes they don't, but inspired by Dr. Frank and Ben Weasel and riding a wave of successful touring, being clean, and just kicking ass, they cut what I think is the band's best album.

To help craft the album, some of Joe King's musical peers were brought in to help in the form of JJ Rassler—a bandmate of King and O'Neill's from the mid-1980s—and fellow labelmate Lisa Marr of Cub. Marr provided guest vocals on the album's final track, the punk light ballad "I Can't Get Over You."

Lisa Marr (Cub): Cub had the opening slot on an American tour with the Muffs and the Queers in August 1995. Neko Case was drumming for us at that point, and everyone in the bands and the crew immediately bonded in a way I've never experienced before or since. Joe and I cowrote "I Can't Get Over You" through the mail; he sent me a cassette tape with the chorus and the music, and I wrote the verses. It was one of those absolutely effortless songs that seem to write themselves.

Joe King (The Queers): Larry came up and insisted we get Mass Giorgini. We had made a conscious decision to not use Mass, but at least we were in a different studio. He did a great job, but we were adamant that I, Hugh [O'Neill], and JJ produce. We wanted a more raw sound, indicative of the way the band sounded. Once it was recorded, we knew we had a good album. The fans liked it, so it was great. Shows got bigger and reviews were good. It was a good time. Felt good to move on musically too.

Shortly after *Don't Back Down*, the Queers had lunch with Epitaph's Brett Gurewitz while on tour. Although Joe King had been encouraged in the past by Rancid's Matt Freeman to make the move to Epitaph from Lookout!, King had always felt at home with the Queers' longtime label.

Joe King: It was great in my opinion. Lots of good energy, they really liked and cared about the bands—I loved it. We dealt with Larry, and we were really happy with the label. So to be able to go from flipping burgers in my café to playing for hundreds of people who clapped and begged us to play more was quite a thrill. I remember one show in particular—it was at the Trocadero in Philly. The place was packed. We walked onstage, and the lights went down, and the whole crowd cheered really loud. I looked behind me to see who they were cheering for, I was dumbfounded.

Even though the band was comfortable as a top tier band for Lookout!, when the larger punk force of Epitaph came knocking, King and Co. were happy to hear what was being offered. With the massive successes Epitaph had been enjoying, it made sense for a career band to take note.

Joe King: A few months later, they flew me and Hugh out to LA to have a sit-down with them. They put us up at the Hyatt on Sunset, and we yakked with them at the office. Brett got two of his lawyers in to meet us—we decided to do a three-album deal, and we shook hands on it. I remember we had asked Lookout! to fax our contract over, so we could show the lawyers what we owed Lookout!, which was one album. We figured we'd do some outtake album or something, and that would be it. Molly [Neuman] was so upset about us even talking to Epitaph she faxed a paper that said we owed them thirteen albums! It was so over the top. They knew it was bullshit, and of course I knew we only owed Lookout! one album. No one said a word when Green Day went to a major label, but we tried to go somewhere and all sorts of shit started. I was the one dealing with the label, and all of a sudden they started talking to Hugh and B-Face. That was the beginning of the end of that lineup. All sorts of bullshit was said, and my own band didn't believe me; it was a mess. In light of subsequent events, the move to Epitaph would have been a shrewd move, to jump off that sinking ship that Lookout! was running onto the rocks. I remember driving out to our last three shows we ever did together and Hugh and B-Face giving me all sorts of shit, but they didn't know what was going on. They had no ideas or suggestions, but they just didn't like mine. I told B-Face that we had just shaken hands on a three-album deal with Epitaph, and he didn't believe me. I said, "Well, Hugh was right there and he'll tell you." Hugh said he didn't remember shaking hands with the lawyers, and at that moment I knew that lineup was history. We did two out of the three shows around Chicago, drove home, and never played together again. Now what happened with Epitaph was that shortly after we shook hands on the deal and they were getting the contracts together, Brett went AWOL with his girlfriend Gina. They basically disappeared for a year. He had tons of money so apparently—this is the story I got anyway—he went off with his wife and Gina and did drugs and had three-way sex for a year. I have no doubt it's true. I called the other guy at the label and said "Hey what's going on? We're ready to go." He said, "Brett disappeared and we don't know what the fuck is going on. So we're not going to sign any bands for a while." I got pissed and then figured fuck it, I got bigger fish to fry. So I stopped contacting them after a while and never heard from Brett again. He owes me an apology for that one. I ended up going to Hopeless, which was about the worst fucking move I could have made, but hindsight is 20/20.

Chris "B-Face" Barnard (The Queers, Groovie Ghoulies, The Mopes): By the time the band folded, things were pretty tense. The last year or so [was] a big, muddled mess. I can't tell what happened when, but at various times Hugh and I had quit the band, then apparently we were still in, and Joe asked me to leave—later claiming he "wanted to hear what I would say." Finally, I just said "fuck this." I've heard Joe say that I left and Hugh got ill, but that's not how I remember it. Hugh was living here in Boston with a new girlfriend, and neither of us were in the band. We were hanging out all the time, then he went out to LA with Joe for some ill-planned meeting with another label while the Queers were still on Lookout!, so apparently he was still in. But this was all before Hugh got sick. The band was already a complete mess. Joe had to go away for a while, and Hugh got wrapped up in his own problems, and I was asked by the Groovie Ghoulies if I could fill in on guitar for part of their tour.

The Queers managed one more release for Lookout! before moving elsewhere . . . for the time being.

Cub

Cub's *Box of Hair* (**LK 143**) came out right when consumers were looking more towards the "less indie more punk" end of the spectrum. The album was again a co-release with Mint Records and was crammed full of fantastic indie punk melodies that couldn't help but charm the listener.

Lisa Marr: By the time *Box of Hair* came out in 1996, the "punk" explosion had hit the mainstream. The Cub craze was definitely on the wane, but new audiences were discovering us through the They Might Be Giants cover of New York City. We did a big US tour with They Might Be Giants that year as well as shows and tours with a bunch of other bands too, including the Groovie Ghoulies, the Mr. T Experience, Squirtgun, and the Queers. There was definitely a family feeling to that whole mid-nineties era of pop-punk indie bands and the small labels that supported them. Although we were, in theory, on the label through the Mint/Lookout! co-releases, I never felt like Cub was a Lookout! band . . . we were kinda like the country bumpkin cousins from up north. just happy to be along for the ride.

GROOVIE GHOULIES
GROOVIE GHOULIES
GROOVIE GHOULIES
BORN IN THE BASEMEN
BOB

23

New Unions

Groovie Ghoulies

Of the next six scheduled releases, a whopping four of them were by a band new to Lookout!, Groovie Ghoulies. A husband-and-wife team from Sacramento, Jeff "Kepi" Alexander and Rochelle "Roach" Sparman had musical roots dating back to the mid-1980s and came with a perfect mix of sci-fi, horror, pop culture, and Ramones-inspired upbeat pop-punk riffs. The band had carved its own path of DIY ethics with the self-released 1989 album *Appetite for Adrenochrome* and stayed under the radar for most of the early nineties, until their next self-released album in 1994, *Born in the Basement*. Drummer Wendy Powell joined the band for the second album.

Wendy Powell (Groovie Ghoulies): We knocked *Born in the Basement* out pretty quickly. Kepi was a great marketer—we would make these coffins that we sold the first CDs in with little lockets with pics of one of the Groovie Ghoulies—a kinda collect-them-all thing. We were all living together—Kepi, Roach, and I—at the time we recorded that record. We had our basement set up as a practice place, it was fun.

Wendy and Kepi of the Groovie Ghoulies signing their contracts with Chris Appelgren.

We would roll home from work, eat dinner together, and then go practice while doing our laundry at the same time . . . . Everyone would ask me how it was playing with a couple. It was great—I got along great with both Kepi and Roach. Kepi pretty much did everything—he booked the shows, wrote the music, drove us everywhere. Me and Roach helped with merchandise and loading. I can remember maybe one domestic dispute.

Roach signs contracts with Chris.

Chris Appelgren: People had mentioned how good they were, and I happened to see them one night in San Francisco, playing at the Chameleon Club. I was by myself and remember bopping around. It was Kepi, Roach, and Wendy at that point. I talked to them after the show, and I just remember thinking how great they were, unassuming but really good performers, enthusiastic and fun. People watching the show couldn't help but smile hugely.

The band was well received and won Appelgren over, as did their work ethic. The Ghoulies signed to Lookout! soon after. But the trio didn't have much touring experience, and it became hard to sell new fans on them, despite the quality of the music. Another major issue was that Livermore wasn't really impressed with the band or their signing.

Chris Appelgren: Some people were just asking who were the Groovie Ghoulies, and why did they have three records coming out so close to each other? It was too many records too close together, it hurt sales for sure. Larry kind of stayed out of it for the most part and posed some seemingly rhetorical questions about the depth of the band's music, but in the end it seemed like once he actually saw them, he kind of "got it."

The 1996 releases that followed were the *Island of Pogo Pogo* 7-inch EP (**LK 146**), *Appetite for Adrenochrome* (reissued LP, **LK 148**), *Born in the Basement* (reissued LP, **LK 149**), and finally, the Lookout! debut LP, *World Contact Day* (**LK 151**).

Pansy Division

Sandwiched in between all the new Ghoulies output was the brilliantly metal-themed Pansy Division 7-inch—*For Those about to Suck Cock* (**LK 147**). The cover of the record featured a reimagined design of the famous AC/DC LP sleeve of *For Those about to Rock*, complete with cock and balls imagery.

Along with reworked covers of Kiss's "Sweet Pain" and Judas Priest's "Breaking the Law," the clear 7-inch features the Freeman/Ginoli original "Headbanger," an ode to picking up a metalhead in a Guitar Center. The record marked the end of the relationship with another drummer, Dustin Donaldson. Before Donaldson departed, he provided some rockstar power from his acquaintance, Metallica's Kirk Hammet. The famous axman—credited as "Al Shatonia"—played a guest guitar solo on "Headbanger," a fact that remained a secret until it was revealed much later by the Metallica members themselves. Also included on the release was a sticker spoofing MTV's Beavis and Butt-Head characters having sex. The stickers issued in the original release were later all removed by hand following a cease and desist order from MTV.

Fifteen

After a three-year break from Lookout!, Fifteen returned for **LK 150**, the *Ooze* 7-inch EP (with *There's No Place like Home (Good Night)* as the CD version).

Jeff Ott (Crimpshrine, Fifteen): The label was still mainly Larry at that point, but as *Dookie* came out there was tons of money all of a sudden, which led to Larry getting harassed a lot by *MRR* and others. I sensed that he was sick of it all, but that's just my feeling about it. Before Larry left, I could show up early and say, "Larry, I need to get paid before royalties are due because of this or that," and he would do it. Once or twice I went to get paid and he would be like, "I just pressed a zillion Operation Ivy CDs, and we don't have money for a while," and the bands would be fine with it. It was really casual and understanding all the way around.

The Phantom Surfers

The Phantom Surfers were already San Francisco–scene veterans by the time **LK 155**—*The Great Surf Crash of '97* LP—and the **LK 156** *Istanbul* 7-inch were released. Led by Mel Bergman, the Phantom Surfers had ten years of history, a vast release schedule, and had crafted a niche with their garage/surf/punk ditties by the time they jumped to Lookout!.

Mel Bergman (The Phantom Surfers, The Go Nuts): We were pals with the Hi-Fives, and they stayed at my house in LA when they were opening for Green Day on the *Dookie* tour. So my wife and I got to tag along to the shows. The Hi-Fives endured a shower of shoes being thrown at them in Phoenix.

John Denery (Brent's T.V., Judy & The Loadies, Ne'er Do Wells, The Hi-Fives, The Bomb Bassets): There were several thousand upset, disappointed, and angry fans who saw nothing redeeming in us. We made some change on stage from the quarters being pelted at us.

Mel Bergman: I saw lots of booing in LA, but that crowd was there for their heroes. Elvis would have got booed. That's where I met Chris.

Chris Appelgren: I already had the Phantom Surfers Estrus [Records] releases and was a fan; in fact, I thought of them as the premiere surf band. I felt like, of the garage scene at the time, the Phantom Surfers were the most interesting and visionary of the bunch—I really did appreciate their irreverence, and I felt it was totally right for the label.

Mel Bergman: We had been offered a contract from Rick Rubin's American Recordings that year. They pulled every sleazy record company tactic under the sun, so we passed. We were making pretty good dough selling our own records, and we had no intentions of being a full-time band. We would have lost all rights to our name if we'd signed with them.

Chris Appelgren: I knew there was some deal in the works. I had heard they were talking to American and remember wondering why they would want to talk to another label. I recall wondering why they'd want to talk to Lookout!.

Michael Lucas (The Phantom Surfers): Chris was the driving force behind us getting signed. Molly [Neuman] was fine with it, and she was generally in a happier state of mind at that point. I may have confused what was actually a general depression on Molly's part in subsequent years with a dislike for me. Then again, my joking about her reminding me of Miss Havisham of *Great Expectations* when she was sitting in her dim office might have rubbed her the wrong way.

The Lookout! debut LP and 7-inch carried on the fun tradition of rocked-out surf that the Phantom Surfers had crafted over the previous years. The fantastic cover art was a product of Jack Davis, original artist for *Mad Magazine*. The releases were great party soundtracks and proved to be good sellers for a band just starting out at the label.

Chris Appelgren: The record was really fun. I liked how the title worked well with the idea of the Phantom Surfers signing to Lookout! and loved the Jack Davis artwork. I felt as though Lookout! signing the Phantom Surfers was part of the punk scene intermingling more with other underground scenes that had been sort of their own distinct communities previously. I may be oversimplifying things a great deal but at least in the Bay Area, it seemed like two different groups of folks.

Mel Bergman: Most people were indifferent, many hated it, and a small amount of folks totally dug it. We did however get lots of gigs because we were on Lookout!.

Chris Appelgren: My favorite memories of them are two shows they played with the Cramps, one in San Francisco and one in LA. It was Halloween, and onstage in San Francisco at the Warfield—a huge venue—they had a friend come onstage as the dead Bill Graham, sort of a zombie version of the famous San Francisco promoter. The venue staff cut their sound and kicked them off the stage. It was hilarious.

Mel Bergman: Then there was the time we opened for Fugazi. That was one uptight crowd. They were polite and all, but were very perplexed by the Phantom Surfers. We got hired to go to Norway because they had a Screeching Weasels fan. We played some gigs for this guy who was a Screeching Weasel fanatic. We were all he could get. We also played with the Queers and Vanilla Ice. It was bad until we played the intro of "Ice Ice Baby."

A Surf Wedding

In June 1996, Chris Applegren and Molly Neuman had the cool, underground punk wedding of the year. Along with the usual suspects, there were musician guests: Fugazi, Green Day, Bikini Kill, and Rancid, with live entertainment provided by the Phantom Surfers. It had been four years of spending time together in the punk rock scene, working on the label, being with bands 24/7, and touring together in their own band. Appelgren was twenty-three years old.

Chris Appelgren: We had both been young, maybe too young to be married, but I think we both also grew a great deal because of the experience. It was pretty exciting to do all this cool stuff with someone you loved.

Rop Vasquez (Rice, The Peechees): The wedding was like a who's who of early indie rock, and it was held in this weird structure boat. But it was one hell of a wedding, I remember laughing—going "This is out of control," both my bandmates and coworkers were getting married in this big deal, and we were supposed to be punk kids, and it's like a circus of people getting wasted. I was one of Christopher's best men, and I spent most of the wedding helping out, seating and showing people where the gifts went and making sure the gifts got back to their house, just helping with almost everything. I figured since I never had any money that my gift was to help with the wedding.

Mel Bergman: They hired us right after we signed. Now it is well known that we are batting zero percent at weddings. We played, the guests danced their asses off, Billie Joe's kid, Joey, played drums—I think he was two or three years old at the time—and Molly and Chris ended up happily ever . . . well . . . hire us and a divorce is in the cards. We don't play weddings anymore for that reason, that, and no one asks us anymore.

Sweet Baby

In 1997, eight years after its original release on Slash Records, one of the early blueprint pop-punk classic albums was reissued on a CD-only release by Lookout!: Sweet Baby's *It's a Girl* (**LK 157**). Although signed to a high-profile label, Sweet Baby had essentially run its course in 1987, with the four members' interest waning and itching to move on to other projects.

Sweet Baby announced its final show, supporting the Lazy Cowgirls, to a capacity crowd at 924 Gilman Street while still in its infancy. As 1988 rolled around, Dallas Denery found himself on the receiving end of a surprising phone call from producer Kevin Army.

Dallas Denery (Sweet Baby, The Bomb Bassets): Without telling us, Kevin had sent a tape with songs he had recorded by Operation Ivy, us, and some other bands to Matt Wallace, his friend who worked at Slash Records. For whatever reason, the folks at Slash loved our songs and wanted to sign us. We convinced Sergie [Loobkoff] and Rich [Bucher] to join up again and after some horrendous showcases to convince them we could play live, they signed us. Once this happened, either because word had gotten out or people had finally wised-up, Larry asked if Lookout! could sign us, and Tom Flynn from Boner Records asked as well. By this point, we had more or less agreed to go with Slash, who had offered to put up something like $10,000 or $20,000 to record us. Larry just wanted to give our demo an official release, and Tom was offering a very small budget to record. The idea of recording our stuff properly was pretty hard to pass up. We needed the recording money, and we ended up recording the entire record twice before it sounded right.

Chris Appelgren: It was pretty easy, we just had to pay a royalty to license it as well as contact the Warner Bros. folks to see if they were interested in doing their own reissue. Since Billie Joe had mentioned Sweet Baby being a great band or something, the president of the label wanted to see if they had an overlooked treasure.

Dallas Denery: Matt [Buenrostro] and I had some songs to write, we wrote them, we performed them, recorded them and went on to other things. We weren't musicians and never imagined ourselves having some career as musicians. To be honest, as things became more professional, we became less interested. I love music, but I never wish I was still performing or still had a band.

PUNK
SCREECHING WEASEL
FEATURING...
THE KEEPER OF THE GREENS
18
BARK LIKE A DOG

Lawsuits & Record Stores

Weasel vs. Livermore

Screeching Weasel somehow re-formed for a third time and began work on a new album, *Bark Like a Dog*, with demos already recorded. The relationship with Lookout! was strained from the Riverdales debacle, and so, with the intention of working out a new deal with the newly re-formed band, Appelgren traveled to Chicago with Cathy Bauer to renegotiate Screeching Weasel's contract. The offers were made and a new deal negotiated. But when they got back to Lookout! HQ, the deal was quickly sidelined by Livermore, who would not entertain the new terms. The trip had been a waste and strained the relationships further. Still, trying to salvage the partnership, Lookout! flew the band out to California and put them in a Berkeley hotel to discuss the details of the proposed album. The band proposed an advance of $50,000 for the yet-to-be-recorded LP. Lookout! declined, proposing—in their eyes—a more reasonable deal. Ben Weasel scrutinized the existing contracts, with his emphasis placed on inaccurate accounting.

Lookout!'s royalty agreement appeared generous but was hard for the bands to comprehend. Both costs and profits were split 60 percent to the band and 40 percent to Lookout!. But the arguments, as always, were in the details. Lookout! apparently had a policy of unnecessarily overnighting packages and would split the expenses of each package based on whose records were inside of it, determined by the proportionate weight of each album. Ben Weasel was apparently under the impression that the elaborate mathematics were an effort to cheat him.

Chris Appelgren: It was over a kind of convoluted part of how royalties were calculated by Lookout!. . . . Our deals were normally 60/40 in the band's favor—a profit split. The only deduction from the gross income for an album was the manufacturing cost and a small extra charge deducted from each record sold. This extra charge was just for, according to Larry, operating expenses. Ben didn't want to be responsible for anything that wasn't specifically spelled out and accounted for as an expense. So, we decided to split the difference and say, let's leave out that charge and adjust the royalty rate. Larry offered 53/47 with 53 percent to the band. Ben said that it should be 54/46. Our contracts limited this charge to no more than 10 percent of the lowest wholesale price of an album, so Ben's thinking was to split that 10 percent 60/40. But Larry said the math didn't work the same way and really would not go for it being less than 53/47. So everything broke down. Seriously, over one percentage point, those two were not friends for years.

No matter the cause, Weasel and Livermore created a feud between label and band, which Livermore feared would harm Lookout! in the long run. The bitter back-and-forth negotiations were not helped by Weasel's questioning of previous contracts. The members of Screeching Weasel, one by one, made a move of no confidence concerning Livermore and Lookout!. Concerned that Weasel could potentially cause a legal war with the label and damage it, Livermore decided to strike first and file a lawsuit. Livermore wanted to get the contracts in front of a judge to determine if the label was, in fact, breaching agreements. The financial ramifications proved to be more than Weasel wanted to invest and only caused alarm on his side of the fence.

Robert Eggplant (Blatz): I assumed in 1996 that both Larry and Ben were too occupied by chasing money to care about the scene as a microcosm. When they first met, Larry and Ben clashed a bit. They are both very self assured about the righteousness of their own opinion. But in 1988, they had enough of a mutual liking for bands like Op Ivy and pop-punk in general to encourage them to work together. Larry also worked his ass off in the years leading up to leaving the label. From what I've read of Ben, I think he can respect that tendency even through his reflexive dislike towards anything hippy.

Chris Appelgren: It was a big weird bummer, and I was totally disillusioned by it myself. The whole staff was confused by what was going on, and I had become friends with Ben and confided in him that I was upset about the lawsuit. I mean, I was really bothered. Our contracts all had a point about treating each other with trust and respect and that had flown out the window here. I felt like we had an obligation to work things out with Screeching Weasel. I told him I was thinking of quitting.

Weasel had already made inroads with Fat Mike at Fat Wreck Chords while recording Fat Mike's guest vocals on *Anthem for a New Tomorrow*. It seemed a natural fit to jump ship to Fat, who quickly took the band up on its $50,000 album proposition and was also interested in the next stage of the Riverdales saga.

The fallout of the lawsuit reverberated to the loyalties and ideals of Joey Vindictive. During the rehearsal, writing, and demo stage of the Vindictives' debut Lookout! studio album, *Rat-A-Tat*, Vindictive approached Livermore with the news that if the lawsuit wasn't settled or dropped, Lookout! would lose the Vindictives.

Joey "Vindictive" Volino (The Vindictives): Involving the law in what I felt were the inner workings of the punk rock world was against all of my ethics. I saw Lookout! as this DIY indie utopia, and Larry was a hero of mine. So it was quite a blow to the spirit when that happened. Being on Lookout! while that was going down made me complicit, so I had no choice but to leave.

The Lookout! Store

In November 1996, during this drama, Lookout! embarked on another ambitious move: opening their own record store. The idea was hatched because of an empty storefront below the Lookout! offices. The store stocked everything Lookout!-related, as well as other punk releases, many from local bands. Mail orders were also run out of the space and helped pay the store's expenses. After moving from Minneapolis to Oakland, artist Erika Grove handled mail-order duties. She became romantically involved with Patrick Hynes, and a visible face at the label. Adopting the nickname "Crumbly" from her own zine, Grove created a niche, was endeared to many, and became a much-needed component of Lookout!'s public relations. Lookout! celebrated the store opening with a big party and a live appearance by the Potatomen as well as a lineup of John Denery, Chris Imlay, and Chris Appelgren riffing on some Brent's T.V. songs.

Chris Appelgren: It was fun for parties and for in-stores, though there were neighbors on the floor between our store and office that complained about noise, often. The Donnas, Auntie Christ, the Peechees, the Potatomen, the Hi-Fives, and a handful of others all played in-stores. We hired Jane Taatjes to manage the store—she had worked with Cathy [Bauer] previously at a vintage clothing store in Berkeley—and they were roomies. Erika Grove, Rop Vasquez, and Tim Tsuda were the mail-order department—they worked out of the back of the store. We had some part-timers in the store and on mail order—Jesse Townley, Monica Deaner, and some of our interns worked down there too.

Lookout!'s merchandise machine was working overtime, with no end of shirt designs in sight. Cinder Block continued to handle shirt printing for the label, and instead of working directly with the label, Cinder Block was now also licensing and selling all of the Lookout! designs that they printed. One of the big sellers of the time was the Queers' "All Stars" design, a variation on the Converse logo. After many shirts were sold in the nineties, Converse eventually issued a cease and desist order.

Chris and Cathy hang a new banner in the Lookout! store.

Strife

The Wynona Riders

The end of 1996 and leading into 1997 produced another long string of releases, including a run of 7-inch singles such as the Queers' *Bubblegum Dreams* (**LK 158**), the Hi-Fives' *It's Up to You* (**LK 159**), Squirtgun's *Mary Ann* (**LK 164**), as well as the already established the Crumbs self-titled album (**LK 161**) and *Shakespeare* 7-inch (LK **166**). The Bomb Bassets released an album, *Take a Trip with the Bomb Bassets* (**LK 165**), as did Squirtgun with *Another Sunny Afternoon* (**LK 167**) and Pinhead Gunpowder with *Goodbye Ellston Avenue* (**LK 168**). While the 12-inch EP was represented by the Potatomen's *All My Yesterdays* (**LK 160**) and the Wynona Riders' *Artificial Intelligence* (**LK 162**), a release that had already been added to the Lookout! catalog and advertised just prior to the band breaking up.

Chris Appelgren: They broke up as it was being released, and I remember being really frustrated by that because Dave [Henwood had] asked for an advance to buy a new drum set. I believe he knew they were splitting up but wanted to get the advance before I found out, knowing I would not agree to it if I knew they weren't a band. That suspicion was never confirmed, however. Before the record came out, we knew, but not before they finished making it. The drums—that was a sore point.

Joe Selby (The Wynona Riders): Why did Lookout! even release that record? There was no band to tour to promote it. And it didn't sound like *J.D. Salinger*. It's funny, Larry and I have had a lot of stupid internet arguments over the years and disagreed on a lot of things, but I've always maintained that Larry at least honored his commitments and promises and didn't do downright ass-headed things like release records no one wanted or buy a drum kit for a drummer in a band that had broken up. *Artificial Intelligence*, in any sensible world, would never have been made, let alone released. I think the excuse would be that we were their friends, and they didn't want to let us down. It wasn't in our best interests to have something else charged against our account—and trust me, that's all a record contract is, an account. Plus, Lookout! should have said to us,"Hey, you guys really can't break up. You still have expenses to pay off for *J.D. Salinger*. Take a break for six months, relax, and then give it another shot." But that kind of thinking takes maturity that was totally absent from the building.

Chris Appelgren: Maybe it was that I didn't have the foresight to know that what they wanted to do was a bad idea. I felt like the Wynona Riders had been kind of a mess, that members of the band had misrepresented what was happening. I don't recall us cross-collateralizing expenses from that album against *J.D. Salinger*, except maybe in the case of Dave Henwood's drum set. It's possible that we saw that as an individual expense and not as an album expense—but as I recall, that was probably sanctioned by the band who didn't think that the album should be responsible for buying him a new drum set. I wasn't asked to give an opinion on the band breaking up, and so I didn't offer one up. By the time they finally ended, it was sort of clear that the band didn't have the internal drive to do anything. I encountered a lot of bands that seemed to be waiting for something to happen to them, and I got that feeling working with the Wynona Riders over the years.

Furious George

George Tabb was an old-time punk veteran by the time his band, Furious George, crossed paths with Lookout!. A native New Yorker, Tabb had been writing for *MRR* for many years, as well as knocking out punk rock in Roach Motel, Iron Prostate, and False Prophets. Ben Weasel and *MRR*'s Tim Yohannan recommended that Tabb check out Lookout!. Tabb had already had some firsthand experience working with Livermore during a battle against skinheads at 924 Gilman Street in the late eighties. After working with dead-end labels over the years, Tabb believed Lookout! was the cool and trustworthy label he was seeking and, on his peers' recommendation, sent a demo to the label. Chris Appelgren responded with a letter, extended his praise for Furious George but passed on the band, citing a full roster. Even though Lookout! didn't seem like a prospective home for Furious George, Tabb continued to make personal contact and keep them updated about the band.

Chris Appelgren: I do remember George sending us stuff, and I also remember really liking him. He was a personable, friendly, and sweet guy. I also did sense his persistence. Not a bad quality to have in a band leader at all.

Eventually, during a visit to California, Tabb met with Chris Appelgren and Molly Neuman. They outlined a plan for Furious George and Lookout! to work together in some form, and Tabb headed back to New York, excited for the future. With Furious George on a lockdown rehearsal schedule, a contract was faxed to Tabb in New York that included plans for the band to work on an EP for Lookout!. What impressed Tabb the most was the inclusion of the infamous Lookout! "respect clause."

Chris Appelgren: Lawrence wrote that final clause, and it was the only item that carried over from his original lawyer-free artist agreement, like the ones signed by Green Day and Operation Ivy.

The band's next contact from Lookout! was a call from a concerned and nervous Molly Neuman: when Livermore found out about the label's new signing, he saw red, partly because he'd been left out of the loop, and partly because he felt the band didn't deserve to be signed.

Chris Appelgren: Larry was adamant against the band being on the label but did not want to be the bearer of that news, refused to, in fact. Molly [and I] both handled communications with bands, but Molly had been more nuts and bolts with Furious George.

The EP went ahead as agreed, but merchandising was on hold until the label could internally negotiate the release of the band's full-length. With expectations being everything, and this chain of events not seeming to match the respect clause, a disappointed and angry Tabb reconfirmed with Neuman about the release of the band's debut album, and was advised to record the EP for a forthcoming release on Lookout!.

The *Goes Ape!* 7-inch EP (**LK 163**) was released in September 1996, featuring guest vocals Dee Dee Ramone on "Betty Crocker, Punk Rocker." With the band relieved and on a high, they continued working on their debut full-length for Lookout!—which had a confirmed Joey

Ramone appearance. With a constantly stalling Molly Neuman and many unreturned phone calls, the band became anxious. During their appearance at the Lookout! showcase in New York, Molly didn't catch up with Tabb, leading to more frustration.

After several more weeks of miscommunication, Tabb was advised to contact Livermore. After several unsuccessful attempts, Tabb wrote a long email to inquire about exactly what was going on with Furious George and Lookout!, and the status of the full-length. The response from Livermore was frustrating at best, suggesting that Tabb wasn't going to make any headway by approaching the "top of the ladder" at Lookout!. Increasingly angry and frustrated, Tabb indicated that Neuman had directed him in Livermore's direction, and Livermore directed him back to Neuman. He was finally told that the LP wasn't going to happen. There were apologies for stringing the band along for many months, but no real explanations.

Tabb proceeded to write a long-form column for *Maximum Rocknroll*. The column outlined in great detail the entire story behind the circumstances with the band's dealings with Lookout! Records and its employees. The issue's cover depicted the Furious George monkey mascot being nailed to the cross by Lookout!. The full article and cover would have lasting effects for the label.

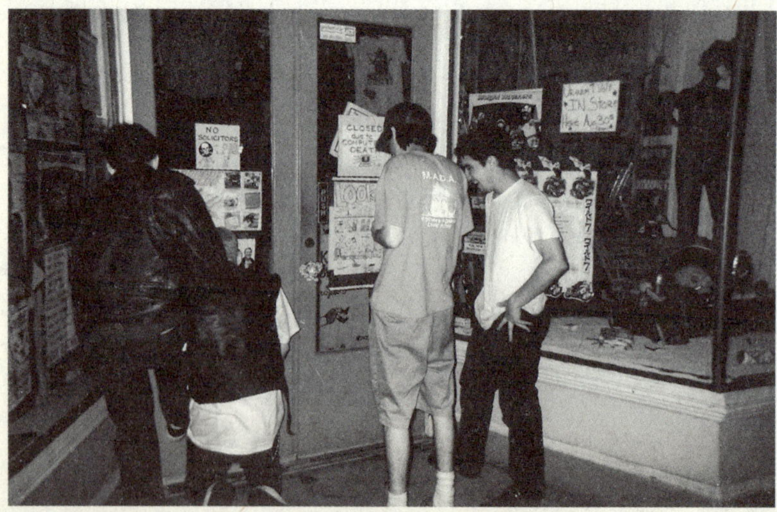

Furious George visits the Lookout! store

George Tabb (Furious George): The cover of the Furious George monkey on a cross was meant as a joke but was taken way too seriously. The next month or so there was an article called "The People vs. Larry Livermore" or something. Larry forged some instant messages making it look like I was trying to pick up on very young girls. It was all a lie and very hurtful. I'm glad it's all over, and we are friends. Needless to say, Lookout! was furious with me over the column. At first, when I wrote the *MRR* article, all the bands hated me. They told me I ruined "their label." Other Lookout! bands were furious with me at the time, saying I was going against their friends, and I was the liar. The only band that didn't give me shit was Pansy Division, who told me they kind of felt the same about the way Lookout! was heading. The Queers called me out as a liar, as did some other bands. Later, they called, apologized, and said I was right and they were sorry. It was all very sad. We all trusted Lookout! like an indie label, not a major label that fucks over bands. That's where the hurt was. Larry was always a standup guy. That's why all of this was

so surprising. Larry apologized to me years later. It did cause a short rift between Joe Queer and me, but that ended quickly. I think everyone felt like I betrayed them. All I did was tell my story. Not theirs. I don't know theirs.

Joe King (The Queers): I was sticking up for Lookout! and sort of stepped on his toes a little, but we were never fighting. I always liked George. He's a damn good writer, and I always loved his columns in *MRR*. Plus, he's a Ramones' freak [and] that love conquers all.

Chris Appelgren: We didn't respond directly to the criticism ourselves, but I feel like bands such as the Queers, MTX, Avail, and others did defend the label in interviews and directly to fans on the road. What gets sort of overlooked in George's column is that internally we were discussing this a lot, weighing our feelings about the band, sense of responsibility to the verbal commitments we'd made, and trying to balance that with Larry's very real distaste for the band. I know that George felt we dicked him around—and the label did. Larry's reasoning was that it was our fault for making this decision without him. I remember feeling like the cover was a really crummy thing to do and feeling glad that we hadn't signed the band when the issue of copyright infringement came up. We would have most certainly been named in a suit if we had signed them.

Shortly afterwards, publisher Houghton Mifflin Harcourt, a parent company that owned the famous Curious George character, filed suit. Tabb fought a battle of seven years with the company and ultimately lost.

George Tabb: I had a conversation with Ben [Weasel] about Lookout!. I told him I was disappointed things worked out the way they did, and he said he was sorry too. That was it. I was not on a crusade against Lookout!, I was just hurt. When the Houghton Mifflin thing came along, I sank my teeth into that because that was an unfair fight.

Promo Woes

These incidents continued to demonstrate the communication and internal management problems within Lookout!, which were starting to erode various relationships and unmask Appelgren's lack of decision-making experience. Tim Yohannan and *MRR* always scrutinized the punk scene, scaling back their involvement with any bands or labels the zine felt were not representative of their own narrow take on the music world, and around this time *Maximum Rocknroll* severed their relationship with Lookout!.

Chris Appelgren: They started discriminating against releases they didn't think sounded punk enough and wouldn't review or accept ads for releases that were not punk in their eyes. It also seemed to somehow be connected to the East Bay/West Bay rivalry of tearing others down in the same scene. It happened a lot back then and probably still does. We started doing ads in other zines.

As *MRR* scaled back its Lookout! coverage, Lookout! bands started expecting more promotion. Expectations were higher now that the underground had seen mainstream success, and bands wanted advertising on par with the likes of Green Day, Bad Religion, the Offspring, and Rancid.

Chris Appelgren: We had achieved a great deal of success without doing it, the thinking was that we'd do even better by doing lots of promotion. It's hard to know if we were right or not, but it felt as though there were lots of labels that were growing up, so to speak, and competition was increasing. It was initially something the bands wanted that we didn't do much of, but because it became the status quo, it got to a point where it was hard or even impossible to wean ourselves off of doing promo campaigns that involved sending out 500–1500 copies of a new release. Having a good picture and bio was really something the label needed for magazines, websites, and venues. For a while it was like, we've done this well while not doing anything, how well might we do if we did this extra bit?

After Lookout! dipped its toes into the sea of videos with the shelved Riverdales video, the label began to test the waters once more with film clips as a promo tool.

Chris Appelgren: Videos were expensive. It wasn't ever a policy, but Lookout! paid all the upfront expenses of the album, videos, and promo, even merchandise. We had good results with our videos getting shown on MTV and other local video programs. We did the Riverdales, MTX's "Ba Ba Ba Ba Ba," then Squirtgun's "Mary Ann."

Joel Reader of the Mr. T Experience, Grant Lawrence of the Smugglers, and Chris Appelgren

Rocking the Boat

Livermore Says Farewell

Following failed negotiations with Screeching Weasel, morale amongst management reached an all-time low while disagreements about company management reached an all-time high and eventually, an impasse. The three owners simply could not agree on how to resolve their disputes and expectations regarding Screeching Weasel.

Appelgren took a weekend trip to Los Angeles to play a couple of out-of-town shows. With encouragement and assurances from Ben Weasel to help him in the next phase of his career, Appelgren was planning to resign upon returning to the Lookout! offices. He felt the situation had escalated beyond the means and morality of an indie punk label, but as Appelgren walked into the Lookout! office after his trip, he was greeted by an even bigger surprise.

Chris Appelgren: Larry had written a long letter to the staff, basically resigning and explaining that Patrick was also resigning. He also stated he was confident that I could continue in the same spirit we had worked in and make the label a success. I was sort of surprised but honored and felt like it was an exciting opportunity, one that I wanted, and that I would have the chance to do right by the bands in ways that I didn't think Larry was inclined to. Which is sort of ironic since I kind of fucked up a number of important relationships myself later.

Livermore had been talking about leaving the label for years, so the day-to-day operation didn't rely on him, but he was still active in terms of decision making and management, so it struck a blow to morale. Livermore had, in fact, contemplated shutting down Lookout! completely.

Chris Appelgren: It wasn't a surprise, considering how acrimonious things had gotten with Screeching Weasel and then Furious George, that he finally decided this was too much and maybe it was time to move on. It was a little surprising that Patrick decided to cash in his chips so to speak, but he had always sided with Larry on business matters, so whatever Larry's concerns might have been, it was not a stretch that Patrick felt the same way. What Larry told me in meetings was that he and Patrick had seen our income plateau and basically felt like the business was going to take a downturn, stop growing, and that they didn't want to lose on their investment, but that by leaving their money in the label, they were destined to lose some of it. It wasn't really anything I could argue against. I did say that I felt we had a responsibility to the bands we'd signed to continue and, in a way, if it had been shut down, the financial benefit that both Larry and Patrick received would have been significantly reduced.

Although Hynes agreed with Livermore's financial forecasting, he continued to work for Lookout! after selling his ownership shares. In fact, Hynes stayed on for the long haul as an employee, covering bookkeeping, royalty payments, and handling the increasingly important web issues.

Chris Appelgren: Larry has repeated that he could have sold Lookout! for tens of millions of dollars—he's absolutely wrong about that. Even at the time, he could not have done any such thing—that would not have been allowed by our operating agreement. It took a few months to figure out the mechanics and what was dictated by the form of business Lookout! is structured in. We took a snapshot of the value of their ownership in the business and paid that amount out over time to each of them. With an LLC—limited liability company—at the time, not more than 50 percent of a company's ownership could be transferred in a year, so we had to pay it out over time. Lookout! paid the money to Larry and Patrick over four years or so. We needed the label to be able to afford sizable chunks of our profit being directed as payments to previous owners, and that was challenging over the years.

Robert Eggplant (Blatz): It doesn't take much to see that playing music is a lot more fun than sustaining a record label. After Blatz broke up, Larry seemed less interested in the Gilman scene and me as a person. By then, he seemed most interested in Aaron Cometbus, Billie Joe, Lint and the up-and-coming types. He was also adjusting to a lifestyle change. It was quite inspiring to see an adult in his forties go and finish college. I think he just had a "later with all that" attitude.

Alongside Appelgren, Molly Neuman and Cathy Bauer immediately became acting owners and, a couple of years later, they became legal owners. Livermore gradually moved out over the coming months. And Appelgren found his days becoming even fuller as he juggled band relations, meetings, phone calls, going to shows, visiting studio sessions, working on album artwork, drafting agreements, advising and interacting with the label bookkeeper, and troubleshooting issues that came up from any department. With the new management in place and ongoing payments to be made to Livermore and Hynes, the label began to feel pressure to create new successes to ride into the future.

Chris Appelgren: I trusted that we could weather another turn in the business cycle. Now when I look back, I am not sure what I based that trust on. I was very young and had no real business experience. I think we were always focused on what was fun and interesting about our inspiration, our bands, our partners, but I definitely felt new pressure and had to do things like reach out to bands about Larry's departure. A lot of band people that Larry had been close to were concerned that there wasn't enough support for them at the label. Larry had used a good cop/bad cop approach to some band dealings that had often cast the rest of the label staff as bad cop—so with groups like Avail, I remember having to work to overcome the idea that we didn't like their music, and I really loved that band myself.

Ernst vs. Green Day

With Green Day now several years into their upswing of worldwide punk stardom, Andy Ernst, producer of their original Lookout! albums, approached the band asking for a percentage of profits from the recording he had helped create. In a letter to Billie Joe Armstrong, Ernst pleaded his case, asking the band to consider his request. In a follow-up phone call with an offended Armstrong, Ernst was told that he should take up his issues with Lookout! Records.

Andy Ernst: I called Larry, and after over an hour of pounding my head against the wall trying to get him to understand my point of view, he told me he'd be willing to give me a percentage—as long as Green Day did. It seemed like a convenient catch-22 position to put me in, since I'd just told him that Billie didn't want to pay me anything, but I didn't have any options. So, I called Billie back, but his number had been changed. I wrote him a few letters and got no response. The amount I should have received and the amount of producing I actually did was always debatable. Unfortunately, there was never any debate.

As the Nineties Wore On . . .

The Sampler

The birth of the internet created instant access to anyone in the world who was interested in up-to-the-minute news about any band that existed, which made promotion a whole lot easier—for *any* band, no matter how good or bad.

As more and more bands got signed or released records after the 1990s punk explosion, more and more releases flooded the market, bewildering the record buyers. Now more than ever, with the relentless release schedule of many labels, a new marketing tool was born: the sampler. Epitaph Records released the hugely popular *Punk-O-Rama* sampler, highlighting its powerhouse roster from the mid-nineties for only $3.99 retail in the US. It made perfect business sense—a CD could introduce a listener to the B-list of bands on a label's roster and be sold on the merits of their A-list for a few dollars. Lookout! stepped boldly forward into the world of the sampler, with its first of many being *Heide Sez . . .* (**LK 169**) in 1996. Samplers mostly contained nonexclusive material and were a huge step away from the much-loved compilations of old. Thrown-together artwork on lifeless CDs from labels became increasingly common, killing the value of, and desire for, actual compilations.

The Criminals & Adeline Records

Jesse Townley had been busy since 1992 with the Gr'ups, but **LK 170** was the debut from his new band the Criminals. Produced by Billie Joe Armstrong, 1997's *Never Been Caught* indicated that old relationships were still valued by Lookout!, and Townley still trusted them.

Chris Appelgren: I liked Jesse and remember seeing the Criminals as an East Bay punk band from the time that was, for lack of a better term, keeping it real. The Criminals wanted to do what punk bands did—tour, make records, put on a good show. They didn't seem to be positioning themselves for some abstract large-scale success [or] worried about making videos.

Jesse Townley (Blatz, The Criminals): The price was right—close to free—so we recorded *Never Been Caught* in Billie's home studio, in his second home post-stardom. The Criminals recorded in three of his home studios over the years.

Brady Baltezore (The Criminals, Black Cat Music): Billie was always a pretty rad guy given all the bullshit that got stirred up from them getting big, and the recording session felt like a "real" studio, even though it was at his house.

With cover art by Jesse Michaels, the Criminals' debut album is twelve tracks of Townley's trademark "Fuk" song titles. The tight rhythm section is a wide mark away from the band's earlier releases or the shambling punk of Blatz.

Following heavy touring, the Criminals were sinking into a sea of debt with constant van replacements, and they attempted to work out a financial plan with Lookout! that never came to fruition. Despite being content with their place in the punk rock food chain, the Criminals were feeling like they were being lost in the cast of bands on the label who were jockeying for a position that would move them onto bigger things.

Jesse Townley: Billie Joe had recorded *Never Been Caught* and was obviously a fan, so he called me one day and asked me if we wanted to do our next record on Adeline. I said "Fuck yeah" and that was it. We were the fourth release on the label.

Named after the Berkeley street of the same name, Adeline Records was put together in 1997 by Billie Joe Armstrong along with his wife Adrienne and fellow Pinhead Gunpowder member Jason White. The early releases demonstrated the intention of the label, capturing local bands from the punk scene, also including AFI, Pinhead Gunpowder, and One Man Army with their classic debut *Dead End Stories*.

Jesse Townley: A really cool time to be a part of that label, and, like at Lookout!, we kind of became part of the crew of bands. We played label showcases, tried to set up shows with each other. They were really picking up the ball, looking for grassroots East Bay punk from their large circle of friends that Lookout! had strayed from. The Criminals played Billie's birthday party at the Bottom of The Hill. All I remember is that Billie was drunk enough to play covers for hours! It was a real hoot, and I met Winona Ryder. She liked our band and saw me naked when we played!

Furious George Tabb

About a year after the Furious George and Lookout! debacle in 1996, George Tabb struck up a deal with San Pedro–based Recess Records. The label had issued the band's *Bananas* 7-inch picture disc and was following it up with the *Gets a Record* LP.

George Tabb (Furious George): As soon as we signed to Recess, I asked Lookout! to discontinue our EP with them. They said they would, but then I started seeing European pressings. When I asked them about it they told me it wasn't them. Whatever, I never saw a cent or got a royalty check from any of it, not that I care. I just found it interesting that at the time the label was claiming to be so DIY and honest, they weren't. All that Green Day money must have come in, and I think greed just took over. I think everyone as individuals were nice people, but they found themselves in a herd mentality.

Chris Appelgren: I don't think there was any money to speak of. EPs aren't really profit generators, also it was a bit much that he called and talked to our distributor and such. That was my one concern at the time, that the band would be very high maintenance. All of the showboating wasn't necessary—he didn't need to introduce Molly and Cathy to Dee Dee or Joey Ramone in order to make the deal happen.

Furious George followed the releases up with a two-week California coast tour alongside Recess Records owner Todd Congelliere's own band, F.Y.P. With the tour taking its toll in the form of too much beer, not enough food, and sleeping on floors, an exhausted Furious George found itself heading to 924 Gilman Street.

Michael Harper (Furious George): Just before the gig, I was trying to sleep on the bare floor of the van. I was woken up just in time to go through the side door and to the stage. George began his nightly inciting the crowd with insults. This time, however, the crowd came prepared. Once we started into our set, we got blasted with all kinds of crap like mayo, fish, some kind of liquid, and who knows what else. Angrily, we all stopped playing and went hunting. I walked in and out of the crowd, not knowing what I was going to do even if I actually did find someone. There are pictures of Evan [Cohen] brandishing his bass like a lance, and I saw the end of what was George tossing someone out the side door. We wiped up, finished our set, and got off the stage. I remember going back to the van and drinking whiskey.

The band confined themselves to the van while F.Y.P. hit the Gilman stage, convinced that the attack—reportedly no different than how any out-of-town band was treated—was a personal one as payback for the *MRR* and Lookout! drama.

Michael Harper: As we were heading out of Berkeley, ready to leave that scene behind, someone pointed out that we were about to pass by the Lookout! store. I'm not sure who thought of it first, but as with all great ideas, everyone instantly got on board. We were going to pull over and do something to it, like piss on the sidewalk or on the door. Best of all, we saw that they had an old-style mail slot in the door that dropped the mail right onto the floor of the store. Great! We'd piss in the mail slot. So each of us took a turn, opening the mail slot on the front door, sticking our dicks in, and pissing a puddle on the floor. I realize it was a really immature thing to do, and I'm not especially proud of it, but it had been a long week and a rough gig. We were tired, sick—I was drunk—and had a long drive in front of us.

Chris Appelgren: It's a bummer that Furious George would pee through our mail slot, and I never knew about that. I guarantee that no one from Lookout! was responsible for any kind of heckling. I will say that kids did typically throw dumpster-dived food at bands, it was not a mean or negative thing—they were just being punk or chaotic.

George Tabb: The "liquid" they were squirting at us at Gilman was urine in Super Soakers. That, and the dead fish, really got to me! Looking back on it, it was a silly thing to do, pee in the mail slot, but at the time, it was fun, and I was *very angry* at Lookout! for the about-face they pulled. I am

George and Michael find relief in the Lookout! store mail slot

certainly not proud of myself for being so immature, but I was younger and less wise. I did throw a kid out of the club by partly picking him up and also partly pushing until he was out the door. No fists or hitting. That night, after the Gilman "riot," Tim Yohannan told me it was the best show he'd ever seen. It was also his last. He passed away shortly thereafter. While he was dying, he thanked me for the most "entertaining show" he'd seen in years. That made it all worth it. It wasn't until the next morning, and we were 300 miles away, did I get a chance to bathe. The hotel we were to stay at wouldn't let us in until the afternoon, and I *stank* like fish and piss and was miserable. Kind of serves me right in hindsight.

Tim Yohannan

Tim Yohannan, founder of *Maximum Rocknroll*, passed away on April 3, 1998 after a battle with non-Hodgkin's lymphoma—he was fifty-two years old. Even though he was well known for his difficulties with many people, his argumentative nature, and his unyielding opinions, his death was also the demise of an extremely important figure in the underground music scene.

Chris Appelgren: I used to run into Tim at the Berkeley post office where the *MRR* PO Box was, the Lookout! box was there too. He would sometimes give me a ride to the Mordam warehouse in San Francisco in his Volvo station wagon. I had been friendly with Tim but hadn't really had much of a relationship with him. I always felt hurt that he refused to consign my zine, *Puddle* at Epicenter because the name was across the bottom of the cover rather than the top, he told me no one would know the name and thus not buy it.

Clumsy Paths

As the nineties wore on, and the second wave of mainstream punk began to deflate, Lookout! continued on a sometimes sure, sometimes clumsy path. With heavy schedules and busy label management—most of them actively playing in their own projects—communication was also often lost.

Dave "Parasite" MacKenzie (The Parasites): They signed us for an album, then pulled it right after Larry left, even though they had a release date up on their site. [Later], Chrisoffered to do the LP, but we turned him down, and then he offered to do the next one, and we turned him down again.

Chris Appelgren: Gosh, not sure I remember it that way. I recall the Parasites thing as Lookout! put out a 7-inch, and it didn't do very well. Folks like Joe King and Dr. Frank were sort of vaguely friends with Dave, but I don't remember it as he does.

Dave "Parasite" MacKenzie: We were touring six months a year back then, so there were no issues with us not being active, and they even said we should do shorter tours, and yes, I can be a handful to work with when I am treated like crap and lied to.

Chris Appelgren: While Joe King advocated for them to a certain degree, it just seemed too complicated, all the different band members, weak art, etc. I was also not a fan, except of maybe the first album. It's possible that I wasn't good at saying "Sorry Dave, I am not into it. We're not gonna do it." I always understood it more as a case of "We'll see."

The Royalty Advocate

In 1997, Jesse Townley began working for Lookout!'s mail-order operation, spurred on by the addition of Jane Taatjes—who Townley later married. Over the coming months, Townley created a new role and title for himself: royalty advocate.

Jesse Townley: Since Lookout!, like many independent labels, was often too overloaded to stay up to date with the accounting of smaller and medium-sized bands, there was a fair amount of grumbling and fumbling around royalties while I was there. Even though I worked there and had two bands on the label, I still had to go upstairs and bug Chrisser [Appelgren] for my band's accounting. There were people who had moved from the address or phone number that the label had on file but were still very much involved in the scene and easy to find. Yet, the label didn't, before me, have the extra pair of hands to go collect the information for these people. Some hadn't been contacted by the label since the late

1980s. I was also able to add an explanation to the infamously confusing royalty statements, and we even had a little band-only newsletter that went out with the statements for a few royalty periods. Part of the reason I pushed for and created the royalty advocate position is because I was on both sides—working for the label and also in two bands on the label. I was seen as someone who could bridge the gap and perhaps help heal and improve relations with band members who felt ignored or ripped off. Non-automated royalty accounting can be incredibly tough and time consuming, especially if non-royalty costs are not being well managed.

Townley felt the relationships of the staff tested, however, when one member of the team was discovered skimming money from Lookout!'s mail-order department—and it was someone close to both management and staff.

Jesse Townley: This created some tension because some of the other friends of this guy held his firing against Jane—as it fell to Jane to drop the hammer—and the rest of the mail-order department, even though he was the one who was stealing. He was a "bro" and some of his friends thought that firing him was too harsh and uncool. I think some of the people involved had never had a "real" job, or a job where they were actually a part of the decision-making process, or a job that was actually independent and offered a fair amount of freedom in a cool, laid-back atmosphere.

Chris Appelgren: When Jane, his manager, suspected what was going on and kind of confronted him about it, she was also weirdly worried about him taking legal action against the company. I felt very much like I was in a position where the people I worked with wanted to be reassured that he wouldn't be let off too easily—i.e., have me put my friendship before the wellbeing of the company.

Jesse Townley: Still, we all hung out and had work lunches at Triple Rock Brewery, and Secret Santas, and all the rest. Most people worked in the third-floor offices, while the mail order and retail store were on the ground floor. Mail order and retail hung out all the time with each other, along with a couple of the "upstairs people." There was a slight divide since we physically worked separately, but nothing too major—even the dustup mentioned [earlier] faded in importance.

MTX Starship

The MTX Starship returned to follow up the popular *Love Is Dead*—the album that had essentially brought them into the wider mid-nineties punk consciousness—with *Revenge Is Sweet and So Are You* (**LK 180**). Post-Livermore, the Mr. T Experience steered its way through the choppy waters of the coming years of Lookout! Records in its own comfortable position.

Frank "Dr. Frank" Portman (MTX, The Bomb Bassets): Seventy-five percent of the company's capital just disappearing was to have long-term effects. I didn't involve myself in the politics of it though; I just wanted to put out what records I could, and, in that regard, those days of Lookout! fit in pretty well with my interests. I think there was also a bit of vigilance about being respected and treated well, and Chris tried really hard with all the bands on that score.

With the Mr. T Experience having been so varied in sound, production, and style with each release, their new full-length took a strange turn: not exploring new territory. The album was solid, with some powerful pop tunes, but it felt like a rehash of outtakes and second servings from the previous album . . . which made the whole thing feel a little like one thirty-minute song.

Frank "Dr. Frank" Portman: *Love Is Dead* was our first successful venture, and of course there's pressure to "keep it going." I felt that it was its own entity as a collection of songs, and that that kind of got lost. I had ambitions for the songs and the arrangements and the whole character of the album that I felt I just wasn't allowed to do. I had a different vision for that album than everybody else did—band members, producer, and label—which was basically *Love Is Dead II*.

Ghoulies Changeup

After the departure of Wendy Powell, Groovie Ghoulies snared the rhythm skills of Screeching Weasel's Dan Panic, who had become resident skinsman for various bands. With a far more accomplished and solid third wheel, the couple went full steam ahead with the next album in their spooky cannon: *Re-Animation Festival* (**LK 182**). With Mass Giorgini on their side, the band created an album with equal parts humor, schlock horror, and melody, capturing a powerful, deep sound.

Mass Giorgini (Squirtgun, The Mopes, Screeching Weasel, Common Rider): I remember having a great vibe the whole session—it was a ton of fun, and it went fast and smooth. The band was strong with Panic backing them—who I knew already before that—but it was that album that gave me the chance to get to know Kepi and Roach, who was not used to being asked to resing things a million times.

The Next Big Thing

Meanwhile, four teenagers had been busy making a name for themselves in their hometown of Palo Alto, California, in 1997. Barely over eighteen, Maya Ford, Brett Anderson, Allison Robertson, and Torry Castellano had forged a strong bond in high school, time-tested by playing punk-influenced rock and roll together since 1993. Originally, they played their first show at thirteen under the name Screen, then they changed their name to Ragady Anne, and then again to the Electrocutes, adopting an adolescent rock and roll look.

Maya Ford (The Donnas): We were always trying to escape extreme ridicule. Nobody liked us so we had to trust each other, and we had each other's backs. Even as seniors in high school kids would throw erasers and paper at me and Allison in art class. We were so mad because we were even older than some of those kids. But because we didn't fit in anywhere, everyone would always pick on us and give us shit. Everyone always yelled at me and asked me if I sewed my own clothes—I wish I did, but I'm bad with sewing machines!

The Electrocutes' music was raw and stripped 4/4 punk, not totally out of place in the realm of early Lookout! releases such as Blatz or Raooul. The defining sound was a wall of rock guitar, courtesy of Allison Robertson.

Maya Ford: We were really excited to play with Raooul in Oakland, but we were fourteen or fifteen and none of us had driver's licenses. So, we had to get our moms to drive us to the show. When we got there, it had been canceled, but no one [had] bothered to notify us. I think there was some band rivalry going on. So, we ended up just playing at the Clam Bucket—where we had parked trying to find the club. We played all the songs we knew and then switched instruments and played Guns N' Roses covers.

The Electrocutes created an alter-ego band, dressing more street punk, visually complementing the rock image they had already established. Influenced by the Ramones, but taking the opposite approach to a family identity, the four teens each went by the same first name, Donna, and became the Donnas.

Chris Appelgren: I saw them play with Groovie Ghoulies at Bottom of the Hill in San Francisco, having already heard about them. There was sort of a buzz about this teenage band that, like the Ramones, had the same name and played cheeky, fun, simple punk songs with lyrics that referenced drugs and sex in cheeky humorous ways. When I saw them, I realized I had actually seen their "other" band Ragady Anne play in Berkeley on the college campus. I was pretty much an instant fan. They were fun and played well and really elicited a great response from the crowd.

Maya Ford: The Donnas was a side project. The songs were super easy, and we never thought we would play them live. We were just having fun and making friends. Our high school was super lame so it was rad to hang out with older cool kids in garage bands.

Guitarist, producer, and Super*Teem! Records owner Darin Raffaelli soon guided the band, in a relationship often compared to that of young seventies rockers the Runaways and Kim Fowley.

Chris Appelgren: I think there was controversy around the idea of him being sort of a Svengali figure à la Kim Fowley. Funnily enough, we got a long voicemail message at the office for the Donnas from Kim Fowley in '98 or '99. It was just a strange invitation to connect with him and a verbose description of his accomplishments, totally unexpected.

Maya Ford: I went to a grindcore show, and I met this nerdy guy Eric who was in a surf band called the Vulcanears. We started hanging out. I went to see his band play at the Hofbrau, and he introduced me to Darin. So then Darin came to see us play and asked if we wanted to record some rock and roll.

Raffaelli proceeded to oversee the band's direction, committed to the band as a surrogate member. Releasing the band's debut self-titled full-length on Super*Teem! in 1997, Raffaelli wrote the entire record for the band. With a typical Ramones-type black-and-white gang photo and a crude marker-pen logo, the LP sleeve captured the essence of four adolescent street punks banging out tracks with titles like "I'm Gonna Make Him Mine," "Get Rid of That Girl," and "I Don't Wanna Go." The album was, musically, a step up from the earlier Electrocutes recordings, with more emphasis on catchy punk melodies and leaning toward surf-inspired guitar playing. The Donnas began getting small tastes of success. Traveling to Japan, they were unexpectedly greeted with a growing fan base.

Maya Ford: We played in Japan when we were seventeen, and this guy had been selling our 7-inches at his tiny store. He flew us over, and I don't remember if we even got paid, but we played to these really big crowds, and they knew all the lyrics and brought us presents.

With the band beginning to make its mark, Raffaelli, aware of his own limitations, reached out to further the band's journey. Through the Phantom Surfers' Michael Lucas, Raffaelli connected with Lookout!.

Chris Appelgren: Michael asked us to meet with Darin and talk about the Donnas. I thought it was a meeting about Lookout! maybe distributing his label Super*Teem!, but as it unfolded he was more interested in us just signing the Donnas—of which he was a full member. I didn't know they would want to be on Lookout!, we were all just fans, but I was really excited about the idea.

Michael Lucas (The Phantom Surfers): Darin? What can I say other than he's a great guy. Too good for his own good. I've often said that Darin would give you the shirt off his back, even if you were already wearing a shirt.

Maya Ford: We thought he was funny because he kept calling us "kid" and was so excited. Darin is the funniest person I have ever met, all he wants to do is eat and laugh. So then he said he was going to go with Michael to meet with Molly and Chris. We were super excited, although we never had any expectations really. I think we just thought everyone thought we were hella lame, so it would probably always be that way.

Chris Appelgren: I remember how great it was that Darin felt like he wanted to help the band grow but reached the extent of what he could do on his own.

The Donnas were officially signed to Lookout!, where they worked on their second full-length, putting emphasis on it as a transitional record—with more attention going into the band's songwriting. Along with the songwriting—which Raffaelli still contributed to—the band was encouraged to add its own touches stylistically and find their direction. Originally more of a social club for the four friends, they were shocked when the local scene picked up on the band, creating a healthy following. Leaning more towards the hard rock and metal world, the Donnas let loose with the 1998 *American Teenage Rock 'n' Roll Machine* full-length (**LK 191**).

With the members all wearing customized shirts sporting each one's Donna identity on the cover, the budding rockers had a young rebel look. While keeping their lo-fi sound intact, they let the traditional hard rock influences rise to the surface. Robertson's lead guitar riffs began to emerge in the fore; it was obvious the Palo Alto teenager had been refining her guitar skills on a steady diet of KK Downing and Robbin Crosby.

One other notable difference from the rest of the Lookout! catalog was that, while they were fans of the catalog, these young women came from a very different social scene, set of influences, and upbringing than the majority of bands from the first ten years, drawing a confused and wary response from longtime fans of the label.

Robert Eggplant (Blatz): I traced their climb into acceptance in the local scene and felt good about it. Well, until they got ultra-glossy—but oddly, at the time there was this cross-dressing starting to happen between the underground and corporate art. It's very hard to claim purity . . . if that's your thing.

Chris Appelgren: It definitely was more eighties metal than their first album and singles. I wanted to be very cautious. The band was definitely popular in the Bay Area, but I wasn't sure how or if that would translate to the rest of the country. I was happily proven wrong. Despite my title as the Nero of Lookout!, I did try to rein in spending when possible. This

was one instance where I rallied—promo budgets, advertising, and if I recall correctly, recording too. Some people thought that Lookout! was sort of responsible for the band's success—like we somehow prioritized the Donnas over other bands. That was not the case at all. They went out on tour in support of the album with Groovie Ghoulies, and the response was really positive: there were indeed fans outside of California. The Donnas did have kind of a polarizing effect, I heard things that did seem to indicate that bands or fans thought we decided to "put our money on" the Donnas at the expense of other great bands. This was not true. It was, at the time, a new and unknown direction for Lookout! to go in, and I think some people reacted badly to that. Why the Donnas? But they were great, always positive, fun, and not dragged down by any of the bullshit that came up. Plus, all of them were so psyched about Lookout!, they loved the other bands, releases, and the staff.

The band created a bond with Molly Neuman from the early days. They had been fans of Neuman's bands pre-Lookout!—heading out to see the Peechees play at Stanford College radio station in Palo Alto during the beginnings of their own musical endeavors. With a lot of attention already directed at the young women, it was obvious that someone needed to help them navigate being a young and up-and-coming band. Striking up a rapport, Neuman began to help organize the growing requests thrown at them. The role of managing was gradual, but before long, Neuman managed them full time.

Ten Years and Counting

The Lookout! Records ten-year anniversary get-together on January 8, 1998, was more of a blowout than the tragic, fire-swept five-year Gilman show. The celebrations were over the course of four nights, with no less than fourteen Lookout! bands stretched across the parties—the Donnas, the Hi-Fives, Black Fork, the Smugglers, the Bomb Bassets, Auntie Christ, MTX, the Go Nuts, Phantom Surfers, the Criminals, Tilt, Pansy Division, Uranium 9 Volt, and Groovie Ghoulies. Each night was held in a different venue with shenanigans at the Cinder Block and Punks with Presses warehouse, 924 Gilman Street, Slims, and Bottom of The Hill. They featured some inventive activities—beyond live sets and out-of-control drinking, there were karaoke, barbecue, and auditions, in which twenty young bands got to try out for Lookout! with five minutes of stage time.

Chris Appelgren: I have lots of fun memories of that weekend; it was crazy.

Mel Bergman (The Phantom Surfers, Go Nuts): The tenth anniversary was where the Go Nuts ruined the PA system with powdered sugar, and all the money raised for various charities went to pay to replace it. The same weekend, the Phantom Surfers were hosts of a Lookout! party at a miniature golf course, and we were the emcees. We caught a kid sneaking in, had a cop mess with him, then sprung the Donnas on him.

Jon Ginoli (Pansy Division): The tenth anniversary seemed to be the peak for the label in terms of visibility and optimism about the future. It was shortly after this that things started going downhill. At this time, we felt that some of the bands on the label were stuck in a Ramones-y rut with nowhere to go, but we had just recorded the album that marked a big shift for us, *Absurd Pop Song Romance* [**LK 198**], and were waiting for it to come out. So for this show, we played nothing but songs from our upcoming album because we wanted to show off how much we had improved and evolved, and blow people away.

A Changing of the Guard

Avail

Avail had been mining their way through tours year in and year out since the band's union with the label. They blazed through towns, and the label sold more albums. While many bands were demanding more promotion from Lookout!, Avail appeared happy with the basic principles of tour, record, and sell albums, with seemingly little interest in the way of extras such as promotional videos. But when they visited a friend who was working for a major label, the discussion sparked a new idea: there might be interest beyond indie labels now that they'd laid the groundwork of successful independent touring and sales.

Chris Appelgren: It came as sort of a shock at the time, and it became clear that the stuff they had never seemed interested in was actually important to them. They weren't just satisfied to do things the way they'd always done them and didn't want to miss out on the chance of growing their success. So, I talked a great deal with Joe Banks on the phone and decided I should go to Richmond and hang out with the guys for a few days and see if we could come up with a plan that would keep them on the label.

The trip helped decipher where the band was heading and how Lookout! could help them get there. They aired their concerns to Appelgren about things like not having much in common with the other bands on the label until, finally, they struck up an agreeable and workable plan.

Chris Appelgren: This was just sort of the process of figuring out the record that became *Over the James*. Ultimately, they decided to record it close to home. So, they recorded the album in Virginia, and we didn't feel it was quite the record we hoped for, sonically. It wasn't that it sounded bad, it just didn't have the production to get more mainstream airplay and attention, but I liked the album a great deal. They were so great live, and we thought if they could capture that energy, they could have been bigger. It did somewhat better than the previous album but didn't quite hit the mark we hoped for. I think they were getting bigger with each release but only incrementally, and they were seeing other bands seemingly shoot by them and got a little frustrated I think.

Memories of this period differ between various parties, with Avail feeling that *Over the James* (**LK 195**) wasn't necessarily on the list of priorities for Lookout!.

Beau "Beau Beau" Butler (Avail): We were told that they would put out the record, but they had "pushed" the last record and now it was another band's time for a "push." Also, they were so excited about the Donnas getting big—not a lot else seemed to matter. At the time, out of all the bands that were on Lookout!, we were one of the only touring bands on the label, and we thought that they should get behind us because of that, and well . . . they didn't. I knew Chris was really upset about Screeching Weasel leaving the label and was worried about us leaving.

Chris Appelgren: It was not something we wanted to happen. The Donnas were new and not really selling a lot at that time, and I didn't want one of our biggest bands to split. The Queers had gone to Hopeless, or at least were not actively doing anything for Lookout!, and Screeching Weasel was on Fat [Wreck Chords]. I think we were all left with a sense of disappointment—the band and the label. We had collectively upped our game but didn't have anything to show for the extra effort.

Beau "Beau Beau" Butler: When we joined Lookout!, we didn't sign, we became part of a family. It was Larry, Chris, and Pat in a one-room apartment running a label. By the time we left, Lookout! was trying to become a record company, and we were told that we weren't as important to them as some other bands were.

Following the album's release, Avail cemented the relationship they had built with Fat Wreck Chords, possibly sensing more common ground with Fat's roster. Lookout! did not bid against Fat to keep Avail on the label.

Chris Appelgren: Joe called and told me they had decided to sign with Fat and that, basically for them, it came down to distribution. Their albums weren't available in chain record stores and they believed that Lookout!'s distribution held them back. I am sure there was more to it than just distribution, but that was the reasoning. They had always been concerned about distribution and I was constantly having conversations with Avail and Ben Weasel about Mordam Records. Avail didn't feel that they did a good enough job and felt like there were lots of missed opportunities.

Pansy Division

Not long after, Lookout! took another blow from one of the label's most prolific and time-tested bands, Pansy Division. The Lookout! mainstays released their final work for the label: the *Absurd Pop Song Romance* full-length (**LK 198**). While working hard on a new sound for the album, the band also found itself struggling with the idea that the label was not as committed as it once was. The record marked a change in style with the band leaning towards a more mainstream alternative radio sound, hoping to speak to a broader audience.

Christopher Freeman (Pansy Division): By 1998, we had made five albums and found the most amazing drummer and guitar player. We really felt like we were on top of the world. We were also very tired of being labeled a joke band, and since we were still working on a relatively empty playing field of gay rock, we felt we could tackle whatever we wanted. Lyrically, we looked more at the relationship side of being gay which, to a certain extent, can be very introspective. We felt we could also keep expanding our musical palette and not stick to any particular genre; just try to write the best songs we could without having to worry about being pigeonholed. Lookout! had nothing to do with our artistic direction or ambitions, and actually tried to discourage us from going with Steve Albini.

Chris Appelgren: We loved the record. But like many bands that try to change styles mid-career, it is a real challenge to retain old fans and gain new ones from people who already think they know what your band is about. The album was great, but it was a hard sell.

More ambitious than ever, *Absurd Pop Song Romance* is epic in more than one way. With violins, cellos, and trumpets, the album's fun punk edge is sanded down. Still, the album was strong and, although more introspective and personal, the songwriting still had the tongue-in-cheek charm of classic Pansy Division.

Cathy Bauer: When I started working at Lookout!, there was a strong history between Pansy Division and the label. Each album and 7-inch single that came our way, I embraced and threw my best towards, each one. As far as *Absurd Pop Song Romance* goes, I really loved that record and thought it was a strong and sonically great album. I did think it was a mistake to try to move away from using the term queercore when they basically invented and defined the term. To me, it would be like Bikini Kill saying they are not riot grrrls any longer.

Pansy Division had become increasingly concerned that interest had been waning at Lookout! HQ. With the departure of Livermore, a sense of changing priorities had them feeling left in the lurch. With the label's shifting roster and the departure of other longtime bands, it appeared that Pansy Division was on their way out.

Jon Ginoli (Pansy Division): Larry wanted to put out records; I don't think he wanted to deal with press or schmoozing or that stuff. He was really in it for the music and to help create a kind of scene. Everyone was nice to us, and it wasn't until after Larry left that we heard about Lookout! employees who didn't like us or our music. That said, we sometimes were kind of demanding of their staff. We'd call them and ask them to do stuff on short notice—we were touring constantly then—and I think we were the first band who really expected them to be competent about this stuff. It is important to note that we were older than most of the other bands on the label, and more professional in some ways.

Christopher Freeman: The support we received from Larry was awesome, all the way. We really did feel free to do as we wished, and we were having a blast. But once Larry had sold the label, we only had Chrisser, Molly, Tristin, and Cathy to rely on. In 1997, we asked the label for an advance for the first and only time: Two thousand dollars to pay for a rear axle replacement on our van that had broken down in St. Charles, Louisiana, while we were on tour. We felt like we were groveling. Most of the time when Jon would call, it would be to complain that our albums were not in stock in the local record store of a town where we had been playing on tour. We were out busting our asses on tour, promoting an album, and they hadn't even bothered to ship albums to any music outlets. That was really hurtful. They dropped so many balls it was pathetic, especially in 1998. The worst part was hearing later that they hated the record we were so proud of, *Absurd Pop Song Romance*. They even lied right to our faces, saying they loved it. Very disheartening.

Chris Appelgren: I have to say I totally disagree with that. Why would we sabotage a record that, in addition to the band spending lots of money on, we spent lots on too? Lookout! never dictated what stores would carry Pansy Division records. I would love to have every store carry every Lookout! album. We always acted on Jon's calls about records in certain stores. I remember specifically talking to Chris [Freeman] about how much I loved the album.

Cathy Bauer: I can't believe that any artist would believe that we'd sabotage our own business in such a way. It just makes no sense that we would not try to do everything to sell records, promote the band, and engage all possible outlets to sell records. That's fundamental to what we do at the label. I was on the front lines of our distribution relationship in the US, and whenever a band came to me with any complaints or questions about their records being in stores, I acted swiftly to remedy them. We even put someone in charge of calling stores directly to follow the tour routing to make sure that records were stocked and posters were put up.

As communication was breaking down, further problems arose. The band had released thirteen records for Lookout!, which may have created some saturation. With weaker sales on this release, band and label were reassessing their respective relationships.

Chris Appelgren: They were definitely our most serious band at the time in terms of trying to build a career, even on an indie level. We had put out a lot of Pansy Division records in a relatively short amount of time. They had a real crazy schedule and then suddenly, made a dramatic left turn in favor of less overt lyrics, I think hoping for a more mainstream success.

Christopher Freeman: The only time we felt Lookout! had really ponied up huge advertising dollars was for *Wish I'd Taken Pictures* [**LK**

133] in 1996 while Larry was still there. We did a video for $5,000, had trading cards made, got a ton of press, it was great. He really wanted to see us succeed. Keep in mind also that advertising costs came out of our royalties first and were split 50/50 with the label. We didn't get paid until the advertising had been recouped. The Donnas definitely got the advertising dollars later on, after Larry had left. I'd like to know where the advertising money went for us in 1998. Posters?

Chris Appelgren: The simple fact remains that if Pansy Division wanted to be groomed for mainstream success, they should have signed with a major label—we just did not have the resources or experience to accomplish such a thing. That said, we busted our asses to sell records, get airplay, and support the band. The times that Lookout! Records tried to create demand, we usually failed. The times when we succeeded were when we forged strong connections with bands that were clearly making music that people cared about and ultimately paid for. Bands always feel like a certain song should be a hit, but reality does not necessarily follow that logic.

Jon Ginoli: After *Absurd Pop Song Romance* came out in 1998, we didn't do anything for about three years. During that period was when it began to unravel. We didn't look to leave, but they turned down the album *Total Entertainment!* when we proposed it to them.

Chris Appelgren: After *Absurd Pop Song Romance*, it seemed like Pansy Division was done. Chris was in LA, Luis [Illades] was in another band, and it seemed like they were basically over. But then when they regrouped after what seemed like at least a year, I think we didn't have a lot of enthusiasm—especially as the demos seemed more like pre-*APSR* Pansy Division. We also didn't have the heart to just say, "No thanks." We dragged our heels, and I am sure that contributed to the feeling of not being valued much.

Jon Ginoli: When we parted ways, they gave us the boxes of our albums, CDs, and singles that they still had left in lieu of royalties owed to us. That was what our contract entitled us to, but we'd rather have been paid too. They claimed we owed them $5,000, which was nonsense, since we'd broken even on every release we'd ever done with them, and been paid royalties, be it single or album. Their accounting was pretty eccentric.

Weasel Redux

With Livermore out of the picture, Appelgren reached out to Ben Weasel with a peace offering. He would drop the court case and proposed a new record label funded by and affiliated with Lookout! and run by Jughead and Weasel. With Appelgren now the majority partner, his intention was to start fresh with Weasel and company and move ahead, past the problems that had created the bad blood. Lookout! would manufacture and distribute the new label, provide Weasel and Jughead a one-time "gift" of $30,000 meant to set up the new label—Panic Button Records—and renegotiate Screeching Weasel's contracts with a much simpler royalty equation.

John "Jughead" Pierson (Screeching Weasel, The Mopes, Even In Blackouts): Ben had a better grasp on what would do well. He was like Livermore in that respect and had an eye for punk talent. Mine was more a connection on a personal level. I liked people and wasn't such a good judge of what would sell. It was a strange arrangement; we were attached but separate. We had to fit our releases into their release schedule, which was fine when they were with Mordam, even though many people at Mordam didn't like Ben. Chris was never very good at standing up against Ben, and when it came down to it, Ben knew more about punk rock than Chris.

The first release for Panic Button was Screeching Weasel's return, its first with Lookout! since *Kill The Musicians*. The band still had an active following, having released *Bark Like a Dog* and *Television City Dream* with Fat Wreck Chords and a 7-inch, *Formula 27*, for Vermiform Records. During their absence from Lookout!, Weasel recruited new members following Dan Vapid's departure after *Bark Like a Dog*. Dan Panic had also left, leaving Jughead and Weasel to recruit Squirtgun's drummer and bass player, Dan Lumley and Mass Giorgini.

Mass Giorgini (Squirtgun, The Mopes, Screeching Weasel, Common Rider): By the time I joined the band, I had been producing Screeching Weasel for several years. They needed a bass player—and one who was not only capable but also truly enjoyed and respected the style of the band. Nobody outside the band was as involved with them as I was.

In fact, I had been working with Ben and John from the beginning in various ways.

Taking over second guitar from Weasel was Zoinks! singer and guitarist Zac Damon. The Reno, Nevada, local had relocated to Lafayette, Indiana, for the gig, moving in with Mass and working at the Sonic Iguana Recording Studio.

Zac Damon (Screeching Weasel): Ben wanted a solid guitarist and backup vocalist. Mass suggested me. I got a totally unexpected call from Ben, and a couple weeks later I was packed up and headed out to the Midwest. It was a huge deal to me at the time. I am honored and thankful to have gotten the chance to be a part of the history of that band, but working with Ben wasn't the easiest task in the world.

During the nineties, Weasel's agoraphobia had reached a breaking point, with little tolerance for touring and live appearances, which added to the strain on band members. Screeching Weasel basically became a studio back, and even rehearsals were replaced with passed-on demos of new material.

A young Screeching Weasel, left to right, Brian Vermin, Ben Weasel, Dan Vapid, Jughead

John "Jughead" Pierson: It ranged from panic attacks to claiming that we would be an old, best-of band limping on stage. But I always said, "Well, if we played out more consistently we would be considered a band and not a reunion."

Zac Damon: I would say it was definitely the least amount of fun I've had playing in a band. We all got demo tapes from Ben. I was tasked to come up with guitar solos and back-up parts, but most of them ultimately got changed by Ben.

Mass Giorgini: I assumed I would have no say at all, but I had a great deal. I ran rehearsals and arranged the musical parts. I was running things the way I believed Ben would want them—I was very familiar with his tastes and preferences.

John "Jughead" Pierson: I hated that. That was ultimately when things went awry with me and Ben. Playing live is what makes you good, not sitting in a studio.

Mass Giorgini: Well, we always rehearsed with Ben once we got things together. But that was the height of his agoraphobia, and I did all I could to keep his stays in the rehearsals as short as possible. The only real downside to all of this was the increased marginalization of John.

The studio contained some claustrophobic recording sessions, with mood swings from Weasel, but they eventually emerged with the *Major Label Debut* 12-inch EP/CD (**LK 190**). The 1998 release was everything expected from the new lineup, including a much more clinical approach to songwriting unlike the varying personalities of the nineties version of the band. One song does stand out on the record, however, a hostile track aimed at an unnamed antagonist. The track was "Hey Asshole!" and it was painfully obvious in whose direction the explicit lyrical content pointed.

Zac Damon: I remember Larry getting upset with Mass for playing on "Hey, Asshole!" but the funny thing was that Larry's name was never mentioned in the song.

John "Jughead" Pierson: Ben was just very very angry at Lawrence, and that's how he vents.

Chris Appelgren: I was sort of shocked, but I didn't feel responsible for it. We were a punk label and didn't dictate song subjects or lyrics. I never talked with Larry about it.

The Green Day Bump

Another associate, who was on friendly terms with Ben Weasel, joined the Lookout! team in 1998. Applying for an ad as a bookkeeper for the label, Bill Michalski was previously acquainted with Weasel through anarchist publisher and distributor, AK Press.

Bill Michalski (Lookout! bookkeeper): [Lookout!] was in pretty good shape as far as I could tell when I first started, though over time I realized that they were spending like the Green Day bump was a permanent thing. For months afterwards they were literally getting millions of dollars from sales of the first two records. That had already dropped off significantly by the time I started. Also, as far as I could tell, the paperwork was in pretty good shape. Xandi, the previous bookkeeper, had worked with an outside accounting consultant to set up the accounting software and organize a workflow and stuff. It was actually very well organized when I started.

Indeed, it appeared that Chris Appelgren and Lookout! were financially set for life, with the icing on the cake of Green Day's sales being the additional 500,000 copies they'd sold of Operation Ivy's *Energy*. Indeed, the label boasted ten million dollars in sales in 1995, according to the *East Bay Express*.

Ernst Part Two

With Chris Appelgren trudging through his first year as president of the label, producer Andy Ernst once again reached out in hopes of compensation for his work on the earlier Green Day recordings. After a discussion between the two, Appelgren agreed to a royalty payment for Ernst of half a percent per album from Lookout!'s net income, thus avoiding any impact on the band's earnings.

Chris Appelgren: I don't know why I made this decision exactly. I don't think there was any lack of understanding at the time of the recording as to what Andy would or should be paid. Lookout! had never done any deals with producers; instead, we paid for their time and all studio costs. Many other bands recorded with Andy, and this was never an issue. I guess I just wanted to resolve what seemed to be a rift between the band and Andy, even if it was mostly one-sided.

Andy Ernst: I could only conclude that either I was paranoid, or that Green Day wanted to make sure I got nothing from anybody, ever. I assumed that they thought I was a greedy blood-sucking leech, and I assumed that they were greedy self-righteous capitalist pigs. But I really never learned the truth because I never had the chance to talk about it. I went to a show where AFI opened for Green Day. AFI knew how I felt, and they specifically asked me not to start any trouble, so I didn't. It was cool talking to Green Day about the old days, but it sucked that I was on leash and couldn't say everything I wanted to.

Chris Appelgren: The same kind of thing came up with Kevin Army about Operation Ivy. I remember once being at the Lookout! office when Kevin made the argument that he should get a percentage, and it turned into a big verbal fight between him and Larry. The difference being that Larry had actually offered Kevin a percentage of *Energy* if he would give Lookout! a discount on the recording cost. Kevin said no thanks and that he needed to be paid his whole fee upfront. Larry paid it, even though it was challenging for the label at the time. So later, after the fact, when Kevin advocated for being cut in, Larry was adamant that it was too late.

Smugglers

In celebration of ten years in the line of duty, the Smugglers set about documenting their high-energy live spectacle for the 1998 live album *Growing up Smuggler* (**LK 199**)—again in conjunction with Mint Records. Recorded in Madrid, Spain, the twenty-track release is a fine example of a band in its prime, working a club audience into a frenzy with its charming mix of visual rock and roll, punk rock energy, and charismatic performances.

Grant Lawrence (The Smugglers): If anything, we're very tight and fast on that record. That record is worth it for the liner notes alone, and it was one of my greatest achievements in rock and roll—I got a Canadian, American, German, and Japanese label to release it! Around this time we also noticed what seemed [like] outrageous spending beyond the means of an independent label. I remember being shocked, when around 1999, I went down to San Francisco for John Denery's wedding and both Molly and Chris had brand new Volkswagens! I could only think of the many bands scraping by on Lookout! and the new owners both driving brand new cars! They could have gotten the cars through other means besides Lookout!, but it raised eyebrows. Chris is a very kind soul and a huge supporter, but he was Lookout!'s Nero.

Chris Appelgren: Molly and I did lease VWs, but I don't think that has anything to do with the label. I worked hard and earned a salary and leased a car. I realize that bands on the label could not necessarily afford to do that from their share of whatever royalties they were earning, but I don't think that the two things relate. In that instance, what is not taken into consideration is that you are paying from a salary, and I also think it could be a very ignorant statement to assume that other people's cash is being used for personal effects. At other times, I have put my own money and resources into the label as were needed. I basically gave up on college and devoted myself to Lookout!, and I always had people in the scene—who weren't raised by a parent on government welfare as my mother was—that told me I should not take a salary from the label. I just was a lower-class kid who felt very fortunate to be able to do such an amazing thing as a job, but I also felt entitled to think of it as a job for myself and for other employees. We provided a retirement 401(k) and healthcare to employees, but I was not able to do the same for bands.

Supergroup

Getting together in their downtime as a project band, the Mopes were a "punk supergroup," featuring members of Screeching Weasel, the Queers, Squirtgun, Groovie Ghoulies, and the Riverdales. The side project was just meant to be fun for the members. While touring together, Dan Vapid and B-Face had begun trading some ideas and worked up a handful of songs. Lookout! quickly jumped on the new project and agreed to release the new recordings as the *Lowdown, Two-Bit Sidewinder!* (**LK 202**) CD-only release.

Chris "B-Face" Barnard (The Queers, Groovie Ghoulies, The Mopes): I think we only rehearsed with equipment once, and then did one more practice session with no amps and Lumley using cardboard boxes, where we came up with "Wipeout on the Dunes" on the spot. It was just us having fun, screwing around and realizing we had a little spare time to do this.

Dan "Vapid" Schafer (Screeching Weasel, Sludgeworth, The Queers, Riverdales, The Mopes): I was intrigued with sixties novelty groups at the time, like the Trashmen. So, songs in that vein were coming out. I thought it would be fun to do a project with these types of silly sixties novelty songs for an EP. Nobody in the Mopes lived in the same state at the time. We had members residing in Washington D.C., Boston, Lafayette, and Chicago. We got together and rehearsed just one time and went into the studio. I was gambling that the performances would turn out fine, and they pretty much did. It was meant to be a one-time thing.

Chris "B-Face" Barnard: I think some younger Lookout! fans weren't aware of that genre and only knew that this band had members of other Lookout! bands in it and were expecting the same stuff. Almost across the board, though, the older people who I talked to about it "got it."

The Queers

After the release of *Don't Back Down*, Joe King and the Queers were still committed to one more Lookout! album. Despite a potential offer from Epitaph and subsequently signing with Hopeless Records, the band put together a CD-only compilation of old tracks to fulfill their obligation to Lookout!, *Later Days and Better Lays* (**LK 216**). It was the end of any era for the band in more ways than one when, in early 1999, longtime drummer Hugh O'Neill developed a brain tumor and died. O'Neill and Joe King had been divided by personal rifts following the golden-era Queers lineup.

Joe King (The Queers): Me and Hugh had gone to different rehabs and sobered up. There was still bad blood between us guys. After a few months, I had this urge to call Hugh. Not sure why, but I just picked the phone up and called his folks' house to see what was up with him in the sober house. I was always good friends with his parents. His mom answered and said they had a tragedy with Hugh—he had a brain tumor. His folks, being great people who also have some money, got the best doctors in Boston, but none of them could do a thing—they hadn't caught it in time. So, he slowly drifted away over the course of the next year. I talked to him a few times, and we buried the hatchet. He told me to keep on playing with the Queers as we had a good thing going. So I kept in touch with him to the end. Last time I saw him, I was on my way to Logan Airport to fly to Italy for some shows—by this time I had new guys with me. He was in some nursing home and really couldn't talk. So I hung out for a half hour and shot the shit as much as possible with him. I did all the talking basically. Finally, I had to bail for Logan, and all he could say was "You gotta go?" over and over. I'm trying not to start bawling out loud in front of him because I know deep down he was scared. I finally left and just hung out for a few minutes in the lounge, half-crying—we went through a lotta shit together. I ended up flying home exactly two weeks from that day for his funeral, which was on a Monday. He lasted a week and a half. I still think of that guy quite a bit.

The New Lookout!

Return of the Avengers

When punk rock was in its infancy in 1977, four young musicians—drummer Danny "Furious" O'Brien, guitarist Greg Ingraham, bassist Jimmy Wilsey, and Penelope Houston—formed the Avengers, a visually striking classic, female-fronted punk band with attitude. Almost twenty years after the band's split, a new iteration of the band formed. With Danny Furious in Sweden and bassist Jimmy Wilsey essentially unheard from, Penelope Houston and Greg Ingraham reunited with MTX's Joel Reader and Lookout! regular Dan Panic to form the scAvengers. The scAvengers played some reunion shows with Pansy Division, ripping up the band's tunes penned by Houston twenty years before, and then entered the studio with Kevin Army to record three new tracks—"I Want In," "Crazy Homicide," and "The End of the World"—all previously finished but unrecorded songs from the band's original days. These new recordings, along with fourteen other live and rehearsal tracks, a 1978 studio track, and a name change back to their roots made up the Avengers' *Died for Your Sins* (**LK 217**) full-length. The band was then inactive until 2004 when a new lineup emerged featuring Pansy Division's Luis Illades as a drum replacement for Dan Panic.

Luis Illades (Pansy Division, The Avengers): Pansy Division had played with the Avengers on their first reunion show, which is where I first met Penelope. I was surprised that the band remained so relevant. I think the whole Avengers experience has been phenomenal, seeing the reactions of people at the shows, be it in San Francisco, Los Angeles, New York, or even the Midwest or Europe was very timely and vital. You're talking about a time when we had Bush and a Gulf War and lyrics reflecting Reaganomics, and 'Restless Youth" might as well have been written that day. People were feeling it.

The Donnas Go on Tour

The Donnas spent 1998 playing alongside Groovie Ghoulies and then the Smugglers in the early part of 1999. The new LP and band were still picking up speed, and if the band had been taken by surprise with their early successes, it would appear things were just warming up.

Maya Ford (The Donnas): Well, I guessed something was going on because we decided it was a good idea to put college on hold and go on tour. Everyone was talking about our "nubile breasts" and matching T-shirts. It was totally crazy, not like the Beatles—but really weird.

Before long, the Donnas were receiving more press than all other post–Green Day artists combined.

Tristin Laughter: I can't explain the Donnas phenomenon, they were just a big deal out of the gate. I wish I could take credit for their press success, but I can't. I remember I was on a panel at CMJ after the Donnas came out, and literally someone did that weird fake worship thing on the carpeting to me about how much press they got, and it gave me acid reflux because I knew that if that was the perception, that I got them all that press, then there was a correlation to the question of why I didn't do that for the other acts.

Although only a year had passed, the Donnas had already shed their adolescent rebel girl look in favor of a newer rocker look—gone were the pastel-colored matching name shirts, and in came the black rock uniform for the cover of their follow-up album, *Get Skintight* (**LK 225**).

Chris Appelgren: I have always thought of them as girls, but there was always a sexual element to their music, as they grew up they grew into it in a way. The second album was definitely better produced, and they had gotten to be better at their instruments and more confident songwriters. I recall how it was funny to me that the Donnas were honestly into hair metal, and when I had been their age I was violently opposed to it, and here I was releasing—and really liking—a Mötley Crüe cover.

If the Donnas' Lookout! debut had begun to lean into the hard rock realm, their follow-up continued the trend, as the four young women developed their act into straight-up rock. The vintage Donnas sound was now gone, with extra riffage from Allison Robertson. Her new confidence on guitar pushed the band's sound to new heights, with the music increasingly becoming centered around classic hard rock lead soloing and the new wave of British heavy metal–influenced riffing. With the new record out, the Donnas spent the rest of 1999 on tour, with a lengthy US and Canadian trail, along with UK festival appearances before more US dates. By October, they were back in Europe and the UK and then headed to Australia just before Christmas and millennium celebrations. With such a dedicated live campaign over the last year before Y2K, the Donnas were going out on a high.

American Steel

Keeping a baby toe planted in their classic East Bay punk roots, Lookout! signed American Steel, a band with a healthy dose of rebellion-fuelled, anthemic, underground rock. While still fresh-faced, they had spent a few years working the scene by the time of their 1999 Lookout! debut album, *Rogue's March* (**LK 231**).

Cathy Bauer: Seeing them on and off stage—before I really got to know them—was so different, they really put so much on the stage, which was so powerful. I remember them coming by for a meeting, all four of them, and being really struck by how young and magnetic they were. They were going back to the spirit of something that we had been touching years before, and historically, I think that was really important. Maybe it was new in the scheme of the other bands on the roster, but they just tapped right into what had been happening before—something that I was really grateful for.

Robert Eggplant (Blatz): Gilman had space for new talent to blunder on the stage, cut their teeth, and get kinda good. American Steel was part of the in-crowd because they worked at or hung out at the club. They had some good songs. They would probably be more relevant in my universe if I hung out with them at a house show or on the street in town. By the time they had a record on Lookout! there was an air about them that resembled the yuppie invasion.

American Steel's explosive energy paired with new labelmates, like up-and-coming Ann Beretta, gave some people the feeling that a new wave of Lookout! bands was moving into the forefront. Ann Beretta had also formed—not long after American Steel—in 1996, when Rob Huddleston and Russ Jones put together a new project after their previous outfit—Inquisition—had split up.

Rob Huddleston (Ann Beretta): The energy around the Bay Area in the mid-nineties was just so amazing. It was a goal of mine to put a record out with Lookout!, and I really wanted to be in a band that could put the Lookout! logo on the back of our shirts. We were actually in the studio, beginning to record our second record, when I got a call from Chris asking if they could release the record.

The 1999 *To All Our Fallen Heroes* album (**LK 234**) emerged around the time of American Steel's *Rogue's March*. With Avail now having jumped ship, it would seem the gap the band had left on Lookout! was being filled by some new blood.

Chris Appelgren: Even though we were actively looking to find great punk bands to work with then in the late nineties, Lookout! was being accused of moving away from its punk base to only hybrids—Avail moved to Fat—the Donnas, MTX were our top-selling artists. We loved punk and felt like Ann Beretta and American Steel were more classic style bands that seemed to have the personality and unique qualities that set earlier Lookout! bands apart.

Rob Huddleston: We toured with American Steel as we both had records coming out around the same time, and at the time we were both being called the new faces of Lookout! and the new generation of punk bands on the label. I think it was really exciting for us all. I really loved American Steel more than any other active Lookout! band at the time, and as dudes, they were and still are the best.

MTX

Like the slower and mellower direction that Pansy Division had taken, another longtime Lookout! band also evolved a more low-key approach. On 1999's *Alcatraz* (**LK 232**), MTX Starship took its last voyage, and a cast of revolving guest musicians was brought in. Although Dr. Frank always had a knack for stepping outside the box lyrically and musically, *Alcatraz* was a new kind of departure. The band's tight, energetic bursts were replaced by layers of trumpets, organs, and piano. The album marked an evolution in their sound, breaking out of the basic pop-punk formula. While many fans rejected it outright as an MTX album, time isn't as cruel towards it, and it doesn't actually stray too far from the update tunes MTX had perfected.

The stance the label took was that—like any other healthy, creative band—MTX should be free to play however they wanted in whatever style, and when it came down to it, Lookout!'s opinion was that Dr. Frank was a unique talent and didn't want to force what he was doing in any boxes. While writing *Alcatraz*, Dr. Frank had distanced himself from the other members, almost to the point of keeping the new tracks under wraps.

Joel Reader (MTX, The Bomb Bassets, The Avengers): Unbeknownst to me at the time, Frank had apparently been pretty unsatisfied with the way *Revenge Is Sweet* had turned out. Despite his best efforts, most of the songs wound up with those very same pop-punk arrangements and sounding far too much alike. For *Alcatraz*, Frank was determined to see his vision through. So, for the first time, he started recording home demos of all the songs where he would play all of the instruments. Then, he would want us to replicate those parts as faithfully as possible once we were in the studio.

Frank "Dr. Frank" Portman (MTX, The Bomb Bassets): The *Alcatraz* reaction was similar to the *Milk Milk Lemonade* reaction: why do you have all these guitar solos, I thought you were a punk band. At the time, people were kind of personally wounded by the guitar sounds. I even talked to people who were in tears over it.

Joel Reader: I'm pretty sure that part of what Frank thought was causing our songs to sound too similar to one another was me overdoing it and singing way too many harmonies. So he did what he felt he needed to do in order to achieve his vision, but it also had the unintended effect of making me feel a lot more emotionally divorced from the material than I'd ever felt before. *Alcatraz* didn't feel as much like a band album; it felt more like Frank's thing, and I certainly didn't feel as much personal ownership with the final result. So, in hindsight, that might have been the start of me pushing, or being pushed away from the band.

With only moderate sales, the album was not the success that Lookout! had planned. Reader —who had also put together his own band, the Plus Ones—still went on the tour but found himself feeling further and further from the band's inner circle.

Joel Reader: It seemed like fewer and fewer people were turning up at the shows, and those who did come out didn't seem nearly as enthusiastic about the new material. Plus, Jym [Pittman] and I, who roomed together on the road, weren't getting along all that well. In any case, it was not a positive place for the band to end up and, for the first time ever, playing shows hadn't been fun for me. We basically had one—totally civil—debate to decide the issue over the course of one very long, very sad afternoon, but ultimately we couldn't manage to come to an accord. The band that had basically been my entire life for the past five years was over. It was heartbreaking for me, but I'm sure Frank saw the Plus Ones as something of a looming threat. Joining the Mr. T Experience was the most profound event of my entire existence. Nothing I'd done before, and nothing I will ever do, will have the same impact on the course of my life. I really miss those guys.

Digital Distribution

With the advent of digital downloads and new online music sources, Lookout! decided to join in on this new era for music. As the early talk of digital distribution loomed, the label partners began to discuss the next step with Mordam Records, their longtime distributor.

Chris Appelgren: We started hearing from people at companies like Cductive and eMusic. The idea was that these new businesses would be online record stores building groups of exclusive labels, so if you wanted a Lookout! release you'd go to XYZ's site to find our digital music. This was pre-iTunes store, and companies were going out and doing all sorts of deals, and in some cases, handing out sizable cash advances to labels. We were approached and were very interested in doing a deal. Then, when I spoke to Ruth Schwartz at Mordam about it, she said "No way," and we were basically told "We already are your digital distributor." Furthermore, she said "We are your exclusive worldwide distributor," and banned labels from doing licensing deals or exclusive distribution deals in foreign territories.

Ruth Schwartz (Mordam Records): I don't remember Chris telling me about any digital plans specifically. During this time there was a great confusion about digital music, and we all together had great arguments and discussions about what it meant and how to handle it. Ironically, many of those same arguments are still prevalent in the industry today.

Chris Appelgren: Ruth had made some concessions for Lookout! because we were the biggest label she had at the time. We pushed back, and she gave us some special considerations, but ultimately, it felt like we weren't selling enough—or at least that was what our biggest bands felt like—and with not being able to do a digital deal or license our releases, we just felt like it was the right time to consider other options. We took meetings with other distributors and decided to go with RED, who was already dealing with Epitaph and Fat Wreck Chords sales. So in early 2000, we left Mordam, signed a digital deal with eMusic, moved to RED, and also moved into our new building in South Berkeley.

The new building was five thousand square feet and set the label back approximately $400,000. Located in South Berkeley, the new Lookout! HQ was half a block from a punk house that had housed members of Alkaline Trio, Rancid, American Steel, and Econochrist. With a new location and more conventional record distribution, Lookout! began to build a relationship with RED and take more control over how their products were sold.

Chris Appelgren: With RED we could set the retail price, with Mordam we were only able to set the wholesale price, meaning the stores could charge whatever they could get away with, creating wildly fluctuating prices. It was a more conventional distribution situation, and we were able to do foreign deals, digital deals, and licensing.

Ruth Schwartz: I have much love and admiration for Larry and Chris and Patrick and Molly and the rest. We grew up together. I was very sad they left. It was quite a ride. Larry was always a good friend and a provocative debater even if his demons were in his way. I have fond memories of Gilman shows and bands in our warehouse. I fondly remember Chris drawing wacky pictures of our staff to put on our catalogs. He used to come visit my family in the country. My daughter loved him. He was like my little brother. I always thought that RED would eat them alive. I think the legacy is that Lookout! ate themselves alive.

Tristin Laughter: There was an element of distrust in the San Francisco and East Bay punk community of Lookout!. When I started, *MRR* had run a hostile piece about the label and then later when we switched distributors, I had to go with Molly to Gilman for a meeting on whether our bands would be allowed to play there or not because our new distributor made us a "major label" potentially in their eyes. So there was a theme of that distrust, and it seemed to me to be mostly just about money. Since Green Day had made so much money, the punk community really did and maybe still does have this anti-capitalism theme. And I

Cover art for the 1994 compilation assembled by Ben Weasel that this book is titled after.

think there was this misperception that the Lookout! people had huge amounts of cash and [those in the community] had resentment about it. But in reality, it was my impression that the label did not have the kinds of resources that people imagined it had.

Ruth Schwartz: I went to war with Tim Yohannan over his attacks in *MRR* about them mistreating bands. I was always available to work with bands when labels weren't kind, but I hated to see Tim take them to task publicly.

After twenty-two years in business, a slew of successful releases, and highs and lows spanning three decades, Ruth Schwartz sold Mordam Records to Lumberjack Distribution in 2005—a company owned by Doghouse Records' Dirk Hemsath, who had purchased Lumberjack in 1997 from Eric Astor and Rich Kraemer of Art Monk Construction Records.

Ruth Schwartz: Lookout! had absolutely nothing to do with the end of Mordam. That failure is the direct result of me selling the company. Selling the company to Dirk Hemsath was a bad idea. In fairness to Dirk, it is a terrible time to be in music distribution. I sure didn't want to be there anymore. But he trashed it. He gets the credit for that. I get the credit for selling it to him. I have no hard feelings toward anyone at Lookout!. I always had a policy that we would make exits as graceful as possible and always do the right thing even if we don't feel like it. We made their transition as easy as we could. There was some push by RED, but in the end it was all handled very professionally on all sides. As far as RED is concerned, I really hate them. I had bad dealings with their management team when they were important. I pulled our catalog when they changed their business model.

Shifting Tastes

Lookout! had not only survived the 1990s, it had thrived to heights never dreamed of in 1987. The saturation of independent releases and access to instant updates about any band via the internet hit overload by 1999 and forced a change that shook the industry. Bands were being discovered and shared through bootlegged downloads rather than only through trusted labels. The ever-evolving musical landscape was shifting away from pop-punk and toward lo-fi indie.

Chris Appelgren: I think it was just the era of the indie label. The nineties—Epitaph, Fat, Lookout!, Jade Tree, Sympathy for The Record Industry, Estrus, Sub Pop, Matador, Merge, No Idea, Johann's Face, and many more. It died out because of there being too many bands, too much access, and the role that labels played as curators of what bands were interesting was no longer as important. People had the access to make that determination on their own. I would tell bands who handed me their CD as a demo to get signed—why do you need me? It used to be that being signed to Lookout! meant a band could get a booking agent, a merch deal, etc. Now that can all happen without a band being signed, in fact, if a band has a manager or better—or worse—a lawyer, they're advised to do as much as possible without working with an indie, [and] instead hold onto the lion's share of any income and wait for the biggest deal possible.

The Turn of the Century at Lookout!

Bratmobile

In 2000, Erin Smith, guitarist of the recently re-formed Bratmobile, made the move from Washington, D.C., to join her bandmate Molly Neuman at Lookout! in Berkeley.

Erin Smith (Bratmobile): I moved to California in May of 2000 to do Bratmobile more regularly—we'd always been on two coasts before—and I started at Lookout! in July of 2000. I took over doing radio promotion and reception from my roommate in California, Vanessa Gates, who had just quit. My college major was Radio, Television, and Film, so it was perfect because radio is what I studied. I went on later to do radio, video, and tour promotion, then was promoted to promotion director.

Following the breakup of the Peechees, and while busily involved in Lookout!'s business affairs, it wasn't long before Molly Neuman reunited the highly influential Bratmobile after a half-decade hiatus. Neuman's endeavors from the early nineties onward cannot be understated, from the Riot Grrrl movement—a term coined by her fanzine—to the music she made with Allison Wolfe and Erin Smith in Bratmobile. The band's original existence—from 1991 to 1994—was a short yet exciting time for anyone immersed in the band's surrounding scene.

Erin Smith: We did more touring with the re-formation, but our singer Allison was still living on the East Coast. All three of us never lived in the same place. We did some great Donnas tours after we re-formed, they had been fans of ours early on when they were in junior high/high school. We first toured with them in the fall of 1999—it was a European tour, 100 percent female, even our tour manager—and it was just an incredibly fun time. We would stay upstairs from where we had just played a show, ten of us or so. Weird guys would try to head upstairs to the band apartment above the venue. The Donnas definitely got it worse than us—I just remember a drunk German guy ambling up the stairs after the show and getting thrown out.

The Pattern

As Y2K marched over the starting line, and the punk peak was now descending, Chris Appelgren decided it was time to get back into playing music after a two-year break following the end of the Peechees. The band had ended unceremoniously when Rop Vasquez moved to New York in 1998. During this time, the stresses of running a successful label while playing in an active band had affected Appelgren, and was compounded by being away from the office when on the road. After being invited to a dinner party by Andy Asp of Nuisance, the seeds of a new musical project—soon to be called the Pattern—were sown.

Chris Appelgren: Jason Rosenberg was at the dinner party, who had been in the band Engage, from Santa Rosa, whom I also knew a little bit. Through Andy, he asked if I might be interested in being in a band that he was trying to form. A band that he hoped would be sort of a summer fun bombastic rock and roll band, like Free and the Who.

Andy Asp (Nuisance, The Pattern): I ran into Jason Rosenberg on the street, and he asked me if I knew how to get ahold of Chris—he wanted a singer for his new project. I agreed, but only if he'd take me on as second guitar.

Chris Appelgren: The three of us met for drinks, realized we were all into the idea, and then we set about finding a drummer and bass player.

Andy Asp: I mentioned it to Carson [Bell] at the Ruby Room, and he said he wanted onboard too.

Chris Appelgren: We tried a few drummers and settled on our friend Jim "[Jim] Nastic" [Andersen]. Carson Bell had been in the band the Cuts and was a friend of Andy's and mine. We started practicing and quickly had about eight songs. Within three weeks of settling on a lineup, we played our first show, a summer party in Oakland. Everything aligned quickly for the band, we started playing a lot, asked friends and local labels to put out some 7-inches, and it just seemed to build in momentum. It was a lot of fun, and we seemed to be up for anything.

Andy Asp: We played mostly punk shows early on and then began doing more club stuff. There was yet another resurgence of "rock," as it were, and we just happened to be in the right place at the right time.

Chris Appelgren: We ended up touring in England and playing Reading and Leeds Festivals in 2001. We had good shows and audiences definitely were responsive.

The Ghoulies

Groovie Ghoulies were also back on the scene, following the 1999 *Fun in the Dark* (**LK 220**) LP with another new lineup. The band had recruited a new touring drummer, nineteen-year-old Amy Cesari, a school friend of the Donnas.

Amy Cesari (Groovie Ghoulies, The Donnas): I was sitting in the Donnas' van in 1999 in front of what used to be the The Edge rock club in Palo Alto—formerly the Keystone. The Donnas had just played a show with the Ghoulies, and we were hanging out in the van with Kepi, and I said "Hey Kepi! If you ever need another drummer . . . you know where to find me!" Apparently he remembered that and found me later.

With a new drummer on board, Groovie Ghoulies returned to their constantly busy schedule. With the upcoming release of the full-length *Travels with My Amp* (**LK 246**), they approached Lookout! with a particularly ambitious tour concept: fifty shows in fifty states in fifty days.

Chris Appelgren: A great idea but hard to pull off, and, for a punk band and a punk label, it had a limited appeal as a "story." It got pared down because it was logistically super challenging. We just weren't as enthusiastic about the idea as they were, and it was disappointing for them I think.

The band had also become disappointed with the label because of the diminishing returns for all their hard work. They'd seen slower sales and smaller attendance at shows with each subsequent year—which could be attributed to the fact that they didn't evolve with the changing musical landscape of the times.

Tristin Laughter: I did the exact same work for the Groovie Ghoulies [that] I did for the Donnas, I just got very different results. Artists are putting themselves out there in a personal way, and when the results of the promotional efforts let them down, it's natural to be frustrated with the people doing the promotion. I would never presume to tell any band that they have an inherently limited appeal, and I believed in the Groovie Ghoulies. I liked them and tried as hard as I could to get them what they wanted and deserved, but the reality of doing music PR is that you send people records, and you beg them to listen to them. You harass them, asking them to review it positively or preview the show, but you have no control over the end results, and I think that expectations of the bands were probably thrown off. How could they not be, by first having Green Day outsell Nirvana?

Chris Appelgren: I felt like we were putting forth the same effort and getting smaller returns with each new release and tour. I felt like the band was kind of blaming that on the label—maybe it was our fault, maybe our enthusiasm was waning, but I did love the band. I guess I just felt like if we could scale expectations down, we could all be happy. The first album did the best, and each successive album did a little less than the previous one. I'm not saying it tracks to quality, I think that the later ones are stronger songwriting- and performance-wise, but I felt like they were afraid to take a break. They really put everything into the band. Ultimately, Kepi and Roach quit their jobs and even had to move out, and I guess sell their house, which seemed super sad. They didn't talk to me about whether that was a good idea, and of course on one hand we wanted them to do as much as possible to support the records touring-wise. But Kepi was always two steps ahead, planning albums and tours way before we could ever think to suggest them. I would see Kepi and Roach—they would come to the office to get their statements and royalties and we would chat, but it was uncomfortable, more from Roach than Kepi. I really felt like she was disappointed or felt let down by Lookout!.

Lookout! bookkeeper Bill Michalski was also coming to the end of his time with the label after two years, in which time he witnessed some questionable business practices, as well as a declining relationship with the Ghoulies.

Bill Michalski: They extended way too much credit to the Groovie Ghoulies for tour merch, resulting in the band owing the label tons of money and creating bad feelings all around. I also was not privy to the negotiations between the band and label. But I think it was a combination of a lot of things on both sides. But in the end, responsible management wouldn't have let the situation degrade to the point that it did, so ultimately, I guess you could blame the label. More generally, they just spent more than they had—way too many employees. The biggest, most obviously dumb decision was the Warped Tour.

They had nowhere near enough money to do it properly and it ended up being a huge disaster, losing the label tons of money.

Farewell to the Donnas

Since their beginning only a few years prior, the Donnas had already made huge inroads by the time of 2001's *Turn 21* (**LK 255**) album release. With their success growing each year, they were clearly on a path that would reach further than the punk label they called home.

Chris Appelgren: It was very exciting and felt like we were building an important success. The staff was really behind the album, and we all worked hard to make *Turn 21* as big of a release as possible. We also knew there was interest, and sales were growing with each album, and it seemed like only a matter of time that leaving would happen. There were lots of A&R people interested in the band, we knew that because Molly [Neuman] was managing them, so she was having those conversations. The Donnas were mostly interested in finding a label that could be a home for them the way that Lookout! had been.

With Lookout!'s blessing, the Donnas entered the world of the majors, signing a deal with Atlantic Records. *Turn 21* had eventually shipped 75,000 copies, upping the ante and leaving Lookout! with no doubt that they didn't have the resources to handle further releases. Although the Donnas had moved on to bigger things, they certainly hadn't bid farewell to Lookout!, with Molly Neuman still on board as band manager.

Back Again: Screeching Weasel

Following almost fifteen years of ups and downs in various forms, Screeching Weasel's tenth studio album in 2000, *Teen Punks in Heat* (**LK**

257), was released on Lookout! Records/Panic Button. The album was the final nail in the coffin of the original lineup. The band remained inactive on the live circuit, aside from the odd showcase event and anniversary shows following the release of *Teen Punks in Heat*. One of those rare shows was a packed house at the House of Blues in Chicago, in October 2000. Mass Giorgini attempted to negotiate a follow-up tour, to get a lineup he was excited about back in front of audiences, but his efforts fell flat.

Mass Giorgini (Squirtgun, The Mopes, Screeching Weasel, Common Rider): I worked hard on a tour that never happened. I did all of the legwork talking to Flowerbooking—Susanne Dawursk, who had also booked Common Rider, set up a two-week mini-tour, and went the extra mile to try to satisfy all of the demands put on her by Screeching Weasel. She had something put together, but then it was all canceled.

The divide between members was so great, and Weasel's agoraphobia so active, that the writing was on the wall.

John "Jughead" Pierson (Screeching Weasel, The Mopes, Even In Blackouts): I think it's a great record, but I don't think it is a Screeching Weasel record as much as it is a Ben Weasel record. I was a performer and a negotiator between band members, but we were just studio musicians by that time. So it has much less importance in my history of the band than say, *Boogada[boogadaboogada!]* or *Wiggle*. In terms of a band getting into rehearsal and coming up with songs, it really fell apart when we let Vapid leave. Ben wasn't there for *Bark Like a Dog* or *Television City Dream*, and *How to Make Enemies* was a recovery record from losing Vapid. *Anthem for a New Tomorrow* was the point when we were touring the songs the most, but Vapid wasn't writing with Ben anymore. Ben would show us the songs, then disappear. It was disconcerting seeing that now he had more control but less appearance in the studio. That bridge has been sadly burned. I don't play with people who aren't friends.

Mass Giorgini: I recall John and Ben being involved in a dance of death. It turned into a death roll, and John was shoved aside; it killed the band.

Divorce & Ann Beretta

After Ann Beretta released their second album for Lookout! in 2001, *New Union...Old Glory* (**LK 262**), and the initial boost from Lookout! had passed, they found themselves beginning to run out of steam. One reason was that the label they had left, Fueled By Ramen, was growing rapidly, making them feel like they'd jumped ship at the wrong time. This feeling was made more real when they watched Lookout!'s latest garage band signings and felt out of place.

Rob Huddleston (Ann Beretta): We were signed on, as was American Steel, as the "new face" of Lookout!, and that was a huge honor and was exciting. It just didn't end up happening that way. Then, suddenly, the label started signing garage rock bands, and the people running the label seemed more interested in putting out their own records. We also took a gamble with the second record by asking for a large advance—thinking that it would force them to work harder to promote the band, but it just backfired. Plus, I'm not sure that the *New Union* record was all that great, so it's my fault there I guess. A lot of our friends in other bands as well as [the members of Ann Beretta] were beginning to become unhappy with the label and the direction it was moving in. We felt slighted a bit. The label was opting to leave us out of events like SXSW and CMJ at this point, and they didn't seem to really care about us at the time.

Chris Appelgren: I was really only a few years in as the one responsible for the label, and I was too involved in trying to address those challenges and create success to look back on the label's prior decade. Everything was going through an evolution. We moved out of our office, changed our physical distribution partner, and then my marriage was breaking up. Molly and I endeavored to collaborate on many things in our lives, working together, forming a band, and becoming business partners. We were very young when we started dating, and in lots of ways we grew up together, and the challenges of business were a strain on our personal relationship. We felt like the label staff and bands were sort of a family, and it made any fluctuations in our personal lives more difficult to admit or deal with. We grew up and grew apart, but the fact remains that we were close friends and tight allies. I moved out in February 2000 then moved back in for a month later that year and then moved out again.

During the early millennium, the personal life of Appelgren and dealings within the label were changing quickly.

Rob Huddleston: I tried to talk to [Chris and Molly] about [problems with the label] and never really felt like they were being straight up with us. I really did and still do love and respect everyone there as people and maybe that even made things worse. I eventually wrote Chris a long email letting him know how much I loved the label and how much of a dream it had been to release a record with Lookout!, but also how disappointed I was in what the label was becoming. I really love Chris and Molly and miss them—but I also think they made poor business decisions at times and lost focus on the magic that the label was.

Ted Leo

Appelgren tried to view this period as a clean slate, despite the public's feeling of ownership over the label and its history. One man and his band were finally won over and changed perceptions and direction of the label. Talks had begun with Ted Leo in 1999 as he began to make waves not only in underground punk, but more widely.

Theodore Francis Leo's roots burrow deep in the DIY punk world. Leo's beginnings can be traced back to legendary New York hardcore band Citizens Arrest in the late 1980s before splintering into the band Hell No. He then took part in a couple of other small-time bands before forming Chisel, the band that came to define his future songwriting and sound.

Chris Appelgren: I really loved Chisel, and when a band I was playing in shared a bill with them in San Francisco, we hung out in the basement backstage area. I really loved Ted's phrasing, melodies, and energy. I was actively looking for something that seemed to have the electricity I experienced seeing the early Lookout! bands but was also as forward facing as those bands had proven to be. So we began talking about doing an EP and then Ted called and told me they'd broken up.

With Chisel now a well-loved memory, Leo soldiered ahead, creating a new identity for his addictive mod, pop-punk tunes—Ted Leo and the Pharmacists. Ted spent the next year working out the direction of his new outfit, all while talking to Chris Appelgren about a Lookout! project.

Leo released his first solo effort on Gern Blandsten—the *Tej Leo(?), Rx/ Pharmacists* LP. The record was a far cry from what he would evolve into with the Pharmacists as his backing band.

Chris Appelgren: I remember seeing him on tour by himself in San Francisco, playing with an electric guitar and an Echoplex only. It was good, but I wasn't sure if it was right for Lookout!. Maybe he had to tear it down to start building again—I loved some of the songs but felt like with the first record I had to listen through certain things to uncover what I really liked.

Released in the summer of 2001, *The Tyranny of Distance* (**LK 268**) surprisingly made little impact upon arrival and became a slow burner. It took the better part of six months for the word to get around, but as it did, the record grew through word of mouth and Leo's hard work, especially on the live front. The record weaved melodic folk tales through fine musicianship and energetic performances. Leo's passionate songwriting made for compelling listening and also showed a songwriter and performer unbound by the constraints of labels and genres. Understanding that Lookout! was having financial troubles, and quite happy with their relationship, Ted Leo began "forgiving" royalties to try and help.

Marriage

Although one Lookout! marriage had been coming to a slow end, another was just beginning, Patrick Hynes and Erika Grove were married in October 2001.

Chris Appelgren: The wedding was outside in a Berkeley hotel near the waterfront, then the reception was indoors and was lots of fun, all of the Lookout! staff, local friends, families—a really great time. I was very proud of Patrick. They were together for a long time and when they got married it seemed totally right.

The Queers

Following a tumultuous relationship with Hopeless Records, the Queers had slipped back into the fray with Lookout! in 2001 and released the

Today EP/CD (**LK 260**) and 2002's *Pleasant Screams* album (**LK 270**). The obvious tip of the hat to the Ramones' *Pleasant Dreams, Pleasant Screams*, it was a solid album with some of Joe King's finest vocal work, fitting in well with the feel of *Don't Back Down*, especially on tracks like "I Don't Get the Girl." The album also featured nods to various punk scenesters cowriting with various punk rock royalty. In the eyes of Appelgren, it was a return home for the band that had previously cut ties with Lookout!.

Chris Appelgren: We had kept talking after the *Today* EP, which was kind of a one-off. When Joe asked if we wanted to do their next album, I checked with the gang and said yes. It was relatively cheap, and I felt like it was kind of vindicating after they'd been on Hopeless—a homecoming.

Pleasant Screams sold moderately well, but fate stepped in again and it wouldn't be until five years later, in 2007, that the Queers would release a new album—the *Munki Brain* LP on Asian Man Records.

Chris Appelgren: The record did okay, but the touring around it wasn't consistent, and I wasn't sure if Joe was in the best place personally. I mostly talked to him on the phone or saw him when they were in town, but there seemed to be problems with the band, and we just didn't pursue doing anything after that.

Joe King (The Queers): Well, they did zero promo for *Pleasant Screams*. Not one thing. No ads. Nothing. They were pushing the Donnas' new album, which wasn't even on Lookout! The ad was like "Check out the new Donnas album! It's amazing. Check out our other new releases too!" That was it. About the time I saw that I said fuck it. *Pleasant Screams* was a kick-ass album, which would have made them a lot of money, and they didn't even push it. We were touring and playing. Of course we were. We always are. So that sucked. No one would tell you the fucking truth, and it was like watching a train wreck. About the time they bought the new building it was really going badly. They were hemorrhaging money left and right and turned their back on the bands like us that made them the money. So I was pissed, but whatever. All water under the bridge now, I always still kept in touch with Chris and Larry. Through thick and thin we've all been pals. Still are.

Cashing Out

Pretty Girls

Seattle-based band Pretty Girls Make Graves was an unexpected success story for the label, stretching its reach beyond the ever-evolving Lookout! world. Pretty Girls Make Graves had pooled its members from various indie scene bands—Killsadie, the Hookers, Murder City Devils, and the Death Wish Kids, with vocalist Andrea Zollo and bassist Derek Fudesco having previously worked together. With releases already in the marketplace—EPs for Dim Mak, Sub Pop, and Sound Virus Records—Appelgren and Neuman approached the band with the offer of a Lookout! full-length release, a truly appreciated opportunity from the band members who had been weaned on the label's releases over the years. After the release of the 2002 *Good Health* (**LK 279**) full-length, the band hit the ground running with its combination of angular and flowing melodic lead guitar riffs, D.C. post-punk-inspired rhythms, and Andrea Zollo's sung and shouted vocals all layered upon a highly energetic and musically relevant sonic landscape.

Tristin Laughter: I definitely didn't expect Pretty Girls to be as big as they were. I remember when Derek played me their demo in my rental car at SXSW. I mean, they are a great band, but I didn't realize they would be a big deal.

Chris Appelgren: It was a big sounding record, and the band [members] were very charming and interesting. All in all, it was an easy deal, but I was not surprised when the record and band were successful with us. I was also not surprised when Matador wanted to buy out their contract with Lookout!.

Andrea Zollo (Pretty Girls Make Graves): The move to Matador was nothing more than to try something different. We loved everyone at Lookout! so much that it was hard on a personal level. I always thought that we didn't sound like a typical Lookout! band but also liked that. I felt the same way on Matador; we were not the typical Matador-type band. In fact, I don't know where we particularly would have fit in 100 percent.

Hit the Panic Button

With Panic Button's solid back catalog and established street cred, the creative duo of Weasel and Jughead started running into business problems and decided it was time to step down from Panic Button. They felt the label had been damaged in the transition from Mordam to RED.

John "Jughead" Pierson (Screeching Weasel, The Mopes, Even In Blackouts): I had to ask myself if it was affordable to put out a Jackie Papers record, if RED would take enough to make it so we didn't lose money. That was when I knew we were done. When ma and pa record stores started calling me and saying they could only get our records if they bought more products from RED, and RED would only print more if we bought ads for Coconuts and other corporate record stores. It was getting out of hand.

Chris Appelgren: Ben called and said they wanted to sell Panic Button. I entertained the idea thinking it would be a way for Lookout! to keep the Screeching Weasel catalog intact. It wasn't a shock, we were already manufacturing and distributing the label. I went out to Chicago to discuss the deal with Ben and then the process involved lawyers drafting up paperwork. John was there for part of the time, but it was really Ben leading the conversation. It was kind of a mess but not too shabby. We never got all the tapes and original album art that we were buying, but we'd already been handling manufacturing, so it wasn't much to take over the rest, and as we were actively in contact with Ben and John, it didn't seem like a big deal. We did, however, pay a lot more than it was worth, a few hundred thousand. The Lillingtons didn't really want to have Lookout! take over the albums, so they ended up leaving with their records, and when we turned down doing Enemy You's second album, they also asked to have their first back. The recording for the second record was great, but they couldn't and wouldn't tour. We were trying not to put out bands that weren't willing to play and tour—"trying" being the keyword to bear in mind. We had ten or so people working at the label, so selling two thousand copies of a new release was not enough to sustain the business. We were in a position where we had to sell more.

Unmet Expectations

Although excitement was high for some of Lookout!'s new releases between 2002 and 2004, several albums and new bands were underperforming or underwhelming the public, drawing a lot of criticism about the direction of the label—what many emotionally invested fans felt was an institution falling into ruin.

Shaun Osburn (The Cost): I think there were expectations of what a Lookout! band should be, and we weren't it—which, looking back, seems so strange as there were plenty of Lookout! bands in the early days that weren't pop in sound. Nobody ever criticized us on tour for being on Lookout!; however, we were asked constantly by other bands "So, what does Lookout! do for you?"

Brady Baltezore (The Criminals, Black Cat Music): I feel like if you picked up our records because you liked the stuff Lookout! used to put out, there was a fifty-fifty chance you'd be bummed out. The last tour we did was pretty dismal—whereas kids used to show up because they were fans or hadn't seen you, it seemed now like they didn't show up because they didn't like the tinny MP3s of your band that they stole off the internet.

Roman Kuebler (The Oranges Band): It is always hard to say whether people came out to see our band or not. We didn't do a lot of headlining things, and the ones we did do were generally pretty weak. We weren't selling any records and still not seeing a lot of people out to our shows.

Chris Appelgren: None of the newer releases were generating any real profits—the Oranges Band, Communiqué, the Reputation, the Washdown—I love those records, but they didn't make money for the label, and they definitely cost money. The Dollyrots' album [*Eat My Heart Out*, **LK309**] was the first Panic Button release after Ben and John threatened a lawsuit because we were slow with the final payment to them for the label purchase. That was the big last piece of the financial misstep that was Lookout's purchase of Panic Button. We had a payment plan with Ben and John over time for Panic Button, and the last one we didn't really want to pay. We had not gotten much value from the catalog sales. Some of the bands were not enthusiastic about the transfer of ownership—notably the Lillingtons—and we had a clause in our agreement that allowed the label to revert [back] to them for nonpayment. We decided it might be best to default and let John and Ben take the label back over. I can't remember all of the back-and-forth, but essentially, we told them we couldn't pay that much, maybe asked for a reduction in the final payment, and they said no. Then they said we had damaged the value of the label and didn't want it back. Ultimately, they hired a lawyer and either threatened or filed suit for the balance, and we ended up settling for a slight reduction, and we were then the full owners of the label.

But around this same time, perhaps as a result of the Panic Button purchase and buying out Hynes's and Livermore's ownership, Lookout! had fallen behind on their most basic royalties owed—the ones to Green Day and Operation Ivy, the bands that were floating their entire catalog and allowing them to have cash flow for new releases in the first place.

Chris Appelgren: [Buying Panic Button] was really the final straw in many ways, and in all honesty, that money should have gone to Green Day and Operation Ivy. We had been in contact with bigger bands about payments on back royalties, but then to have to say a payment is on its way and then not make that payment but offer up some promise of making it at a later date . . . it was more damage to fragile relationships. I did worry about the label in general, and it was tough to balance the financial troubles with the need to be doing new things and creating new successes.

Lookout! signed two new bands: Illinois's Troubled Hubble and Minnesota's Hockey Night, but the deals did not include big cash outlays, aside from the costs of promoting the releases. Appelgrean was overwhelmed by the cost of keeping the business going and began experimenting with anything he could to get costs down. The lack of cash flow began impeding Lookout!'s ability to fulfill promises they'd made to bands, leading to the same failure to meet expectations that shatters any relationship. Appelgren's lack of business experience combined with being propelled into the driver's seat of an organization that had a lot of pressure to keep growing during a changing time in the music business created a bubble that seemed ready to burst. But if that wasn't bad enough, Small Brown Bike, Engine Down, and Troubled Hubble all broke up shortly after Lookout! released their albums.

Chris Appelgren: It was really when I spoke with Pat Magnarella, Green Day's manager, that I realized we had to make a significant change. We had been talking to the band Mates of State and had to pull our offer. I knew that, essentially, this was the end of the label operating as it had. It was sort of a relief while at the same time supremely scary.

The Dollyrots

With their song "Feed Me, Pet Me" featured in a 2002 Hewlett-Packard ad campaign, a vinyl deal, some heavy L.A. radio play, and their full-length album already recorded and self-released, the Dollyrots signed with Panic Button and re-released *Eat My Heart Out* in 2004.

Luis Cabezas (The Dollyrots): We had some traction in L.A. because of the radio play. Indie 103 set up these showcases at the Viper Room. I don't know how the word got to Lookout!, but all of a sudden there was interest. And it was primarily based on the fact that they had acquired Ben Weasel's label, Panic Button, and I guess the thinking, from our perspective, was like "Alright, I guess we don't fit on Lookout!, but they think that we'll fit on Panic Button.

Kelly Ogden (The Dollyrots): They explained to us that Panic Button was gonna be their pop punk label.

Luis Cabezas: And at the time I'm thinking to myself, wait, aren't *you* [Lookout!] the pop punk label? But they said, "No, we're gonna make Panic Button the pop punk label, and Lookout's gonna be these other bands." So, Jeff [Oppenheimer, who was managing Panic Button] came down to see us at one of these Indie 103 showcases, and we fucking killed it. At the end of the show, we tackled each other off the stage. It was a magnificent ending. And so, basically, the show ended, and we were all standing outside on Sunset Boulevard, and Jeff was like, "You guys wanna be on the label?" and we said yes, and that was it. They sent over a contract, and it was a reasonable contract that didn't promise anything. Like, there wasn't much of a marketing budget.

Kelly Ogden: They did give us something for tour support.

Luis Cabezas: Yeah. It was a standard deal at the time, and we were happy to take it because it meant, alright we get to be in stores everywhere. I think it was Mordam and then Lumberjack distribution. It was great. They were reasonable with us—we already had an entertainment attorney, and he took one look at the contract and was like, "Um, you're not giving them worldwide perpetuity ownership of your release. If they can do a license for it, then that's better." And they agreed to that. We just did like a five year license.

Kelly Ogden: And we already had a deal for vinyl, and they were fine with that too.

Luis Cabezas: They were really cool about everything. They were cool with the fact that we'd self released, too. So we scheduled a secondary release, a national release for September 2004. We planned some dates. To be honest, it was easier to book a tour being on a label than not being on a label. So that was another bonus. But, you know, we knew going into it that we weren't going to be a priority. And we were okay with that.

Kelly Ogden: It was more that we were playing something that wasn't trendy or cool to them anymore.

Luis Cabezas: This was just our impression—we didn't fit the label, even though we had grown up with the label being our format. But it was clear that things were changing. Maybe they wanted to distance themselves from what they perceived as being like a dying genre.

Kelly Ogden: Then the Warped Tour came, which was a very clear indicator.

Luis Cabezas: Yeah. I remember Jeff was like, "Well, do you guys have a tent? You're gonna need a tent."

Kelly Ogden: We had a super cheap sixty dollar pop-up one.

Luis Cabezas: So Jeff said the Lookout! tent was just kind of hanging out at the office. I was like, "We can take the Lookout! tent on the Warped Tour? That'd be awesome!" and so—

Kelly Ogden: We took the tent and a whole bunch of crap, all these awesome stickers and Green Day posters. And compilations.

Luis Cabezas: The response was interesting. There was a good amount of "What the hell happened to the label?" They [Warper Tour audience members] thought that we worked for the label. I think punk music was changing a lot in general during that time period. My Chemical Romance and Fallout Boy were becoming the hip thing. It wasn't melodic pop punk carrying the genre. It was more like emo or indie-oriented music. I remember a guy came up to me at the tent and was like, "You guys," meaning our band, "are like the last of a dying breed."

Kelly Ogden: I thought, that's real inspiring with our first album coming out.

Luis Cabezas: So we saw out the cycle of the first record, and it was time to record the next record, and we weren't about to get an advance for it. So, again, just like the first time around, we self funded it, and we cut a full album with our own pennies, with the idea that this would be our second release on Lookout!. Our experience had been good enough, especially with Jeff, that we felt comfortable with that. Either way, we'd get a record. And . . . while recording this record we got word that the label was shutting its doors. This was like 2005.

Kelly Ogden: Which was a bit of a gut punch, because we had just spent all of our money thinking that we'd at least have distro.

Luis Cabezas: It was like, Oh my god, we just spent all of our money.

Kelly Ogden: We still had day jobs, thank goodness. And the reasons for shutting down—we started hearing from all sorts of different people.

Luis Cabezas: Money had to have been invested in things that, in the end, didn't make sense. I don't know what the mechanics of that were, all we knew was that we didn't have a label anymore. But, on the other hand . . .

Kelly Ogden: They released us from our deal with them.

Luis Cabezas: We got our first record back, and I heard that other bands got their records back. We had the impression that even though the label folded, they were decent enough to give everyone the rights to their music. At least in our case, that allowed us to do whatever we wanted with that first album. We came out of it fairly unscathed. At the end of the day, that led to us finding a new label.

Kelly Ogden: We took those songs out on Warped Tour; there was an EP of what would become *Because I'm Awesome* that I handed to Joan Jett and months later we got a call from Blackheart.

Townley Parts Ways for Good

Another longtime member of the Lookout! family also decided it was time to part ways for good. Even though it had been four years since Jesse Townley removed Blatz's output from Lookout!, the Criminals' *Never Been Caught* had remained. As a result of concerns Townley was hearing from friends still working at Lookout!, he approached Appelgren.

Jesse Townley (Blatz, The Criminals): I didn't want that record to languish in some bank's vault after a bankruptcy proceeding. Lookout! sent me the remaining copies of the LP—the CD was out-of-print—and the masters and art files all for free. I really appreciated this because the band had racked up a couple thousand dollars of debt when we were a touring band in the 1990s. Back then, Lookout! and the band set up a payment plan, but it failed because our band didn't pay. I think at this point, the Lookout! managers were just happy to get rid of me, and I gotta say, the feeling was mutual. I felt like a weight had been lifted off of me, and I'm glad that we were able to part ways permanently.

Losing Green Day, Losing Face

In what seemed like a surefire way to get back on track during a lean and difficult year, Lookout! had the bright idea to reissue the Green Day catalog. Both full-lengths were to get an overhaul—an enhanced version of *Kerplunk!* and a double vinyl remastered compilation of the band's first three releases, fittingly dubbed *1,039/Smoothed-Out Slappy Hours* that would be **LK 300**. Test presses of the vinyl had been completed when Appelgren got a phone call.

Chris Appelgren: [Green Day] had approved the master, and [the plant] was in the process of doing the vinyl when I spoke with the band's manager, Pat Magnarella. It was decided that Green Day would end their relationship with Lookout!. He left me a voicemail, and I returned his call. Molly [Neuman] and I both were fairly friendly with Pat. He seemed genuinely unhappy to relate their feelings—that although they appreciated our efforts to come up with stopgap solutions like partial payments, calculating and paying interest on any late payments—the band was just not comfortable with how much they were owed and had real questions about whether they'd be paid. Basically, they decided they needed to take control of the situation and find a better solution for their early albums. I said I understood and was really sorry. I also told him how much we had appreciated the long-standing relationship that the band had maintained with Lookout! Records. I told him I would speak with Cathy [Bauer] and Molly, talk to our distributor, and get back to him when I had a handle on how to stop sales.

Years of questionable bookkeeping and a seeming inability to pay bands royalties that were owed to them without being repeatedly asked, had finally caught up with Lookout!. But the real doozy was doing the math and realizing that the amount Lookout! had paid for Panic Button would have been ample to catch up on paying the royalties owed to Green Day.

One of the barbs that stung the most came from Livermore, reported by *Pitchfork* to have said, "No matter how rich a band is, they shouldn't be expected to subsidize a failing label forever, especially when that label isn't doing anything particularly worthwhile." He was seemingly hurt that Appelgren hadn't gone to him for counsel, while Appelgren felt like he needed to prove to Livermore that he could run Lookout! and that it hadn't ceased to be relevant once the cofounder and father figure had left. But, in the end, he had failed to resolve small issues before they had eaten away the entire foundation of the company.

More than the issue of outstanding money owed, Lookout! had violated a much more important agreement: the implicit trust of bands Lookout! worked closely with. And ultimately, that is why Green Day chose to walk away.

A Mint and Lookout! co-release!

THE SMUGGLERS

Selling the Sizzle!

The End of an Era

An Open Letter from Label Prez Chris Appelgren

(Posted on the Lookout! website news: August 5, 2005)

By now most of you that visit the Lookout! Records site are aware of something happening here at the label and I'd like to take this time to let you know a few things and really set the record straight if I can.

There are a lot of questions about the future of Lookout! so I want to say the following. Lookout! Records is not going under or closing up shop. We are however making some significant changes. After over sixteen years of operating, Lookout! has gotten to be quite an operation. We have a staff, a building, big shelves, desks, computers, shipping materials, fax machines, and bunches of records and CDs laying around. That translates into a lot of expense every month, and, frankly, we haven't been selling enough records to cover all these costs. Top that with some of the bad business decisions we've made and you have an understanding of how we got to where we are.

Want examples? Without getting into specifics it was acquiring labels, maintaining our new release schedule, signing bands while not giving enough attention to financial concerns that were not going away. Bad decisions and poor judgment came into play—most strikingly, in hoping that things would all somehow magically work out, that the shortcomings in operating income and the fact that our new bands were not selling as many records as we hoped would all somehow just turn out okay on their own if we just kept working hard and doing the best job we could.

Not all of our decisions were bad, and we honestly tried to turn things around, enjoying some great successes too, including some incredible releases and a great celebration of fifteen years of business in 2003. But the bottom line didn't change despite modest upturns in our sales. My two partners often had a better sense of our problems than I did—I was the source of the naive hope in some of our internal discussions. I probably owe Cathy and Molly an apology for my problem-solving always relying on a big dose of pure luck. We got behind in payments as money that was due to artists was used to maintain our business or in some cases fund new releases. We were in touch with a good deal of our bands as this was happening—although not everyone—and many were understanding and willing to bear with us and this hopefully brief downturn in business, including Green Day.

But the downturn was not brief, and, as has been reported all over, Green Day has decided that they can't bear with us any longer and are taking control of their Lookout! albums. They hung in there with us through thick and thin but now it's time to move on. It has not been a battle and, however insincere it may have seemed in the light of all the hubbub, our statement about friendship, respect and trust between Lookout! and Green Day is accurate. They're one of the greatest bands in the world and we had a relationship with them that lasted longer than many major label deals do. That's something to be proud of even in the face of the truth that it could have continued had Lookout! made some different decisions about our own business.

Coming to this decision and looking at what it meant was a huge wake-up call. I sat down with my two partners to assess what this would mean for Lookout! and a few things were very clear. It was high time to make some hard decisions about how Lookout! will exist in the future. It was also time for us to get to work on meeting our current and past-due obligations before we take on any more. The changes we looked at were not because Lookout! would no longer have Green Day's first two albums, but had to happen because our business was not healthy. Green Day's decision was a result of our internal problems, not a cause.

We looked long and hard at our situation and what we would need to do for Lookout! to continue and build back up to a secure, solvent business. It was clear we had to let our staff go, relocate into a smaller office space, and hold off on any new releases. We're a very small business and we had to start acting like it.

It is heartbreaking that the team that has been Lookout! Records will no longer be here working with each other day-to-day. This is a good opportunity to say thank you to Tristin [Laughter], Erin, Taggylee, Todd, Patrick, Lisa, and Ben for all your time, energy and spirit. The contribution that each of you has made to this company is indelible and I appreciate the years you have given to Lookout! Records—Todd and Erin over five years each; Tristin over eight; Patrick, something like fifteen—but each day that every one of you was here means a lot. We weren't perfect, but we worked hard because we cared about what we were doing and we pulled off some pretty incredible things along the way.

Things are going to change. In fact, they have already started to. We're tightening our belts and getting to work to meet our obligations, do right by our bands and partners, our supporters and even our detractors. I've never particularly been good at taking advice, but now more than ever I need to listen to my friends and peers and learn from my mistakes.

Thanks for reading, Chris

The News Hits

Spensaur Cooper (Intern): My internship was scheduled to end somewhere toward the beginning of September of '05, and in the middle of August, Chris [Appelgren] and Cathy [Bauer] called a Friday meeting. They had full-staff meetings all the time so it didn't seem too out of the ordinary to me, except the fact that Chris brought a twenty-four pack of Tecate into the office. After a couple hours doing whatever work I was doing, everyone came out looking super bummed. I think a couple folks had gotten drunk, some folks were in the back smoking cigarettes, everyone was talking about something, but I didn't really find out until the next morning. Green Day had pulled their catalog, and there just wasn't enough income to continue the label operating the way it had been. As it turned out, the last day of my internship was the entire staff's last day. I can't really remember the last day, but I do remember those last couple weeks had a lot of sad faces around the office.

Erin Smith (Bratmobile): Molly [Neuman] was in town from New York, so we had all gone out for an all-staff lunch at a Thai place. Then, when we got back, there was a pack of beer, and they said we would have a meeting. I am not a big drinker, but I drank a lot of that beer that day. Basically, I moved and left California one month after we all got laid off. Life would never be the same for me there without Lookout!.

Roman Kuebler (The Oranges Band): Cathy called and told me on the phone, and I do remember the phrase "catalog only," it was clear that we were without a label, that they couldn't support our next release, or continue to support this one. At this time, Cathy was our manager, and we had another album with a $15,000 advance on our contract.

Chris Appelgren: When it became clear that this was it, that we had to pull the plug on Lookout! Records as a business that had provided all of us with our livelihoods, it was more mournful than a surprise. I think in a way it was also liberating. For some time I had been wishing we could do more for the staff, but because of our money issues, we couldn't really provide raises and were constantly pushing for people to do more to create success. Admitting that we had gotten to the point of no return and had to take drastic action was like finally taking a breath after all of us holding our breaths collectively. After that, it was Cathy and me in the office and a few interns. I moved from my office down into the warehouse to do mail orders and ship distribution orders. It was a lot of work. I did mail order, which we had a lot of but we also ran Ted Leo's webstore and had our own wholesale online store for small stores and international customers. The big office, the empty desks, the unused computers, the workload—all of it was really sad. My attitude was that we had to put scaling down the business first. We entertained the idea of another music company investing in the label and had an offer on the table for a short time. It was really too late, and I don't know if it would have been possible to make it work. We had talked about how to shrink the costs of running the label for some time—a couple years at least—but it was hard to do while not making it seem like we were in trouble. By having such a public and undeniable thing happen, we were able to accept the truth and finally put our attention into eliminating the extensive monthly costs associated with the business.

Ernst Part Three

One of the small costs, and an ongoing issue relevant to the loss of the Green Day income, was the ongoing royalty payment made to Andy Ernst.

Chris Appelgren: In the midst of this, I remember writing to Andy and letting him know that as Lookout! had elected at our own discretion to pay him a small royalty on the Green Day albums, and considering the fact that these titles were no longer being released by Lookout!, he would not receive any further statements or payments from us. I received a call and a letter from a lawyer representing Andy, threatening a lawsuit against, I guess, Lookout! Records regarding future earnings of the two albums. I told the lawyer what the situation was, that Lookout! had, purely out of consideration for Andy, paid him even though there was no obligation to do so. I ended up having to go to this lawyer's office in San Francisco to meet and discuss this even further. It turned out to be a very negative experience—there was a secretary recording my responses, and the questions led me to understand that what was really going on was that Andy's lawyer wanted to build a case that he was entitled to a royalty on these albums and should be paid by the band or whatever label rereleased the two early records. I was quietly very angry and disappointed on behalf of the band and felt as if I was being used to help build a case. I told the truth—that in my understanding Andy had no claim to any share of any earnings—and was not contacted by the lawyer again. I never spoke to Andy after this and don't harbor any ill will towards him in the slightest. He is a talented, creative, and incredibly economic producer and engineer—he knows his shit. It sounds as if he made his case to Warner Brothers and is now getting some financial consideration from the Green Day records he recorded. Good for him, I guess. Personally, I believe it was the band themselves that deserve production credit on those albums. As young as they were at the time, Billie Joe and Mike were very accomplished musicians who knew what they wanted. Andy's biggest credit is that he worked fast and didn't get in the way.

Andy Ernst: "I was pissed off at Green Day for years, but as time went by I became less pissed off at them and more pissed off at Larry. Larry is the one who asked me to produce, not Green Day, and if he understood my point of view, why didn't he just pay me? Why did it matter what Green Day did? Finally, in 2008, almost twenty years after I first worked with Green Day, Warner Brothers started paying me a small royalty on future sales. Now, when I think about Lookout! I try to think about the poster I still have in my office that shows so many bands that I've worked with over the years. I'm grateful for the business Larry brought me. For the most part it was fun, and the majority of my memories are good ones. But to this day, every once in a while, when I think about Lookout!, I still get a bad taste in my mouth.

Chris Appelgren: I tried to be honest and was hopeful for the process of resolving any issues with bands and partners, but brave? No. It would have been brave to have anticipated a problem and taken action before problems arose—like Touch and Go Records did. In the sense that they did the same thing, essentially announced that they were done releasing new artists, focusing on back catalog, and scaling down the business—but they did so before, not causing them to lose bands or tax any relationships.

Full Circle: Op Ivy

As Lookout! entered a period of inactivity, nearly twenty years from its inception, another blow was struck. Following Green Day's lead, and amidst rumors of a lawsuit brewing from Avail, Operation Ivy also pulled its catalog on May 4, 2006. Although the label had ceased normal operations around the end of 2005, there were many broken relationships to mend and many outstanding royalty payments overdue. With Lookout!'s biggest income source now having disappeared, the situation was crushing.

According to Livermore, Green Day was earning between $10,000 and $3,000,000 annually in royalties for the albums that Lookout! had the rights to for a little over fifteen years. According to Appelgren, Lookout!'s typical royalty rate was 54 percent of profits to the band and 46 percent to the label, which would leave Lookout! with roughly $23,000,000 in profit from Green Day sales alone. Lookout!'s third best-selling album, Operation Ivy's *Energy*, likely added another 5 to 10 percent onto that, plus royalties that were due but never paid to Green Day, unpaid royalties to the remainder of their catalog, and with the profit from the rest of their other 300+ releases, it would appear that Lookout! somehow squandered what may have been upwards of $50,000,000 between 1991 and the time of their bankruptcy filings in 2012.

Chris Appelgren: I feel like Lookout! let Operation Ivy down. In the later years, our royalty payments had not been as consistent with them, but I also feel as though the band had drifted away from the label culturally. After Rancid was popular, Matt [Freeman] and Tim [Armstrong] had a whole different label family and friend bands and not many were associated with Lookout!. In early 2006, Matt came by to talk about *Energy*. They were worried about the label for the same reason that Green Day [had been], that we would fold or do something drastic—like try to sell—and they'd lose the control they had of their records. So the band got together and talked about it and decided it was best to pull it.

Robert Eggplant (Blatz): Even though Lookout! opened a cool record store/social center . . . they were not supporting the new local bands. It was a turd. There was something sleazy and cocaine-laden about the vibe by then. A good example would be found by spending a few minutes with the Peechees. Certainly live—but [even] their records reveal the excess and off-mark expression as much as your worst seventies disco/arena rock example. Punks who had records out on Lookout!—and that were selling—were grumbling about the teeth that had to be pulled to get their promised check.

Press Coverage

In the midst of the maelstrom surrounding the label's now-public business dealings, on September 14, 2005, an article appeared in the *East Bay Express* called "Kerplunk: The Rise and Fall of the Lookout! Records Empire." The article was written by Rob Harvilla, and through interviews with members of the Lookout! Records family such as Chris Appelgren, Jesse Townley, Molly Neuman, Mike Dirnt, Larry Livermore, and Jon Ginoli, the extended piece unravels a passionate story with many people throwing in their two cents about the legacy of one of the most successful independent record labels of all time.

Chris Appelgren: I am not sure how the story got out, but somehow there was a lot of reporting about Green Day pulling their albums and much of it was unfortunate. The band thought we had leaked the story for sympathy or something, but that was far from the case. We let our distributor know, and the staff, when it became apparent that this was indeed going to happen. Someone talked, and it became a story, being reported in *Spin*, *Rolling Stone*, and even on MTV, plus lots of online music sites. It was important to me, when asked, not to lay any blame on the band. They were not responsible, and I felt bad that some journalists tried to spin it into a tale of Green Day "forgetting their roots." Rob, the music editor of the *East Bay Express*, asked if I would be part of a story he was doing on the label and Green Day. I felt like it could be sort of negative, but I figured it was better to be a part of than not to be. Everyone's comments stung of course, but I came to grips with it. I came to understand that while I had to be responsible for my role in Lookout! failing some of its artists, I didn't have to take the whole thing personally. I do think it was the final word for many people, regardless of their opinion of the label. Like, "Appelgren sure managed to fuck up a great label by signing stuff that wasn't like *X* and didn't sell.' Or, "It's a shame that the music industry is so far in the tank that a great label like Lookout! Records had to throw in the towel."

Rob Harvilla (Editor/reporter): I'd been at the *Express* a couple years by that point. I saw the Pattern and the Oranges Band at the Stork Club and had lunch with Molly and Chris at one point. I'd written about Lookout! bands before, but once Green Day pulled their back catalog, it seemed like an obvious candidate for a deeper piece—two huge East Bay institutions splitting up. Public opinion seemed to be in the "not malicious, just poorly run" camp. It's telling that arguably, Ted Leo aside, there weren't any Lookout! bands at that time getting national exposure [or] love on anywhere near the Green Day or Operation Ivy scale. That the label folded I don't think surprised anyone, necessarily. Lookout! meant something to people, represented a DIY/artist-friendly ideal it wasn't able to live up to, and that hurt people arguably more than the late or absent paychecks. I didn't think Chris and the Lookout! brain trust were bad people. They made mistakes, arguably enormous ones, and clearly didn't pay everyone everything they were owed, but who does?

Sad Farewells

As 2005 came to a close, the building that had housed Lookout! for five years at 3264 Adeline Street was sold off to make way for a more modest office space in San Francisco. Moving into the small workspace, Cathy Bauer kept working full time for Lookout! throughout 2006, while Appelgren took an offer to work at the Noise Pop Festival, based in San Francisco. Settling into the small office, Bauer began downsizing the operation.

Chris Appelgren: We would meet regularly to check in on things, and basically she handled artist relations, distribution, royalties, and also some website revisions—moving the store over to Little Type Mail Order.

Little Type had been the brainchild of Patrick and Erika Hynes—the business set up as a home-run mail-order punk record store. Little Type also operated online stores for—amongst others—Ted Leo, Screeching Weasel, and Larry Livermore. The online presence serviced Lookout!'s mail order as well, but tragedy befell the company in April 2009. After a long battle with liver-related complications, Erika Hynes passed away.

Chris Appelgren: When Erika passed away, Patrick had the idea to continue, but ultimately he proved to not be up to the challenge. I can understand that it might have been too sad for him. So much of Little Type's personality was Erika.

Things were quiet on the label front from 2006 to 2009, but then an unfortunate chain of events struck the beleaguered label.

Chris Appelgren: We had a few fires that needed to be put out—like relations with Phantom Surfers getting to a point where they wanted to audit our books. Mike Lucas from the band came into our office and poured over the sales and accounting info for their albums. Then, basically, things started to fall apart in 2009. Cathy moved to NYC, and we lost two partners, Lumberjack Mordam—after a semi-surprising demise—and Little Type. Both went away without paying us; we lost stock and money. We tried to rally by consolidating distribution with The Orchard, who'd been Lookout!'s digital music partner for a number of years already.

With The Orchard taking over distribution and Lookout! losing inventory and having holes in its catalog, a reissue campaign began. Due to their agreement with The Orchard, Lookout! had enough cash flow to recreate some releases it still owned, beginning with a new CD pressing of former Operation Ivy frontman Jesse Michaels's band Big Rig. With new interest in vinyl from college students and adults, other releases were planned as vinyl re-pressings with MP3 downloads, including the Donnas' *American Teenage Rock 'n' Roll Machine*, *Get Skintight*, and *Turn 21*; Ted Leo's full-length albums; and American Steel's *Jagged Thoughts*. Others that were planned never came to fruition, fittingly including the Mr. T Experience's *...And the Women Who Love Them* extended compilation on vinyl.

Before too long, Screeching Weasel, Avail, Pansy Division, the Riverdales, the Queers, Groovie Ghoulies, and virtually every band on the label began citing the unpaid royalties clause in their contract and rescinding their rights and masters from the label. Confusingly, as the ship was thoroughly sunk, the Mr. T Experience still never yanked their licensing agreements.

Frank "Dr. Frank" Portman: I had lots of people say "Why don't you jump ship like everyone else," but that would have just been abandoning one declining label for another—the whole world was declining.

Chris Appelgren: It became increasingly clear that we were not, despite our best intentions, making any headway towards the goals we set. We wanted a smaller, simpler Lookout! Records to better serve the bands that stuck with us. Instead of doing any good, it felt like it was harder, and all we were doing was trying to mitigate potential disappointment or disillusionment from the artists. That's not a good situation to be in. Add on top of it, both of us had day jobs and were not making any money on the label. It just felt like it was time to honestly let it rest, let it end. Maybe that should have been done in 2005, really. Lookout! Records, as a project, a business, a family, a cultural entity, a clubhouse, an idea, has been part of some of the most amazingly wonderful times in my life so far. Running the label and working at the label also challenged me, helped me grow as a person, and was part of some of my saddest, hardest times too. I was a fan, an intern, an employee, street teamer, store clerk, errand boy, artist, designer, secretary, executive, stakeholder, president, co-owner, spokesperson, A&R guy—so many things. Some things I did in service of the label really worked, and other things failed on a large scale, but through it all, I believed in the idea that I was committed to seeing the label through and felt responsible for its legacy. Though that might seem sort of ironic as other folks would say I squandered it. I feel proud of Lookout!'s successes and regret and shame for its failures. Collectively, our hearts were in the right place, despite periodically stepping in shit or doing something extremely stupid.

As of November 2011, Bauer and Appelgren—the current label operatives at the time—decided to officially cease all Lookout! Records business matters. Ownership of the remaining intellectual property and rights to use the name were purchased by Hopeless Records in 2012 but have so far gone unused.

The Lookouting

After a lengthy break the Lookout! family of bands came together once more in January 2017 for an official (to date) big send-off party. Ironically the person behind this was a young fan, not around to experience the heyday of Lookout! Records. Discovering the label around the time of its demise, Alex Botkin did a deep dive into the entire whole catalog and history. Armed with a gifted copy of the original *Punk USA* book in 2014, Botkin penetrated the already long-in-the-tooth East Bay punk scene.

At nineteen, Botkin had begun booking at 924 Gilman, aware that its thirtieth anniversary was approaching.

Alex Botkin: I reached out to Larry Livermore, who seemed like the best place to start, and heard nothing. That was probably mid-May of 2016. In July, I was staying in a hotel in Arcata with a friend and my phone buzzed. It was Larry. I was in shock. He was up for it and thus got the ball rolling. Larry was initially reluctant to the idea, not because he didn't want it to happen but because he was sure nobody would come. It snowballed after that. The idea of one night quickly expanded into two, then a full weekend, and then four shows with weekday evening talks hosted at the Berkeley Public Library for those traveling for the shows. I think the first bands confirmed were Mr. T Experience and the Smugglers. Word started to spread, and there started to be online speculation about who might show up. I posted hint photos, the first one being the telephone in the Powell Street BART station, phone in the receiver. As expected, the debate of MTX or Green Day playing ensued, exactly as I hoped. The increase in attention also helped convince some bands that this was not just some punk kid messing around but a legitimate effort to do something special, which helped get bands like Monsula and Brent's T.V. to reunite. Things started to get serious, and the shows quickly sold out. People flew from all over the world, tickets in hand or not, just for the shows. I think my view of Lookout! from an outsider perspective helped make the shows happen. I asked bands who people thought would never reunite, just because I didn't know any better. Of course, some said no, but the bands we ended up with I could not be more happy with. I still have the voicemail on my phone of Adam LaBelle telling me Nuisance would reunite for it, which was the biggest triumph of the weekend.

The Lookouting brought a host of bands back to Gilman Street at the start of 2017 for a four-day festival, including Lookout! originals Monsula, Corrupted Morals, MTX, Nuisance, Brent's T.V., Kamala and the Karnivores, and Sewer Trout; and mid-era mainstays Wynona Riders, Pansy Division, the Smugglers, Squirtgun, and Tilt along with sets by Groovie Ghoulies' Kepi, Avengers, Black Fork, and more.

Sets were recorded and released in 2018 on a special double vinyl set from Hopeless / Lookout! with profits going toward 924 Gilman Street.

Alex Botkin: If anything stands in my memory, it's the joy it brought to those in attendance. The friends who hadn't seen each other for decades, the musicians who were getting one more chance to play, the people who never believed they'd see their favorite band play. It's impossible to pick a favorite, every band was a highlight. If I can be selfish about it in any way, it's that I got to see bands that I wasn't able to see—or wasn't even alive for—during their tenure. Seeing Ivy from Kamala & the Karnivores sing "Fuk Shit Up" with the Criminals was a total surprise. There's so much variety across the bands on Lookout!, and these shows served not only as a celebration of 924 Gilman and the label, but of that unique musical range. Brent's T.V. and the Smugglers bring a lot of joy and boundless energy, while bands like Corrupted Morals, Scherzo, Wynona Riders, and Monsula capture more of the hardcore sound and dynamics. Surrogate

Brains, Black Fork, Sewer Trout, and Nuisance all defy genre in their own ways. And then there's Jüke. Oh how there was Jüke. There wasn't a dud in the group, they were all brilliant.

Despite the overwhelming success surrounding The Lookouting, it appears for now that this is where the current story of Lookout! finds its footnote.

Discography

lk001 | Lookouts *One Planet, One People* LP
lk002 | Corrupted Morals *Chet* 7"
lk003 | Operation Ivy *Hectic* 7"
lk004 | Crimpshrine *Sleep, What's That?* 7"
lk005 | Isocracy *Bedtime for Isocracy* 7"
lk006 | Stikky *Where's my lunchpail* LP
lk007 | Plaid Retina *self titled* 7"
lk008 | Sewer Trout *Songs About Drinking* 7"
lk009 | Yeastie Girlz *Ovary Action* 7"
lk010 | Operation Ivy *Energy* LP
lk011 | various artists *Thing That Ate Floyd* 2xlp
lk012 | Neurosis *Aberration* 7"
lk013 | Surrogate Brains *Surrogate Serenades* 7"
lk014 | Eyeball *Prosthetic Head* 7"
lk015 | Crimpshrine *Quit Talkin' Claude* 7"
lk016 | Kamala and the Karnivores *Girl Band* 7"
lk017 | Green Day *1,000 Hours* 7"
lk018 | Lookouts *Spy Rock Road* LP
lk019 | Corrupted Morals *Cheese-it* LP
lk020 | Plaid Retina *Pinkeye* LP
lk021 | Neurosis *Word as Law* LP
lk022 | Green Day *39/Smooth* LP
lk023 | Mr. t experience *So Long, Sucker* 7"
lk024 | Samiam *I Am* 7"
lk025 | Cringer *Karin* 7"
lk026 | Fuel *Take Effect* 7"
lk027 | Monsula *Nickel* 7"
lk028 | Lookouts *Mendocino Homeland* 7"
lk029 | Skinflutes *self titled* 7"
lk030 | Filth *Live the Chaos* 7"
lk031 | Blatz *Cheaper Than the Beer* 7"
lk032 | Vagrants *Gone* 7"
lk033 | EAST BAY MUD (canceled)
lk034 | Fifteen *self titled* 7"
lk035 | Green Day *Slappy* 7"
lk036 | Brent's TV *Lumberjack Days* 7"
lk037 | Mr. T Experience *Making Things with Light* LP
lk038 | Monsula *Structure* LP
lk039 | Mr. T Experience *Everybody's Entitled to Their Own Opinion* LP
lk040 | Fifteen *Swain's First Bike Ride* LP
lk041 | Scherzo *self titled* 7"
lk042 | Lookouts *IV* 7"
lk043 | Filth / Blatz *The Shit Split* LP
lk044 | various artists *Can of Pork* LP
lk045 | Mr. T Experience *Love American Style* 7"
lk046 | Green Day *Kerplunk* LP
lk047 | Scherzo *Suffering and Joy* LP
lk048 | Nuisance *Confusion Hill* LP
lk049 | Mr. T Experience *Milk Milk Lemonade* LP
lk050 | Screeching Weasel *My Brain Hurts* LP
lk051 | Spitboy *self titled* 7"
lk052 | Wynona Riders *Some Enchanted Evening* 7"
lk053 | Juke *Don't Hate Us Because We're Beautiful* 7"
lk054 | Fun Bug *Tezbinetop* 7"
lk055 | Monsula *Sanitized* LP
lk056 | Jack Acid *Destroy the Boat* 7"
lk057 | Crimpshrine *Duct Tape Soup* LP
lk058 | Pinhead Gunpowder *Fahizah* 7"
lk059 | Rancid *self titled* 7"
lk060 | Citizen Fish *Disposable Dream / Flesh and Blood II* 7"
lk061 | Tilt *self titled* 7"
lk062 | Screeching Weasel *Boogadaboogadaboogada* LP
lk063 Screeching Weasel *Wiggle* LP
lk064 | Nuisance *Sunny Side Down* LP
lk065 | Fifteen *The Choice of a New Generation* LP
lk066 | Queers *Love Songs For the Retarded* LP
lk067 | Ne'er Do Wells Hello, *It Is I, Thee Intolerable Bastard, Child Genius* 7"
lk068 | Mr. T Experience *Gun Crazy* 7"
lk069 | Pansy Division *Fem in a Black Leather Jacket* 7"
lk070 | Pansy Division *Undressed* CD
lk071 | Tilt *Play Cell* LP
lk072 | Raooul *Fresh and Nubile* 7"
lk073 | Screeching Weasel / Born Against *El Mozote / Janelle* 7"
lk074 | Pansy Division *Touch My Joe Camel* 7"
lk075 | Screeching Weasel *You Broke My Fucking Heart* 7"
lk076 | Screeching Weasel *Anthem for a New Tomorrow* LP
lk077 | various artists *Punk USA* LP
lk078 | Judy & Loadies / Ne'er Do Wells *The Gift of Knowledge* LP
lk079 | Pot Valiant *self titled* 7"
lk080 | Mr. T Experience *Our Bodies, Our Selves* LP
lk081 | Queers *Beat Off* LP
lk082 | Avail *Satiate* LP
lk083 | RANCID / AVAIL (canceled)
lk084 | Wat Tyler *I Wanna Be Billie Joe* 7"
lk085 | Pansy Division *Nine Inch Males* 7"
lk086 | Screeching Weasel *Suzanne is Getting Married* 7"
lk087 | Pansy Division *Deflowered* CD
lk088 | Raooul / Skinned Teen *Jail Bait Core* LP
lk089 | Vindictives *Rocks In My Head* 7"

lk090 | Queers *Grow Up* LP
lk091 | Frumpies *Tommy Slich* 7"
lk092 | Tourettes *Hidden Keys to Loving Relationships* 7"
lk093 | Rice *Fuck You This is Rice* LP
lk094 | Big Rig *Expansive Heart* 7"
lk095 | Screeching Weasel *Kill the Musicians* CD
lk096 | Invalids *Punker Than Me* 7"
lk097 | Screeching Weasel *How to Make Enemies and Irritate People* LP
lk098 | Potatomen *On The Avenue* 7"
lk099 | DOWNFALL (canceled)
lk100 | various artists *A Slice of Lemon* 2xLP
lk101 | Potatomen *Now* LP
lk102 | Brent's TV / Sweet Baby *Hello Again* LP
lk103 | Avail *Dixie* LP
lk104 | Wynona Riders *JD Salinger* LP
lk105 | Pinhead Gunpowder *Jump Salty* CD
lk106 | Mr. T Experience *Tapin' Up My Heart* 7"
lk107 | Couch *This Lifes* 7"
lk108 | Queers *Surf Goddess* 7"
lk109 | Pansy Division *James Bondage* 7"
lk110 | Pansy Division *Pile Up* CD
lk111 | Bomb Bassets *Please Don't Die* 7"
lk112 | Vindictives *Alarm Clocks* 7"
lk113 | Hi-Fives *Welcome To My Mind* LP
lk114 | Queers *Move Back Home* LP
lk115 | Riverdales *Fun Tonight b/w I'm a Vegetable* 7"
lk116 | Vindictives *The Many Moods of the...* 2xLP
lk117 | Riverdales *Back To You b/w I Can't Pretend* 7"
lk118 | Squirtgun *Shenanigans* 7"
lk119 | Peechees *Scented Gum* 7"
lk120 | Riverdales *self-titled* LP
lk121 | Worst Case Scenario *self-titled* 7"
lk122 | Shotdowns *This Party is a Frat House* 7"
lk123 | Citizen Fish *Millenia Madness (Selected Notes From the Late 20th Century)* LP
lk124 | Cub / Potatomen *split* 7"
lk125 | Wat Tyler *Tummy* LP
lk126 | Mr. T Experience *Alternative is Here to Stay* 7"
lk127 | Pansy Division *Valentine's Day* 7"
lk128 | Squirtgun *self-titled* LP
lk129 | Smugglers / Hi-Fives *Summer Games* 7"
lk130 | Queers *A Day Late and a Dollar Short* CD
lk131 | Sludgeworth *Losers of the Year* CD
lk132 | Pinhead Gunpowder *Carry the Banner* LP
lk133 | Pansy Division *Wish I'd Taken Pictures* LP
lk134 | Mr. T Experience *Love Is Dead* LP
lk135 | Hi-Fives *And a Whole Lotta You!* LP
lk136 | Smugglers *Selling the Sizzle* LP
lk137 | Go Sailor *Don't Go* 7"
lk138 | Avail *4 AM Friday* LP
lk139 | various artists *Winter Compilation* CD
lk140 | Queers *Don't Back Down* LP
lk141 | Vindictives *Johnny, Where Are You? b/w Eating Me Alive* 7" picture disc
lk142 | Couch of Eureka *Year of the Zombie* LP
lk143 | Cub *Box of Hair* LP
lk144 | Mr. T Experience *Night Shift at the Thrill Factory* LP
lk145 | Mr. T Experience *Big Black Bugs Bleed Blue Blood* 10"
lk146 | Groovie Ghoulies *The Island of Pogo Pogo* 7"
lk147 | Pansy Division *For Those About to Suck Cock* 7"
lk148 | Groovie Ghoulies *Appetite For Adrenochrome* LP
lk149 | Groovie Ghoulies *Born in the Basement* LP
lk150 | Fifteen *There's No Place like Home (Good Night)* 7"/CD
lk151 | Groovie Ghoulies *World Contact Day* LP
lk152 | Citizen Fish *Thirst* LP
lk153 | Go Sailor *self-titled* CD
lk154 | various artists *More Bounce to the Ounce* 2xLP
lk155 | Phantom Surfers *The Great Surf Crash of '97* LP
lk156 | Phantom Surfers *Istanbul / Tokyo Twist* 7"
lk157 | Sweet Baby *It's a Girl* LP
lk158 | Queers *Bubblegum Dreams* 7"
lk159 | Hi-Fives *It's Up to You* 7"
lk160 | Potatomen *All My Yesterdays* LP
lk161 | Crumbs *self-titled* LP
lk162 | Wynona Riders *Artificial Intelligence* LP
lk163 | Furious George *Goes Ape* LP
lk164 | Squirtgun *Mary Ann* 7"
lk165 | Bomb Bassets *Take a Trip with the Bomb Bassets* LP
lk166 | Crumbs *Shakespeare* 7"
lk167 | Squirtgun *Another Sunny Afternoon* LP
lk168 | Pinhead Gunpowder *Goodbye Ellston Avenue* LP
lk169 | various artists *Heidi Sez...* CD
lk170 | Criminals *Never Been Caught* LP
lk171 | Parasites *Hang Up* 7"
lk172 | Black Fork *Rock for Loot* LP
lk173 | Auntie Christ *Bad Trip / Nothing Generation* 7"
lk174 | Pansy Division *Queer to the Core* 7"
lk175 | Pansy Division *More Lovin' From Our Oven* LP
lk176 | Auntie Christ *Life Could Be a Dream* LP
lk177 | Groovie Ghoulies *Running with Bigfoot* 7"
lk178 | Go-Nuts *self titled* 7"
lk179 | (young) Pioneers *On Trial* 7"
lk180 | Mr. T Experience *Revenge is Sweet, and so Are You* LP

lk181 | Uranium 9-Volt *Wild 7* 7"
lk182 | Groovie ghoulies *Re-animation Festival* LP
lk183 | Phantom Surfers *The Exciting Sounds of Model Road Racing* LP
lk184 | Mr. T Experience *and I Will Be with You* 7"
lk185 | Smugglers *Buddy Holly Convention* 7"
lk186 | Groovie Ghoulies *Graveyard Girlfriend* 7"
lk187 | various artists *The Last Great Thing You Did* CD
lk188 | Potatomen *Iceland* LP
lk189 | Avail / (young) Pioneers *The Fall of Richmond* 7"
lk190 | Screeching Weasel *Major Label Debut* LP
lk191 | Donnas *American Teenage Rock 'n' Roll Machine* LP
lk192 | Avail *Live in San Francisco* CD
lk193 | various artists *All Punk Rods!* LP
lk194 | Crimpshrine *The Sound of a New World Being Born* LP
lk195 | Avail *Over The James* LP
lk196 | Donnas *Rock 'n' Roll Machine b/w Speeding Back to My Baby* 7"
lk197 | Servotron *Entertainment Program For Humans (Second Variety)* LP
lk198 | Pansy Division *Absurd Pop Song Romance* LP
lk199 | Smugglers *Growing Up Smuggler* CD
lk201 | Donnas *self-titled* CD
lk202 | Mopes *Low Down Two Bit Sidewinder* CD
lk203 | Boris the Sprinkler *I've Been Hittin' on a… Russian Robot* 7"
lk204 | Phantom Surfers & Davie Allan *Skaterhater* LP
lk205 | Hi-Fives *Get Down* LP
lk206 | (young) Pioneers *Free the (young) Pioneers Now!* LP
lk207 | Moral Crux *Something More Dangerous* LP
lk208 | Screeching Weasel *Formula 27* 7"
lk209 | Citizen Fish *Habit* 7"
lk210 | Crumbs *Low and Behold* LP
lk211 | various artists *Four On The Floor* LP
lk212 | Citizen Fish *Active Ingredients* LP
lk213 | Screeching Weasel *Beat on the Brat* LP
lk214 | Donnas / Toilet Boys *Get You Alone / You Got It* 7"
lk215 | various artists *Forward Til Death* CD
lk216 | Queers *Later Days and Better Lays* CD
lk217 | Avengers *Died for Your Sins* LP
lk219 | Me First and the Gimme Gimmes *Garf* 7"
lk220 | Groovie Ghoulies *Fun in the Dark* LP
lk221 | Lillingtons *Death By Television* LP
lk222 | Dr. Frank *Show Business is My Life* LP
lk223 | Cuts *Heart Attack* 7"
lk224 | Cleveland Bound Death Sentence *self-titled* CD
lk225 | Donnas *Get Skintight* LP
lk226 | Common rider *Last Wave Rockers* LP
lk227 | Screeching Weasel *Emo* LP
lk228 | Basicks *Little Thing* 7"
lk229 | Jackie Papers *I'm In Love* LP
lk230 | Mopes *Accident Waiting to Happen* LP
lk231 | American Steel *Rogue's March* LP
lk232 | Mr. T Experience *Alcatraz* LP
lk233 | Towards An End *Change and Pass Through* 7"
lk234 | Ann Beretta *To All Our Fallen Heroes* LP
lk235 | various artists *Lookout! Freakout* CD
lk236 | Smugglers *Rosie* LP
lk237 | Enemy you *Where No One Knows My Name* LP
lk238 | Donnas *Detroit Rock City* 7"
lk239 | Screeching Weasel *Thank You Very Little* 2xCD
lk240 | Phantom Surfers *XXX Party* LP
lk241 | Splash 4 *Rules of Life* 7"
lk242 | Jimmies *Let the Fat Men Plunder* LP
lk243 | Go-Nuts *Dunk and Cover* LP
lk244 | Eyeliners *Here Comes Trouble* LP
lk246 | Groovie Ghoulies *Travels With My Amp* LP
lk247 | Gene Defcon *Liz* 7"
lk248 | Moral Crux *Side Effects of Thinking* LP
lk249 | Black Cat Music *One Foot in the Grave* 7"
lk250 | Pinhead Gunpowder *8 Chords, 328 Words* 7"
lk251 | Zero Boys *Livin' in the 80's* 7"
lk252 | Bratmobile *Ladies, women and Girls* LP
lk253 | Zero Boys *Vicious Circle* LP
lk254 | Mr. T Experience *Miracle of Shame* CD
lk255 | Donnas *Turn 21* LP
lk256 | Gaza Strippers *1,000 Watt Confessions* LP
lk257 | Screeching Weasel *Teen Punks in Heat* LP
lk258 | Pinhead Gunpowder *Compulsive Disclosure* CD
lk259 | Lillingtons *Backchannel Broadcast* LP
lk260 | Queers *Today* CD
lk261 | Enemies / Pitch Black *split* CD
lk262 | Ann Beretta *New Union… Old Glory* LP
lk263 | Bis *Music For a Stranger World* CD
lk264 | Alkaline Trio *Hell Yes* 7"
lk265 | American Steel *Jagged Thoughts* LP
lk266 | Wanna-be's *Self Titled* LP
lk267 | Yesterday's Kids *Everything Used to be Better* CD
lk268 | Ted Leo & the Pharmacists *The Tyranny of Distance* LP
lk269 | Black Cat Music *Hands in the Estuary, Torso in the Lake* LP

lk270 | Queers *Pleasant Screams* LP
lk271 | Common Rider *Thief in a Sleeping Town* 7"
lk272 | Eyeliners *Sealed With a Kiss* LP
lk273 | Mr. T Experience *...and the Women Who Love Them* CD
lk274 | One Time Angels *Tricks and Dreams* CD
lk275 | various artists *Lookout! Freakout Episode 2* CD
lk276 | Pattern *Immediately* CD
lk277 | various *Boys Lie* CD
lk278 | Enemies *Seize the Day* LP
lk279 | Pretty Girls Make Graves *Good Health* CD
lk280 | Bratmobile *Girls Get Busy* LP
lk281 | Yesterday's Kids *Can't Hear Nothin'* LP
lk282 | Ben Weasel *Fidatevi* LP
lk283 | Moral Crux *Pop Culture Assassins* CD
lk284 | Cost *Chimera* LP
lk285 | Pattern *Real feelness* LP
lk286 | Washdown *self titled* CD
lk287 | Oranges Band *On Tv* LP
lk288 | Donnas *Spend the Night* LP
lk289 | Communique *A Crescent Honeymoon* CD
lk290 | Ted Leo & the Pharmacists *Hearts of Oak* LP
lk291 | various artists *Lookout! Freakout Episode 3* CD
lk292 | Oranges Band *All Around* LP
lk293 | various artists *Punk Rock 7"s Volume 1* CD
lk294 | Even in Blackouts *Myths & Imaginary Magicians* CD
lk295 | Small brown bike *The River Bed* LP
lk296 | Donnas *Who Invited You 7"*
lk297 | various artists *Turn On, Tune In, Lookout* DVD
lk298 | Ted Leo & the Pharmacists *Tell Balgeary, Balgury is Dead* cd
lk299 | Mr. T Experience *Yesterday Rules* CD
lk300 | Green Day *1,039 Smoothed Out Slappy Hours* CD
lk301 | Washdown *Yes to Everything* CD
lk303 | Evening *Other Victorians* CD
lk304 | Reputation *To Force a Fate* CD
lk305 | Communique *Poison Arrows* LP
lk306 | Smugglers *Mutiny in Stereo* CD
lk307 | Black Cat Music *October, November* CD
lk308 | Lashes *The Stupid Stupid* CD
lk309 | Dollyrots *Eat My Heart Out* CD
lk310 | Ted Leo & the Pharmacists *Shake the Sheets* LP
lk311 | Engine Down *self titled* LP
lk313 | Oranges Band *The World and Everything in It* CD
lk314 | Mary Timony *Ex Hex* CD
lk315 | Hockey Night *Keep Guessin'* CD
lk316 | Troubled Hubble *Making Beds in a Burning House* CD
lk317 | various artists *This is My Bag* CD / DVD